ENGLISH OPERA IN LATE EIGHTEENTH-CENTURY LONDON

ENGLISH OPERA IN LATE EIGHTEENTH-CENTURY LONDON

STEPHEN STORACE
AT DRURY LANE

Jane Girdham

CLARENDON PRESS · OXFORD

1997

Oxford University Press, Great Clarendon Street, Oxford OX2 6DP
Oxford   New York
Athens Auckland Bangkok Bogota Bombay
Buenos Aires Calcutta Cape Town Dar es Salaam
Delhi Florence Hong Kong Istanbul Karachi
Kuala Lumpur Madras Madrid Melbourne
Mexico City Nairobi Paris Singapore
Taipei Tokyo Toronto
and associated companies in
Berlin Ibadan

Oxford is a trade mark of Oxford University Press

Published in the United States
by Oxford University Press Inc., New York

British Library Cataloguing in Publication Data
Data available

Library of Congress Cataloging in Publication Data
Girdham, Jane.
English opera in late eighteenth-century London : Stephen Storace
at Drury Lane / Jane Girdham.
p.   cm.
Includes bibliographical references.
1. Opera—England—London—18th century.   2. Storace, Stephen,
1762–1796. Operas. I. Title.
ML1731.8.L72G57   1997   782.1'09421'09033—dc20   96–28712
ISBN 0–19–816254–5

1 3 5 7 9 10 8 6 4 2

Typeset by Graphicraft Typesetters Ltd., Hong Kong
Printed in Great Britain by
Bookcraft Ltd
Midsomer Norton, Somerset

For Michael, Sarah, and Josephine

PREFACE AND ACKNOWLEDGEMENTS

When I started this project I could find very little published material other than Roger Fiske's pioneering and insightful work, *English Theatre Music in the Eighteenth Century*. I gratefully used his book as the starting-point for my own more focused research. In a book with such a vast base of material it was inevitable that I should find some minor errors and omissions, which I have corrected silently here, and which should not detract from Fiske's achievement. Recently there has been more interest in English musical activities of the late eighteenth century. I hope my work on Storace will illuminate a small part of a complex picture.

I originally chose to work on Storace's operas for my Ph.D. dissertation because he was such a central musical figure in London at the end of the eighteenth century, yet at the same time a young composer managing (however briefly) to move English opera away from its insular roots. As my research progressed, I began to assess the role of music in the playhouses, only to find it had been virtually ignored by literary historians. Chapters 2 and 3 are the result of my viewing a period of theatrical history from a musical standpoint, specifically through Storace's operas. I found a similar gap when trying to sort out the vast number of editions of Storace's music (and I still occasionally find new ones); so I used his operas to illuminate aspects of printing history and copyright use, presented here in Chapter 4.

Storace held a unique position in English music by turning from *opera buffa* to English opera and attempting to take English opera in the direction of the Italian. His lyric gift and strong dramatic sense were appreciated by his audience, but were unfortunately less influential on other composers. I wondered why he had so little influence—though nineteenth-century critics continued to praise him for his achievements—and later writers casually dismissed his operas as pastiches unworthy of intellectual attention. I soon came to realize that such judgements were facile because, far from simply putting together collections of songs to make a show, Storace expended great care and originality in refashioning the music he borrowed. In fact, while he may not hold first rank now, he was perhaps the most successful composer for the theatre of his generation and should not be forgotten.

While working on my dissertation I incurred many debts of gratitude, and in the course of reworking the material into its present form I have accumulated yet more. Thomas Bauman first stimulated my interest in eighteenth-century opera, and Eugene Wolf saw my original project to its completion. More recently, James McCalla has read this typescript with perception and encouragement. Michael Keenan, too, has read the entire typescript and helped me regain perspective many times; he now knows far more about Storace than he ever expected.

One of the great pleasures of research is the helpfulness and generosity of librarians everywhere. I should like to thank the many libraries and other archives whose materials have made my research possible and whose staffs have made it enjoyable, especially the University of Pennsylvania libraries, the British Library, the Folger Shakespeare Library, the Public Record Office, Sir John Soane's Museum, and the Bowdoin College libraries. I have also used material from Bath Central Library, the Huntington Library, the Harvard Theatre Collection, the Royal Society of Musicians, the Worshipful Company of Stationers & Newspaper Makers, and Lord Barnard's personal diaries, which were made available by the present Lord Barnard.

Many people have generously shared their material, ideas, and assistance. I am especially indebted to Stanley Corran, Theodore Fenner, Marjorie Gleed of the Royal Society of Musicians, Dorothea Link, Neil McGowan, Marilyn Murphy, John Platoff, Richard Platt, Deborah Rohr, Rose Theresa, Carolyn Tipping, and Felicity Watts. And Ron Girdham provided research assistance far in excess of the responsibilities of any father.

J.G.

CONTENTS

LIST OF FIGURES

LIST OF TABLES

LIST OF MUSIC EXAMPLES

ABBREVIATIONS AND CONVENTIONS

Biographical Dictionary	Philip H. Highfill, Jr., Kalman A. Burnim, and Edward A. Langhans, *A Biographical Dictionary of Actors, Actresses, Musicians, Dancers, Managers and Other Stage Personnel in London, 1660–1800*, 16 vols. (Carbondale, Ill., 1973–93)
BL	British Library, London
BUCEM	Edith B. Schnapper (ed.), *The British Union-Catalogue of Early Music Printed before the Year 1801*, 2 vols. (London, 1957)
Drury Lane Journal	'Drury Lane Journal 1788–89' (Folger MS W.b. 291)
Drury Lane Ledger	'Drury Lane Ledger 1795–99' (Folger MS W.b. 423)
Drury Lane Paybook A	'Drury Lane Paybook 1789–94 [chronological]' (Folger MS W.b. 347)
Drury Lane Paybook B	'Drury Lane Paybook 1790–96 [name-indexed]' (Folger MS W.b. 422)
Folger	Folger Shakespeare Library, Washington, DC
JAMS	*Journal of the American Musicological Society*
Kelly, *Reminiscences*	Michael Kelly, *Reminiscences of the King's Theatre, and Theatre Royal, Drury Lane*, 2 vols. (London, 1826)
Kemble, Memoranda A	'Professional Memoranda of John Philip Kemble, 1788–1795' (BL Add. MS 31,972)
Kemble, Memoranda B	'Professional Memoranda of John Philip Kemble, 1796–1800' (BL Add. MS 31,973)
Larpent MS	Manuscripts submitted to Larpent (Examiner of Plays in the Lord Chamberlain's office), now in the Huntington Library, San Marino, California
London Stage	*The London Stage 1660–1800: A Calendar of Plays, Entertainments & Afterpieces Together with Casts, Box-Receipts and Contemporary Comment Compiled from the Playbills, Newspapers and Theatrical Diaries of the Period*. pt. 4: *1747–1776*, ed. George W. Stone, jun.; pt. 5: *1776–1800*, ed. Charles B. Hogan (Carbondale, Ill., 1962–8)
ML	*Music and Letters*
MMR	*The Monthly Musical Record*
MQ	*The Musical Quarterly*
MT	*The Musical Times*

ABBREVIATIONS AND CONVENTIONS

New Grove	Stanley Sadie (ed.), *The New Grove Dictionary of Music and Musicians*, 20 vols. (London, 1980)
New Grove Instruments	Stanley Sadie (ed.), *The New Grove Dictionary of Musical Instruments*, 3 vols. (London, 1984)
New Grove Opera	Stanley Sadie (ed.), *The New Grove Dictionary of Opera*, 4 vols. (London, 1992)
PRMA	*Proceedings of the Royal Musical Association*
RISM	*Répertoire international des sources musicales*, ser. A/I (Kassel, 1971–86)

Eighteenth-century British Monetary Units

d. = penny	12 pennies = 1 shilling
s. = shilling	20 shillings = 1 pound
£ = pound	£1. 1*s.* 0*d.* = 1 guinea

All playbills were seen in the microfilm series *Playbills from the Harvard Theatre Collection: Theatre Royal Drury Lane* (Woodbridge, Conn., n.d.). Newspapers were seen in the microfilm series *Early English Newspapers* (Woodbridge, Conn., 1983).

Quotations are given exactly as they appear in the original sources, except for occasional punctuation which has been added to song texts in the interests of intelligibility.

PART I

CONTEXTS

STEPHEN STORACE'S FAMILY TREE

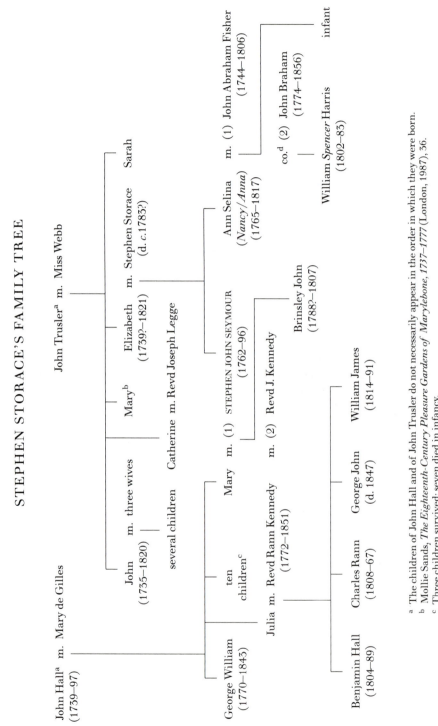

a The children of John Hall and of John Trusler do not necessarily appear in the order in which they were born.
b Mollie Sands, *The Eighteenth-Century Pleasure Gardens of Marylebone, 1737–1777* (London, 1987), 36.
c Three children survived; seven died in infancy.
d Cohabited *c.*1797–1816.

1

BIOGRAPHY

Stephen John Seymour Storace (1762–96) was one of the leading English composers in the last decade of the eighteenth century. Studies in Italy led to opera commissions in Vienna and a friendship with Mozart, then to a career as house composer at the Theatre Royal, Drury Lane, until his early death at the age of nearly 34. His brief career was both prolific and successful. He composed a total of twenty stage works: two *opere buffe* for Vienna and one for London, sixteen operatic pieces in English, and one ballet score. The focus of this book is his English operas, many of which were extremely popular, some of them providing financial support for other less successful productions at Drury Lane. Storace's English operas are works of imagination and innovation, introducing elements from *opera buffa* into the traditional forms of English opera.

Storace's obituary in the *Gentleman's Magazine* summarizes his life and music succinctly: 'His style of composition was formed upon the Italian model; and, in his airs for many voices, and in choral energy, he followed the musicians of Italy with great success. He was distinguished in private life for shrewdness, penetration, and knowledge of mankind.'[1] Said by some to be a brusque man and not shy of speaking his mind, Storace nevertheless showed remarkable tact in his musical innovations. He persuaded a conservative theatre-going British public to accept changes of style in their native opera that approached the integrity of music and drama in *opera buffa*.

Storace's career has always been overshadowed by that of his younger sister Nancy, who was a *prima buffa* in Italy and Vienna before joining her brother at Drury Lane. This emphasis on Nancy is hardly surprising, given the supremacy of singers in the popular imagination of the time. Only Michael Kelly treated brother and sister equally, in his *Reminiscences* of

[1] *Gentleman's Magazine*, 65 (Jan.–June 1796), 353.

1826. Kelly met the Storaces in Italy, sang with Nancy in Vienna, then returned to work at Drury Lane a little before Stephen. The three remained friends and colleagues throughout their lives. Kelly's *Reminiscences*, written with assistance from Theodore Hook thirty years after Storace's death, is one of our most important sources of anecdotal information about Storace. Kelly's long-term memory is sometimes inaccurate but, despite some recent expressions of distrust of his information, he is usually reliable in spirit. He gives a vivid, even theatrical, picture of the life of an opera singer, complete with vivacity and fun.[2]

Our other important contemporary sources of biographical information about Storace are two anonymous obituaries that appeared in the London newspaper the *Oracle* on 17 and 18 March 1796. William Bingley used their information for his *Musical Biography* of 1814, which was in turn used as a source by many nineteenth-century writers.[3] These later essays should be approached with caution as they simply reword and sometimes modify the meaning of the earlier accounts.

No detailed biography of Storace has yet been published. Roger Fiske's sketch in *English Theatre Music in the Eighteenth Century* and a recent book on Nancy Storace, Geoffrey Brace's *Anna . . . Susanna* are the fullest to date. While the present chapter makes no claim to be complete—there are still many unknown aspects of Storace's life that would elucidate his working procedures, for instance—the known facts provide a useful context to his musical career and professional activities.

Family Background

Stephen Storace was a Londoner, born on 4 April 1762.[4] His father Stefano had emigrated from Italy, via Bristol in 1747, to Dublin by 1750.[5] Stefano

---

[2] See Jane Girdham, 'A Note on Stephen Storace and Michael Kelly', *ML* 76 (1995), 64–7. Critics of Kelly's accuracy include Roger Fiske, in the introduction to his edn. of Michael Kelly, *Reminiscences* (London, 1975), p. x; Geoffrey Brace, *Anna . . . Susanna: Anna Storace, Mozart's First Susanna: Her Life, Times and Family* (London, 1991), 46, 48, 129. Alec Hyatt King, 'Kelly, Michael', *New Grove Opera*, ii. 973–5, takes the more positive view.

[3] William Bingley, *Musical Biography*, 2 vols. (1st pub. 1814; London, 1834, repr. New York, 1971), ii. 212–15. See also Lawrence I. Ritchey, 'The Untimely Death of Samuel Wesley; or, the Perils of Plagiarism', *ML* 60 (1979), 53–4.

[4] Storace's date of birth used to be given as 4 Jan. 1763. However, accurate sources include his application to the Royal Society of Musicians in August 1788, which required the production of his birth certificate.

[5] Brace, *Anna . . . Susanna*, 16.

soon Anglicized his name to Stephen, signing himself 'Stephen Storace' in a letter to the *Gentleman's Magazine* in 1753.[6] The letter was headed 'a *genuine* Letter from an *Italian* Gentleman, concerning the Bite of the Tarantula' and included details of his upbringing near Naples, so Storace had no reason to Anglicize his name specially for the occasion. In his letter he tells of being born in 'a small village, called *La Torre della Annunziata*, about ten miles from *Naples*', of studying music in Naples, and of playing the violin. Ten years later he signed his application to the Royal Society of Musicians (which he then withdrew) as Stephen Storace. A story has persisted into the twentieth century that the surname 'Storace' was originally spelt 'Sorace'. This tale probably originated in Joseph Haslewood's *The Secret History of the Green Room*, a publication of theatrical gossip of 1790, which, talking of Nancy Storace, states: 'Storace is not the original name of this Lady; the *t* was added by the family, to give it a more delicate pronunciation.'[7] Given the scandalous comments that follow about Nancy's lifestyle and character, plus the fact that the name is only rude with an English pronunciation, we should dismiss the anecdote as nonsense.

In 1750 Stephen Storace senior was employed by Dr Bartholomew Mosse, founder of the Lying-in Hospital and amateur musician, as leader of the band at the Great Britain-street Gardens in Dublin. In this capacity, he once tried to persuade Sheridan's musicians to play in a series of fund-raising concerts.[8] As leader he would have been a violinist, though by the time he moved to London he was playing the double bass. In August 1751 Storace senior and four other musicians leased the Crow-street Musick Hall for a regular series of concerts.[9] His Irish activities paint a picture of a competent professional musician with entrepreneurial ambitions.

By 1758 or 1759 Storace senior was working in London, playing the double bass at the King's Theatre in the Haymarket for the Italian opera company in the winter season and working at Marylebone Gardens in the summer. As his brother-in-law John Trusler junior mentions briefly in his *Memoirs* (which unfortunately stop in the 1760s), Storace senior was one of twelve members of a clique of performers from the Italian opera

---

[6] *Gentleman's Magazine*, 23 (Sept. 1753), 433–4. See also Timothy J. Rishton, 'Plagiarism, Fiddles and Tarantulas', *MT* 125 (1984), 325–7.

[7] *The Secret History of the Green Room*, 2 vols. (1st pub. 1790; 3rd edn., London, 1793), i. 156.

[8] Brian Boydell, *A Dublin Musical Calendar 1700–1760* (Dublin, 1988), 290. See also Esther K. Sheldon, *Thomas Sheridan of Smock-Alley* (Princeton, NJ, 1967), 145–7. According to Boydell, there is no evidence for Roger Fiske's statement that Sheridan employed Storace when he enlarged the Smock Alley Theatre band in 1748 (Fiske, 'Stephen [Stephano] Storace (i)', *New Grove*, xviii. 179).

[9] Boydell, *Dublin Musical Calendar*, 290; Thomas J. Walsh, *Opera in Dublin 1705–1797: The Social Scene* (Dublin, 1973), 81.

company who would meet after performances as the Order of the Lyre; wearing his golden lyre in his buttonhole one day, and in Trusler's company, Storace was mistaken for a foreign dignitary.[10] Storace also had various provincial engagements, such as the annual Three Choirs meetings in which he performed regularly between 1759 and 1770.[11]

Marylebone Gardens was owned by John Trusler senior, who was soon to become Storace's father-in-law. Here Storace arranged and directed Italian operas for the summer seasons, which were performed in translation as burlettas. His first project was *The Servant Mistress*, an adaptation of Pergolesi's intermezzo *La serva padrona*. It is not clear whether he collaborated with John Trusler junior on the version that was performed seventy-three times in the summer of 1758, but he was certainly responsible for the version performed the following year when Marylebone Gardens staged 107 performances of three burlettas, all of them adaptations by Storace.[12] The other two were *La Cicisbea alla Moda; or, The Modish Coquette*, from Galuppi's opera of that name, and *The Stratagem* from *La strattagemma*, supposedly by Pergolesi. A libretto of *The Coquet* (presumably a revival of *La Cicisbea*) was published in 1771 to coincide with that season's performances; in the preface Storace offered an apology for any weakness in his use of English:

Those who understand musical compositions, and the nature of such an undertaking, will be sensible of the difficulty of finding such English words as would not prove too stubborn for music, originally adapted to the Italian language. . . .

As I am a foreigner, I hope for the indulgence of the candid public, for many inaccuracies in the following performance, and flatter myself there is some degree of merit, in attempting to shew, that the English language is not altogether incompatible with Italian harmony, and expression.

In 1760 one of several problems, financial and personal, related to the burletta performances was the public dispute between Storace and Trusler senior over whose libretti were being sold legitimately. Trusler stated that his were the genuine article; Storace claimed that 'those sold at the Bar are Copies pirated from me'.[13] Despite their quarrel, Storace married Trusler's daughter Elizabeth the following year.

---

[10] *Memoirs of the Life of the Rev. Dr. Trusler* (Bath, 1806), 8.

[11] Daniel Lysons *et al.*, *Origin and Progress of the Meeting of the Three Choirs of Gloucester, Worcester & Hereford, and of the Charity Connected with it* (Gloucester, 1895), *passim.* Instrumentalists are not named every year.

[12] Evan Owens, 'La serva padrona in London, 1750–1783', *Pergolesi Studies*, 2 (1988), 205–10. Warwick Wroth and Arthur E. Wroth, *The London Pleasure Gardens of the Eighteenth Century* (London, 1896), 97, claim it was a joint enterprise. Trusler, *Memoirs*, 57, claimed sole responsibility, but presumably he meant only the words.

[13] Both announcements appear in *The Public Advertiser*, 2 Aug. 1760. See also Owens, 'La serva padrona', 207.

John Trusler senior had at least five children: John, Elizabeth, Mary, Sarah, and Catherine, three of whom were extremely long-lived.[14] According to Kelly, the Trusler family came from Bath, and the Storace family seems to have retained that connection.[15] Trusler senior had enlightened views on education. His son wrote that 'though not a rich man [he] brought me up in the line of a gentleman. Fortune he could not give,—education he did not spare.'[16] Trusler junior's education, which included a degree from Emmanuel College, Cambridge, and ordination in the Church of England in 1759, certainly supports his words. However, the fact that the Trusler girls were also educated is more relevant to the Storace family. Elizabeth, though far from an intellectual of her brother's stature, was certainly literate, as we know from her surviving letters. One of her sisters may have been a schoolteacher, the owner of 'Miss Trusler's School at Lancaster' which is mentioned in Nancy Storace's will.[17]

On 16 June 1761, at St James's church, Piccadilly, Stephen Storace senior married Elizabeth Trusler.[18] The Storaces had two children: Stephen John Seymour, born on 4 April 1762 in London, and Ann Selina (usually known as Nancy or Anna) born on 27 October 1765. In 1763 John Trusler senior sold the Gardens, which changed hands again in 1769, this time being sold to the composer Samuel Arnold. Shortly afterwards Storace, who had not been associated with the Gardens during most of the 1760s, returned there to work for Arnold. Each of his benefit performances in 1770, 1771, and 1772 included one of his earlier adaptations. A particularly spectacular occasion was 31 August 1772, with a concert, fireworks with music, a representation of the 'Forge of Vulcan', and *The Coquet*. It also included a performance by the 16-year-old Thomas Linley junior on the violin.[19]

Although the Storaces lived in London, they kept up their contacts in Bath and in particular were on friendly terms with the composer Thomas Linley senior and his large family. As well as Linley's son Thomas, who died at the age of 20, his daughter Elizabeth was also directly connected with the Storaces. Storace senior arranged engagements for her to sing at the Three Choirs festivals before her marriage to Richard Brinsley Sheridan,

[14] The will of Elizabeth Storace (née Trusler), dated 12 Sept. 1817 (London, Public Record Office, PROB 11/1686), mentions Sarah and Catherine (married to the Revd Joseph Legge) as still living. Her brother John, not mentioned in the will, died in 1820. Reference is made to her sister Mary in Mollie Sands, *The Eighteenth-Century Pleasure Gardens of Marylebone 1737–1777* (London, 1987), 36.
[15] *Reminiscences*, i. 95.   [16] *Memoirs*, 24.
[17] Will of Ann Selina Storace (London, Public Record Office, PROB 11/1597).
[18] *International Genealogical Index*, microfiche (Salt Lake City, Ut., 1992). The card 'Storace' in the card file of names at the Society of Genealogists, London, gives the date of their marriage licence as 15 June 1761 at the Bishop of London's Registry.
[19] Sands, *Pleasure Gardens*, 97–8.

son of Storace's old acquaintance Thomas Sheridan of Dublin.[20] Linley senior also had a professional association with Storace senior. For instance, the *Public Advertiser* announced on 12 April 1773 that tickets for a concert by Thomas Linley senior could be obtained 'from Mr. Linley at Mr. Storace's, in High Street, Marylebone'.[21] Later, Stephen Storace junior worked at the Theatre Royal, Drury Lane, which was owned by R. B. Sheridan and Linley senior.

The story of Sheridan's elopement to France with Elizabeth Linley in 1772 is famous. After their return home and marriage in 1773, Sheridan and his new wife stayed with the Storaces at 72 High Street, Marylebone, while looking for a permanent home of their own.[22] Stephen was then 11 years old and already a prodigious violinist.[23] If Kelly is to be believed, his sister Nancy (who was 8 at the time) 'could sing and play at sight'.[24] In October that year, father and both children performed at the Salisbury Musical Festival, young Stephen on the violin.[25] The story that made the rounds of the nineteenth-century dictionaries and encyclopedias comes from Stephen's obituary, via William Bingley:

At an early period of his life he discovered a strong propensity for music; and his father, who was a very able musician, took uncommon pains to cultivate this infantine genius, who at the age of ten or eleven years, was able to perform the most difficult Solo of Tartini and Giardini on the violin with the greatest precision.[26]

We know few other facts about Stephen Storace's early musical education or activities. Kelly, in an anecdote about Stephen's mathematical ability, makes a passing remark that his father 'gave him a bravura song of Bastardini's to copy'.[27] This implies that his father taught him, and that he educated him in compositional styles as well as in performance. Certainly a musician of his father's versatility would consider musical education important. The household in which Stephen and Nancy grew up was well connected with London theatrical life. They both lived in a world dominated by Italian opera, though only Nancy later emphasized her Italian parentage (as any singer with aspirations to singing Italian opera had to). Stephen, on the other hand, considered himself proudly English. He is

[20] Roger Fiske, *English Theatre Music in the Eighteenth Century* (2nd edn., Oxford, 1986), 492. All citations are from the 2nd edn.

[21] Quoted in Richard B. Sheridan, *The Letters of Richard Brinsley Sheridan*, ed. Cecil Price, 3 vols. (Oxford, 1966), i. 79 n. 5.

[22] Thomas Moore, *Memoirs of the Life of the Right Honourable Richard Brinsley Sheridan*, 2 vols. (5th edn., London, 1827), i. 121.

[23] *Oracle*, 18 Mar. 1796.   [24] *Reminiscences*, i. 96.

[25] Betty Matthews, 'J. C. Bach in the West Country', *MT* 108 (1967), 703.

[26] *Oracle*, 18 Mar. 1796. The story is reworded in Bingley, *Musical Biography*, ii. 212–13.

[27] *Reminiscences*, i. 250–1 n.

announced as 'Stefano Storace Inglese' on the title-pages of two early Italian works: his cantata *Orfeo negli elisi* (1781) and the manuscript score of his first opera, *Gli sposi malcontenti* (1785).[28] Three years later a reviewer of his first opera for Drury Lane, *The Doctor and the Apothecary* (1788), wrote: 'The music is by Ditters and Storce [*sic*]—that is partly German, and partly English—for—Storace, one of the most promising composers we know, has the honour to be "English, Sirs, from top to toe".'[29] Stephen Storace certainly underplayed his Italian heritage, although he probably used the Italian rather than the English pronunciation of his name. Nancy definitely pronounced her name in the Italian manner, as it was sometimes spelt 'Storache' or 'Storachi' in contemporary publications. She also affected the title Signora even after years of singing in English at Drury Lane.

Italy

Our first real insight into Storace's musical education dates from the late 1770s, when he was sent to study at the San Onofrio conservatoire in Naples. This was a natural choice for his father, whose family home was nearby, as his brother was a Neapolitan bishop and San Onofrio had probably been his own place of education. Storace's obituary describes his musical activities in picturesque fashion:

It being then the fashion to send our young musicians abroad, for the improvement of their taste, &c. Storace was placed in a *concervatori*, or musical college in *Italy*, where he thought the study of composition much more respectable than *drawing the bow*, or *scraping the cat gut*, having laid the latter aside, and strictly adhered to the former.[30]

He does seem to have dropped the violin as a serious pursuit and is rarely mentioned as playing it later in life, whereas he played and taught the harpsichord throughout his career. Kelly, no doubt with hindsight and affection, called Storace 'a great ornament' to San Onofrio;[31] however, the picture of the diligent student is shattered by Thomas Jones, a painter who

[28] *Orfeo negli elisi di Pier-Domenico Arrighi[.] Cantata a due voci[,] musica del Signor Stefano Storace Inglese* (Lucca, 1781); *Gli sposi malcontenti* (Vienna: Österreichische Nationalbibliothek, Musiksammlung, MS K.T. 425).
[29] *Times*, 27 Oct. 1788.   [30] *Oracle*, 18 Mar. 1796.
[31] *Reminiscences*, i. 96; see also ibid. i. 11 n.

actually knew Storace in Naples. On Christmas Day 1778 he wrote a diary entry (which he later edited for posterity):

Went with Storace to pay a visit to his Father, Mother & Sister who were lately arrived from *England*—with this family we enjoy'd many agreeable Evenings. . . . Young *Storace* had been sent 2 or 3 years before, to study Music at Naples, under the care of a Paternal Uncle, one of the Neapolitan Bishops, Young *Storace* however, at this time, being a giddy, thoughtless young fellow, apply'd very little to his Musical Studies, & being tired of the restraints he felt under his Uncle's roof, lived entirely with the English, & as he was fond of Drawing, was almost always of our parties.[32]

Jones also took sketching expeditions in Storace's company up Vesuvius, through the countryside on horseback, and to Sorrento by boat.[33] According to Kelly, the scenery of Storace's opera *The Pirates* (1792) was painted from sketches Storace made at this period, but no original drawings survive.[34] Jones last mentions Storace on 22 January 1779 when Jones 'made one of a party at Storace's where we danced Country dances in the English fashion'.

Despite his predilection for drawing, Storace also absorbed some musical education in Naples. A manuscript survives of a copy that Storace made of an aria by his teacher Giacomo Insanguine (also called Monopoli) in 1777. It comes from the opera *Adriano in Siria*, which was performed in Naples that year.[35] It may have been an exercise in style study (like the one his father gave him earlier) or intended for practical use. At least one original composition dates from Storace's time in Italy, a cantata for two voices entitled *Orfeo negli elisi*.[36] Storace was already taking composition seriously.

Jones mentioned that Storace's family arrived in Naples in late 1778. Earlier that year, on 27 April, Nancy had held a benefit concert for which 'Miss Storace humbly solicits the favour of her friends and patrons on this occasion, as she is going to Italy the ensuing summer for improvement'.[37] First she and her parents stayed in Naples with Stephen, and no doubt included a family visit to relations. When they moved on, Stephen accompanied them on a tour of Italy, with Nancy singing at various opera houses. In the autumn of 1779 they were in Florence, where Nancy sang in Francesco

---

[32] *Memoirs of Thomas Jones: Penkerrig, Radnorshire, 1803* (London, 1951), 83.

[33] Ibid. 80–2, entries for 29 Oct., 14 Nov., and 16–19 Nov. 1778.

[34] *Reminiscences*, ii. 32.

[35] Otto Albrecht, *A Census of Autograph Music Manuscripts of European Composers in American Libraries* (Philadelphia, Pa., 1953), 278.

[36] Only its text by Pier-Domenico Arrighi survives, printed in Lucca in 1781.

[37] *Gazeteer*, 27 Apr. 1778.

Bianchi's opera *Castore e Polluce* and Stephen played second harpsichord.[38] While in Florence, they met two people whose friendships lasted throughout their lives: Prince Hoare, who later wrote librettos for some of Stephen's English operas, and John Soane, who was to become a prominent architect, and to whom Stephen's son was later apprenticed.[39] Soane became Nancy's confidant when her relationship with John Braham collapsed, and after her death in 1817 he designed her memorial tablet, for which Prince Hoare wrote the verse at Elizabeth Storace's request.[40]

The Storace family moved round Italy in pursuit of operatic engagements for Nancy, arriving in Livorno in 1780, where Michael Kelly first met them.[41] He describes their first meeting with his usual extravagant gestures:

After we had been visited by the officers of health, I went on shore to shew my passport at the Custom-house; I had on a Sicilian capote, with my hair (of which I had a great quantity, and which, like my complexion, was very fair) floating over it: I was as thin as a walking stick. As I stepped from the boat, I perceived a young lady and gentleman standing on the Mole, making observations; as the former looked at me she laughed, and as I approached, I heard her say to her companion in English, which, of course, she thought I did not understand, 'Look at that girl dressed in boy's clothes!' To her astonishment, I answered in the same language, 'You are mistaken, Miss, I am a very proper *he* animal, and quite at your service!'

We all laughed till we were tired, and became immediately intimate; and these persons, my acquaintance with whom commenced by this childish jest on the Mole at Leghorn, continued through life the warmest and most attached of my friends. All love and honour to your memories, Stephen and Nancy Storace![42]

By 1782 Nancy was singing at La Scala, Milan, where she may have started the practice that she continued throughout her operatic career of inserting substitute arias by Stephen into her roles. Either here, or later in Vienna, she inserted an aria entitled 'Compatite miei signori' into Sarti's *Fra i due litiganti*.[43] The aria survives in manuscript, but Storace did not reuse it in his surviving English works, unlike some of his other Italian

---

[38] Claudio Sartori, *I libretti italiani a stampa dalle origini al 1800* (Milan, 1990–), s.v. *Castore e Polluce*.

[39] Stephen Gwynn, *Memorials of an Eighteenth Century Painter (James Northcote)* (London, 1898), 166–7; Dorothy Stroud, *Sir John Soane, Architect* (London, 1984), 42.

[40] Stroud, *Sir John Soane*, 275.

[41] Brace, *Anna . . . Susanna*, 130, gives evidence for the date.

[42] *Reminiscences*, i. 94–5. Fiske, *English Theatre Music*, 493 n. 2, reports that the *General Magazine* for May 1788 states they met at a concert in Livorno.

[43] Brace, *Anna . . . Susanna*, 130, states that she inserted the aria in Milan; John Platoff, in private correspondence, thinks it was probably added after the opera (now called *I pretendenti delusi*) opened in Vienna in 1783.

pieces.[44] At some time while the Storaces were still in Italy, their father died. Stephen returned to England, while Nancy continued to perform in Italy with her mother as chaperone. Mother and daughter then moved to Vienna in 1783 after Nancy was engaged as *prima buffa* at the Burgtheater.

The chronology of Storace's travels and activities in the early 1780s is not precisely known. He spent most of his time in England, probably in both London and Bath, with at least two visits to Vienna in 1785 and 1786–7. The whole Storace family returned to London in the spring of 1787, when both brother and sister went to work for the Italian opera company at the King's Theatre. In the early 1780s Storace's career was still unsettled, even though he was beginning to have some success as a composer. He had already published some small pieces in London: *Eight Canzonetts* and *A New Recitative and Rondo* ('Ah se poro') in 1782. Three of the canzonets were popular enough to be republished individually in about 1785. His other publications during this period included a set of two quintets and a sextet dedicated to Mademoiselle Godsalve in about 1784,[45] and a song 'Ah! Delia, see the fatal hour' from perhaps a year later. At the time he published the chamber works he lived at 68 Great Queen Street, Lincoln's Inn Fields, which was probably lodgings.

Storace's other musical activities between 1782 and 1784 include performances at the annual music meetings in Salisbury in 1782, 1783, and 1784. In 1784 John Marsh recorded that Storace was to 'play the choruses' (presumably at the keyboard), and a piece of his was tried out. He also played the organ for Rauzzini's performance of *Messiah* in Bath in 1782.[46] There is a consensus in the secondary literature that at some point during the 1780s Storace tried to settle in Bath and give up music for drawing. Certainly he did not abandon music for long, as he was commissioned to write his first *opera buffa* in 1785.

Whatever his doubts about a career, Storace used his musical skills to earn a living. We cannot be sure where his teaching practice was (possibly in both Bath and London to judge from the subscription list of his *Collection of Original Harpsichord Music*), but the following notice in the preface to volume 1 indicates that he did have students:

---

[44] 'Compatite miei signori' is included in MSS of Sarti's *Fra i due litiganti*, including Vienna: Österreichische Nationalbibliothek, Musiksammlung MS 17.888.

[45] Miss Godsalve and (separately) J. Godsalve Crosse, Esq., both of Baddow, Essex, are listed as subscribers to Storace's *Collection of Original Harpsichord Music*, 2 vols. (London [1787–9]). Brace, *Anna . . . Susanna*, 33, describes the dedicatee as Elizabeth Godsalve, daughter of an Essex land-owner.

[46] Brace, *Anna . . . Susanna*, 32–3.

S. Storace having been obliged, for the last two Seasons, to give up all his Scholars, owing to his late Engagement at the *Opera-House*, and his two former ones at the Court of *Vienna*; now wishes to inform his Friends, that the ensuing Winter he proposes to teach Singing, Thorough-Bass, (after the Neapolitan Method,) and playing on the Harpsichord, as usual.[47]

He must have spent much of 1785 and 1786 working on his Viennese operas, though we might wonder how he earned a living.

Vienna

In 1783 Nancy Storace and Michael Kelly both accepted contracts to perform at the Burgtheater in Vienna, Nancy as *prima buffa*, Kelly in lesser roles. Still not yet 18, Nancy was chaperoned by her mother. Kelly mentions Mrs Storace in describing the courtship of Nancy by Dr John Abraham Fisher, the violinist:

The harmonious Doctor, however, (who, by the bye, was a very ugly Christian) laid siege to poor Nancy Storace; and by dint of perseverance with her, and drinking tea with her mother, prevailed upon her to take him for better or worse, which she did in despite of the advice of all her friends; she had cause, however, in a short time to repent of her bargain, for instead of harmony, there was nothing but discord between them; and it was said he had a very striking way of enforcing his opinion, of which a friend of her's informed the Emperor, who intimated to him, that it would be fit for him to try a change of air, and so the Doctor was banished from Vienna.[48]

Nancy's short and unhappy marriage is another story.[49] She took Fisher's name only briefly, and on her return to England was known as Signora or Madame Storace.

Stephen Storace went to Vienna for the productions of both his operas at the Burgtheater: *Gli sposi malcontenti* on 1 June 1785 and *Gli equivoci* on 27 December 1786. It was certainly Nancy who influenced Emperor Joseph II into commissioning Stephen to write his first opera, probably out of respect for her professional judgement rather than from any purported intimacy between them.[50] Storace doubtless earned the second commission

---

[47] The notice is dated 1 July 1788, even though the first volume was entered at Stationers' Hall as copyright in 1787.

[48] *Reminiscences*, i. 228–9.   [49] Brace, *Anna . . . Susanna*, 41–7.

[50] Karl Geiringer and Irene Geiringer, 'Stephen and Nancy Storace in Vienna', in Robert L. Weaver (ed.), *Essays on the Music of J. S. Bach and Other Divers Subjects: A Tribute to Gerhard Herz* (Louisville,

by a combination of the quality of the first work, Nancy's persuasion, and the emperor's desire to keep her in Vienna.[51]

The première of *Gli sposi malcontenti* was a disastrous performance, because Nancy, who was heavily pregnant, lost her voice early on.[52] Her baby apparently died of neglect the following month.[53] Storace's next opera, *Gli equivoci*, for which he had chosen both the subject and his librettist, was a success. As Kelly writes:

Storace had an opera put into rehearsal, the subject of his own choice, Shakespeare's Comedy of Errors. It was made operatical, and adapted for the Italian, by Da Ponte, with great ingenuity. He retained all the main incidents and characters of our immortal bard; it became the rage, and well it might, for the music of Storace was beyond description beautiful.[54]

Lorenzo Da Ponte was inclined to dismiss his effort:

Directly I finished 'Figaro', [Nancy] Storace's brother who now knew better what were the abilities of his first librettist [Brunati], had obtained the Emperor's permission for me to write a libretto for him. So to please him and get the matter out of the way quickly, I adapted one of Shakespeare's comedies.[55]

Gli equivoci was never performed in London, though Storace later adapted substantial sections for his English operas.

Storace used his travels to and from Vienna to carry job contracts for the London theatre managers. Kelly remembers his own negotiations with Drury Lane:

I got a letter from Mr. Linley, to say, that he and Mr. Sheridan would be very happy to treat with me for Drury Lane Theatre; that Stephen Storace would soon be at Vienna, and that he would have a *carte blanche* to close an engagement with me, on their parts.

. . . Stephen Storace at length arrived at Vienna from England, and brought with him an engagement for his sister, from Gallini, the manager of the Opera House in London, as prima donna for the comic opera.[56]

Ky., 1981), 237, and Roger Fiske, 'The Operas of Stephen Storace', *PRMA* 86 (1959–60), 32, both think the emperor and Nancy were intimate; Brace, *Anna . . . Susanna*, 45, thinks he simply respected her musicianship.

[51] Brace, *Anna . . . Susanna*, 48.

[52] Ibid. 46–7, states that Nancy's baby later died and that, contrary to Kelly's statement, the Duke of York and Emperor Joseph II were not present at the première.

[53] Count Johann Karl von Zinzendorf, quoted in Brace, *Anna . . . Susanna*, 132.

[54] *Reminiscences*, i. 233–4.

[55] *Memoirs of Lorenzo da Ponte, Mozart's Librettist*, trans. L. A. Sheppard (London, 1929), 144.

[56] *Reminiscences*, i. 259, 262.

On his last visit to Vienna, Storace obtained a book for his uncle John Trusler with help from the British Ambassador Sir Robert Keith, along with scores for the London theatres.[57] When he left England in September 1786, he was asked by Gallini at the King's Theatre to bring home a score of Paisiello's *Il re Teodoro* (and undoubtedly others). Gallini paid him 10 guineas.[58] In a passing comment in a letter from Vienna to an English friend, 'I have made a pretty little collection of music', he suggests that he also bought music for himself.[59]

To modern musicians Storace's most important association with Vienna was his friendship with Mozart, whom he no doubt met through Nancy. Her professional relationship with him included creating the role of Susanna in *Le nozze di Figaro* (1 May 1786). Mozart's other works for her include part of a collaborative cantata (with Salieri and 'Cornetti') called *Per la ricuperata salute di Ophelia*, K. 477a, which celebrates her recovery after she lost her voice in *Gli sposi malcontenti* in 1785. He also wrote the concert aria 'Ch'io mi scordi di te', K. 505, for Nancy with an obbligato piano part for himself. It is dated 26 December 1786, the day before the première of *Gli equivoci*. Our knowledge of Stephen's direct contact with Mozart is limited to an anecdote told by Kelly, the gist of which is well known:

Storace gave a quartett party to his friends. The players were tolerable; not one of them excelled on the instrument he played, but there was a little science among them, which I dare say will be acknowledged when I name them:

> The First Violin . . . . . Haydn.
>   "   Second Violin . . . Baron Dittersdorf.
>   "   Violoncello . . . . . Vanhall.
>   "   Tenor . . . . Mozart.

The poet Casti and Paisiello formed part of the audience. I was there, and a greater treat, or a more remarkable one, cannot be imagined.[60]

Mozart's music was a strong influence on Storace, both in style and form; however, we have no evidence that Mozart taught Storace, even though it would have been natural for Storace to show work in progress to his older

---

[57] Letter from Stephen Storace to Sir Robert McKeith, 3 July 1787 (BL Add. MS 35,538, fo. 258). The ambassador's correct name was Sir Robert Murray Keith (1730–95).
[58] Curtis Price, 'Italian Opera and Arson in Late Eighteenth-Century London', *JAMS* 42 (1989), 93; Curtis Price, 'Unity, Originality, and the London Pasticcio', in *Harvard Library Bulletin*, NS 2/4: *Bits and Pieces: Music for Theater* (1991), 25 n. 29.
[59] Letter to J. Serres, 21 Feb. 1787 (Harvard Theatre Collection, Autograph V 79).
[60] *Reminiscences*, i. 237–8.

and more experienced colleague. Certainly there was no formal arrangement like the one Mozart had with Thomas Attwood, another Englishman in Vienna in the 1780s.[61]

The Storaces stayed in contact with Mozart after they returned to England in 1787, although only musical evidence of their continuing correspondence survives. Storace published several pieces by Mozart for the first time in his *Collection of Original Harpsichord Music*, at least one of which Mozart had composed after Storace left Vienna: the Piano Trio, K. 564. Nancy also performed 'Batti, batti' from *Don Giovanni* in London before its publication.[62] The Storaces tried to persuade Mozart to make a visit to England. Leopold Mozart, in a letter to his daughter, gave his view of the enterprise: 'As I had gathered, [Wolfgang] wants to travel to England, but ... [Attwood] is first going to procure a definite engagement for him in London, I mean, a contract to compose an opera or a subscription concert, etc.'[63] He then explained how his letter of advice had probably discouraged Mozart from travelling. At all events the plan never succeeded.[64]

In early 1787 the Storaces, along with Michael Kelly and Thomas Attwood, planned to return to England when Nancy's contract ran out at the beginning of Lent. What was originally intended as a year's leave of absence for the singers turned out to be permanent for everyone. As Kelly says: 'The Carnival was now fast approaching. I informed Stephen Storace of the leave of absence I had obtained from the Emperor, and that I would accompany him and his sister, and mother, to London.'[65] Shortly before they left, on the night of 20 February, Storace found himself arrested for disorderly conduct. The following day, Ash Wednesday, he passed the time writing to a friend in England:

You might not have recieved a letter from me, so early as this, long good friend— had it not been owing to a ridiculous circumstance that happen'd last night or rather early this morning—to make short of the story—it is some hours since I have been in a guard:house under an arrest—and of course having much leisure I know no better mode of passing my time than devoting it to my friends in England—but to inform you of some of the particulars—you must know that there

---

[61] Attwood's exercises, with Mozart's corrections, survive. See *W. A. Mozart: Neue Ausgabe sämtliche Werke*, 10th ser., 30/1: *Thomas Attwoods Theorie- und Kompositionsstudien bei Mozart*, ed. Erich Hertzmann and Cecil B. Oldman (Kassel, 1965), and Daniel Heartz, 'Thomas Attwood's Lessons in Composition with Mozart', *PRMA* 100 (1973–4), 175–83.

[62] Fiske, *English Theatre Music*, 506.

[63] *The Letters of Mozart and His Family*, trans. Emily Anderson (3rd edn., London, 1985), 906.

[64] For other reasons why Mozart did not come to London, see H. C. Robbins Landon, *Mozart and Vienna* (New York, 1991), 193–200.

[65] *Reminiscences*, i. 270.

never perhaps were so *hard:a going* sett of English in any one town out of England—as are at present in Vienna—we have lived these last six weeks almost in one continual scene of riot—*amongst ourselves*—as long as it remain'd so, nobody could find fault—but lately some of our youths—high:charged with the juice of French grapes—have made their occasional sallies—& exposed themselves to the natives especially at the Ridotta's, or Masquerades—many of which have been given in the course of the newly expired Carneval[.] a few nights ago the Hon^{bl}: Charles Lennox—L^d: Clifford and one or two others—courted some ladies—with rather too much vehemence—which occasion'd an order—that every Englishman that behaved with the least impropriety, at the ensueing Ridotta—(the one last night) should be put under an arrest—It so happen'd that about three oclock this morning as my Sister was dancing a minuet with L^d: Barnard, a Man who was standing by chose to stand in such a manner that Lord Barnard, turning the corner inadvertently trod on his toe—upon which he was rather impertinent— L^d: B took no notice but proceeded—on again coming to the same corner— the Gentleman took an opportunity of advancing still further into the ring & had nearly thrown him down—upon which I who was a stander by—with more spirit than prudence—asked him, 'what he meant by being so impertinent as to attempt throwing down any gentleman that was dancing'—he then immediately chose to use some very ungentlemanlike language—which I (who had rather too much Champaigne in me, though far beneath intoxication) could not brook—inshort words begat words—the whole rooms were presently in a confusion—the report was that an *Englishman had mis:behaved*—we were almost press'd to death—by the multitudes that crowded round:us—my antagonist proved to be an officer— he immediatly apply'd to the officer of the guard—who *sans:cerimonie* put me under charge of a corporal's guard—and I was conducted to the guard-house— from which place I have the honor of addressing to you this epistle—as all the English have taken up this matter warmly—I immagine I shall soon be liberated— and we shall strive hard to bring the aggressor to condign punishment.

   . . . I can hardly refrain from laughing at the Idea of myself *in durance vile.*[66]

Kelly, too, gives a description of the event. The details differ—Kelly was writing some forty years later—but the tenor of the story is the same.[67] Lord Barnard, Nancy's escort, also recorded his visits to Stephen in the guard-house on Tuesday and Wednesday, when he supped with him. On Thursday he supped with Nancy, and Stephen was released from prison.[68] His arrest and release are the most fully documented events in Storace's life.

---

[66] Stephen Storace to J. Serres, 21 Feb. 1787 (Harvard Theatre Collection, Autograph V 79).
[67] *Reminiscences*, i. 271–3. See also Girdham, 'Note'.
[68] Lord Barnard, diary entries for 20–2 February 1787. Lord Barnard's diaries belong to his family at Raby Castle, Staindrop, Co. Durham, and they were consulted by kind permission of the present Lord Barnard.

On Saturday, 24 February, almost immediately after Nancy's benefit concert the previous evening, the travellers set out for England. The party comprised Mrs Storace, Nancy (with her lapdog), Stephen, Michael Kelly, and Thomas Attwood.[69] Kelly says they met up with Lord Barnard in Munich, when he shared his carriage to make the other group's journey more comfortable, but Leopold Mozart's letter suggests they were all in Salzburg together.[70] The two parties may have set out separately, as Lord Barnard wrote that he left Vienna at 2.30 p.m., whereas according to Storace his party was to leave at 2 a.m. If so, they soon met up and travelled most of the route together, listed by Storace as Salzburg, Munich, Augsburg, Ulm (which Lord Barnard does not mention), Strasburg, Chalons, and Paris.[71]

In Salzburg they should have delivered a letter from Mozart to his father, but Mrs Storace mislaid it. Leopold Mozart described their visit in some detail, including their entourage on departure. It is noteworthy that for a second time Nancy performed in the evening before leaving immediately to travel through the night. As Leopold Mozart wrote to his daughter on 1 March:

In the evening [Nancy] sang three arias and they left for Munich at midnight. They had two carriages, each with four post-horses. A servant rode in advance as courier to arrange for the changing of eight horses. Goodness, what luggage they had! This journey must have cost them a fortune. They all spoke English, far more than Italian.

The party followed Storace's itinerary, with an additional stop for the men in Stuttgart before Strasburg.[72] They then proceeded via Nancy to Paris, where they stayed a week and attended the opera, then parted from Lord Barnard. They arrived in London via Boulogne and Dover on 18 March 1787 after a journey of three weeks. Lord Barnard returned to London on April 26.[73]

---

[69] Kelly, *Reminiscences*, i. 274–7.

[70] Ibid. 277. Leopold Mozart described 'another Englishman whom I did not know but who is probably cicisbeo to the mother and daughter' in a letter to his daughter of 1 Mar. 1787 (*Letters of Mozart*, 906).

[71] Storace to J. Serres, 21 Feb. 1787 (Harvard Theatre Collection, Autograph V 79); Lord Barnard, diary entries 24 Feb.–11 Mar. 1787.

[72] Kelly, *Reminiscences*, i. 279–82.

[73] Ibid. 276–89. It is possible, however, that Nancy Storace and her mother stayed in Paris until Mar. 23, on which day Lord Barnard wrote that he escorted unnamed company to Calais.

London: Early Days

On their arrival in London, Stephen and his sister were both contracted to work at the King's Theatre while Kelly was to sing at Drury Lane, the theatre owned by Sheridan and Linley (who was also house composer). Since Storace also knew the Drury Lane proprietors through his family connections, it was natural that he and Kelly should visit Thomas Linley at once. Thus, on the evening of 18 March 1787, Kelly recounts:

Stephen Storace and myself called upon Mr. Linley, at his house in Norfolk Street in the Strand, where I found his accomplished daughters, Mrs. Sheridan and Mrs. Tickell. Mrs. Sheridan asked me if I had seen [Grétry's] 'Richard Coeur de Lion,' in Paris; and on my telling her that I had, only four evenings before, she requested me to go and see it at Drury Lane that evening, as she was most anxious to know my opinion of the relative merits of the French and English pieces. General Burgoyne had translated it, and Mrs. Sheridan adapted it to the English stage.

I and Storace, accompanied by a young gentleman, set off for the theatre, but the piece was nearly half over. . . . I [did not] think much of the vocal powers of the royal captive; and turning to Storace, said, 'If His Majesty is the first and best singer in your theatre, I shall not fear to appear as his competitor for public favour.' Storace laughed, and told me that the gentleman who upon that special occasion was singing, was Mr. John Kemble, the celebrated tragedian, who, to serve the proprietors, had undertaken to perform the part of Richard, as there was no singer at the theatre capable of representing it.[74]

Thus we meet yet another important person in Storace's professional life. John Philip Kemble (who was known as a weak and reluctant singer) became acting manager at Drury Lane eighteen months later, and remained so throughout Storace's time there; he also wrote one libretto for Storace.

At first Storace worked for the Italian opera company at the King's Theatre where Joseph Mazzinghi was music director; however, Kelly also persuaded him to help out for his Drury Lane début on 20 April. Kelly chose to play Lionel in *A School for Fathers* (Dibdin's *Lionel and Clarissa*), and included not only all the original music but also

an Italian air of Sarti's, with English words, written for me by Mr. Richard Tickell, brother-in-law to Mr. Sheridan; and a duet, written by the well-known Doctor Lawrence, the civilian. I composed the melody, and Stephen Storace put the instrumental parts to it. This duet was his first introduction to Drury Lane theatre.[75]

---

[74] Ibid. 289–90.   [75] Ibid. 292.

Shortly afterwards, on 24 April, Nancy Storace made her first appearance at the King's Theatre, playing Gelinda in Paisiello's *Gli schiavi per amore* under her brother's direction. She had previously performed the role in Vienna, where the opera was given as *Le gare generose*. Stephen made substantial revisions and included substitute arias by Corri, Mazzinghi, and himself.[76] As Stephen reported in a letter to Sir Robert Keith in Vienna, this production proved satisfactory to the management and both Storaces: 'We have done the *Gare Generosa* under another title with very great success—it has been performed to near 20 bumper houses—[Nancy] is reengaged for the next season at an advanced salary—& likewise at the ancient concerts—I am likewise to compose an opera.'[77] In the same letter, Storace showed himself to be under no illusions about the Italian opera scene in London: 'My Sisters success in London upon the whole has been as much as we could expect—though she has had great opposition from the Italians—who consider it as an infringement on their rights—that any person should be able to sing that was not born in Italy—at present she gains ground very fast.' Storace was employed by the King's Theatre to arrange pasticcios, and was paid 25 guineas apiece for two.[78] He did not stay at the King's Theatre as long as Nancy, because '[Stephen] Storace obtained great credit for the manner in which [*Gli schiavi per amore*] was produced; but the intrigues of an Italian theatre soon drove away this sensible, able manager.'[79]

Storace kept up an association with the King's Theatre for a while longer. In the following season he composed the aria 'Care donne che bramate' for his sister to sing in Paisiello's *Il re Teodoro*, first performed in London on 8 December 1787, the score of which Storace had brought back with him from Vienna. In 1788 Storace sued the music publishers Longman & Broderip for illegally publishing 'Care donne', and eventually won his case.[80] His own opera, *La cameriera astuta*, received its première on 4 March 1788; it was not a success, though four excerpts were published. Nancy continued her habit of using substitute arias by Stephen. On 9 May 1789 at the first performance of the season of Giuseppe Gazzaniga's *La vendemmia*,

[76] Curtis Price, Judith Milhous, and Robert D. Hume, *Italian Opera in Late Eighteenth-Century London*, i: *The King's Theatre, Haymarket, 1778–1791* (Oxford, 1995), 378–82; Frederick C. Petty, *Italian Opera in London 1760–1800* (Ann Arbor, Mich., 1980), 249 n. 3.

[77] Stephen Storace to Sir Robert McKeith [Keith], 3 July 1787 (BL Add. MS 35,538, fo. 258). The 'ancient concerts' refers to an annual series of subscription concerts run by the society called the Concert of Antient Music.

[78] Price, 'Unity, Originality', 25 n. 29.

[79] 'Memoir of Stephen Storace', *Harmonicon*, 6 (1828), 2.

[80] Price *et al.*, *Italian Opera*, 389–93.

according to the *World*, 'Storace's two Airs are by her *Brother*.'[81] He may have brought the score back from Vienna, along with a number of others.[82]

At the same time as he was working at the King's Theatre, Storace was editing his *Collection of Original Harpsichord Music*, published in two volumes between 1787 and 1789. The collection includes chamber works as well as the solo pieces indicated by the title. Among them are three works of his own and some that he brought back from Vienna, including three pieces by Mozart published for the first time.[83] The subscription list provides information about Storace's circle of colleagues and friends. Fifteen names from Bath and its environs are listed, which include Storace's uncle the Revd Dr John Trusler, and some unmarried women who were probably past students. Some names with London addresses may also have been students. Twelve names from Cambridge (eleven attached to colleges and many of them clerics) suggest Trusler's influence. Fellow musicians include Charles Burney (six sets), Samuel Arnold (two sets), and Thomas Linley, James Hook, Thomas Attwood, and Muzio Clementi.

At the end of the 1787/8 season, Storace further established his professional career when he applied for, and was granted, membership of the Royal Society of Musicians. In the recommendation, dated 3 August 1788 and signed 'S. Arnold', Storace's activities are described as 'teaching the Harpsichord and Singing—Composing and Publishing Musick'.[84] He became an active member of the society, played the violin for its annual benefit concerts, and became one of its governors in 1793.[85]

Storace's other engagements in 1788 include playing in the orchestra for the Salisbury Festival;[86] no doubt he performed on other occasions. All his activities after returning from Vienna indicate that he was establishing his

[81] *World*, 11 May 1789. *Morning Post*, 11 May 1789, does not mention Stephen Storace as contributing to the work. He did publish a duet by Mozart, 'Crudel perche finora', sung in *La Vendemmia* by Benucci and Nancy Storace.

[82] Price *et al.*, *Italian Opera*, 368, 431.

[83] Fiske, 'Operas of Storace', 35.

[84] Recommendation for membership, The Royal Society of Musicians. See also Betty Matthews (comp.), *The Royal Society of Musicians of Great Britain: List of Members 1738–1984* (London, 1985), 139.

[85] Storace's name appears among the violins in an undated notebook which lists members by the instruments they played at the society's benefit concerts. His name was subsequently crossed out and marked 'Dead' (information kindly supplied by Mrs Marjorie Gleed, secretary to the society). Although the *Biographical Dictionary* (xiv. 308) states that he was a governor in 1793 and played the violin for the benefit concerts from 1789 to 1792, Storace's name is not listed in the advertisements for those years. He and his sister donated £100 to the society in 1793, the amount paid by Charles Manners 'as an attonement for an insult offered' (Betty Matthews, *The Royal Society of Musicians of Great Britain 1738–1988: A History* (London, 1988), 47).

[86] Betty Matthews, 'The Childhood of Nancy Storace', *MT* 110 (1969), 735.

career as a professional musician by composing, editing, directing, performing, and teaching. However he still lacked a salaried position.

Storace married Mary Hall on 23 August 1788, after his first full theatrical season back in England.[87] She was the daughter of John Hall, who was historical engraver to the king from 1785 to 1792 and the person responsible for the frontispiece of *Storace's Collection*.[88] The fact that Hall did not complete any further work for Storace's publications should not suggest any distance between them as, according to John Thomas Smith: 'Mr. Hall, when he quitted his house in Berwick-street, where he had resided for a number of years, took one in Cumberland-street, near the New-road, where it is said he never enjoyed his health, from suffering so much for the loss of his son-in-law Storace.'[89] Hall died in April 1797, just a year after Storace.

After their marriage, Stephen and Mary Storace lived in Percy Street, Rathbone Place, round the corner from the Storace family home at 23 Howland Street, Rathbone Place. Later they also bought a house in Hayes, Kent. They had one surviving child, Brinsley John, who was born in 1788 or 1789 and died in 1807.[90] The child's name suggests he was called after Sheridan, but no specific connection is known.

Drury Lane

Storace started work at the Theatre Royal, Drury Lane, early in the 1788/9 season. He soon became house composer in practice, although Thomas Linley retained the official title of 'composer to the theatre' until his death just four months before that of Storace. Linley, however, had always been a reluctant theatre composer and must have been delighted to pass his responsibilities on to someone younger and more enthusiastic. Linley's last opera

---

[87] Fiske, *English Theatre Music*, 500. Storace's application to the Royal Society of Musicians, dated 3 Aug. 1788, states that he is single. In an addendum four days later, signed 'S. Arnold' like the application, his married state is recorded, without an exact date. If his son Brinsley was 19 when he died in Mar. 1807, then he would have been born prior to the marriage. However, the instructions for application would require his birth to be recorded along with his parents' marriage. It is more likely that his age at his death was reported inaccurately.

[88] Ian Maxted, *The London Book Trades, 1775–1800: A Preliminary Checklist of Members* (Folkestone, 1977), 98.

[89] *Nollekens and His Times*, 2 vols. (London, 1828), ii. 390.

[90] Bingley, *Musical Biography*, ii. 214, states that the Storaces had several children, although all evidence points to the contrary. Certainly Brinsley was the only living child by 1797, when Nancy Storace wrote her will, because she left money to Brinsley and to his mother, but to nobody else connected with Stephen's household. Brinsley's date of birth is calculated from his date of death given in *Gentleman's Magazine*, 101 (Jan.–June 1807), 283.

had been *Love in the East* (25 February 1788) with a libretto by James Cobb; Storace's first work for Drury Lane was the afterpiece *The Doctor and the Apothecary* (25 October 1788) with a libretto adapted from the German by Cobb. The following season Nancy Storace joined her brother for his first full-length opera at Drury Lane after the King's Theatre burned down.

Nancy's performance at the première of Storace's *The Haunted Tower*, on 24 November 1789, was her first appearance on the English stage, and Storace took 5 guineas out of the authors' benefit money to buy earrings for her.[91] Thereafter, she and Michael Kelly sang leading roles in almost all of Storace's operas. Neither of them gave up singing Italian opera entirely, though Nancy did turn down a contract in 1790 to perform at the Pantheon because its exclusive nature would not allow her to perform elsewhere, and specifically not in Stephen's operas at Drury Lane.[92]

Storace normally composed two operas per theatrical season until his death in 1796. He also contributed nine numbers to a revival of *Cymon* by David Garrick and Michael Arne, performed on 31 December 1791. A complete list of his stage works is given in Appendix 4. Almost all of Storace's works after 1788 were for the Drury Lane company, though between 1791 and 1794 some were performed at the newly rebuilt King's Theatre and the Little Theatre in the Haymarket while the Drury Lane Theatre was being rebuilt. During this transition period, Storace and Kelly also directed Italian operas at the King's Theatre. Storace directed Paisiello's *Il barbiere di Siviglia* (26 January 1793) and Sarti's *Le nozze di Dorina* [*I rivali delusi*] (26 February 1793), in which he also included his own aria 'Io non era'. His ballet *Venus and Adonis*, with choreography by Noverre, appeared on the same bill. He completed the season by directing Paisiello's *I zingari in fiera* (14 May 1793).

In 1793 English eyes were riveted on the events in revolutionary France. Louis XVI was executed in January, Marie Antoinette in October. Englishmen expressed their support of the monarchy in a wide variety of ways, and Storace made his royalist contribution by composing and publishing two songs about Marie Antoinette, the first after her husband's execution, the second after her own. Storace was not alone in offering musical

---

[91] James Cobb, Receipt of Thomas Westley, Drury Lane, 1 Jan. 1790, 'Receipts and Letters of Jas. Cobb, 1787–1809' (BL Add. MS 25,915), no. 3.

[92] Price, 'Opera and Arson', 66–8. See also Curtis Price, Judith Milhous, and Robert D. Hume, 'A Royal Opera House in Leicester Square (1790)', *Cambridge Opera Journal*, 2 (1990), 1–28; and Curtis Price, Judith Milhous, and Robert D. Hume, 'The Rebuilding of the King's Theatre, Haymarket, 1789–1791', *Theatre Journal*, 43 (1991), 421–44.

tributes, but he was the only composer to mark both occasions.[93] His 'Captivity, a Ballad Supposed to be Sung by the Unfortunate Marie Antoinette During her Imprisonment' was sung by Anna Crouch during the Covent Garden Lenten oratorio season in February and March 1793;[94] his 'Lamentation of Marie Antoinette, Late Queen of France, on the Morning of her Execution' was published in mid-November.[95]

The Drury Lane company reassembled for the opening of the new theatre in March 1794, after being disbanded for over six months, and at the end of the season Storace's involvement with the Italian opera ceased. Drury Lane reopened at the end of Lent with a concert of music by Handel, in which, as the *Thespian Magazine* reports, 'Shaw led the band, Mr. Linley presided at the organ, and Storace played the *Carillons*.'[96]

Even though Storace had now been Drury Lane's house composer in practice for six years, Linley still remained on the company's books. His main activity was directing the oratorios during Lent, though in 1794 he shared the directorship with Storace.[97] Linley did eventually sell his shares in the company. In May 1795 Storace considered taking over a part share, in a plan that was also to include Joseph Richardson, Kemble, and Westley. Nothing came of it.[98] At the beginning of the 1795/6 season Sheridan's new partners were John Grubb and Richardson.

Storace continued his interest in teaching, publishing *Six Easy and Progressive Sonatinas for the Piano Forte or Harpsichord Compos'd for the Improvement of Juvenile Performers* in 1791, in keeping with the fashion of writing such pieces. Throughout his career, Storace's regular income derived from a combination of teaching fees, author's benefits at Drury Lane, and the sale of copyrights to his publisher. His uncle included 'Mr. Storace, (Singing and Piano-Forte)' in an exclusive list of nine 'Ladies' Teachers, the most capital in London', in his *London Adviser and Guide* of 1790.[99]

In the 1790s Storace probably earned most of his income through musical publications. His operas were published in complete form as soon as it was apparent that they were successful on stage (his few failures were never published). Contemporary reports of how much he was paid vary, but the amounts named are all large. The *Quarterly Musical Magazine and Review*

[93] Jane Girdham, 'Marie Antoinette, Martyr: Music, Politics, and Popular Culture in London, 1793' (unpublished paper).

[94] Entered at Stationers' Hall on 19 Feb. 1793.

[95] Entered at Stationers' Hall on 17 Nov. 1793.   [96] *Thespian Magazine*, 3 (1794), 128.

[97] *London Stage*, 12 Mar. 1794, Drury Lane; William T. Parke, *Musical Memoirs*, 2 vols. (London, 1830), i. 185.

[98] Sheridan, *Letters*, ii. 20 n. 1, 29 n. 3.

[99] John Trusler, *The London Adviser and Guide* (2nd edn., London, 1790), 210.

of 1822 reported a figure of £400 for *The Haunted Tower*; in 1791 the *Gazeteer* said he was paid 500 guineas for *The Siege of Belgrade*.[100] According to Busby, 'Longman and Broderip gave Mr. Shield one thousand guineas for his opera of *The Woodman*; and to Stephen Storace more than five hundred guineas, for most of his musical dramas; and often paid fifty or a hundred guineas for a single vocal composition.'[101] During the 1790s, many individual numbers from Storace's operas were published separately. Despite Busby's evidence, it is not clear that he was paid extra for all of them. Busby's statement is at best exaggerated, as Longman & Broderip published only the first three of Storace's operas. Nevertheless, all indications are that his publications brought in a comfortable income.

His benefits at the theatre were another matter, as his expectations of income from Drury Lane often differed substantially from what he was actually paid. Since he was not salaried, his payments came from benefits shared with his librettists. Documentation is sporadic, because—unlike performers' benefits—authors' benefits were not advertised. Authors normally received the profits from the third, sixth, and ninth nights of a run; in addition they might receive a bonus if their work was performed twenty times in its first season. However, authors' nights were not immutably set, and their moneys were not consistently paid. Storace should have earned over £100 for each of his full-length operas, but the Drury Lane account books provide an incomplete record of his benefits and payments. Indeed, an appeal from James Cobb in 1802 makes it plain that he and Storace were often not paid—or were only partly paid—what was owed to them.[102]

In discussing the period when Storace worked at Drury Lane, most contemporary biographers confine themselves to talking about his music; facts about his life are negligible. We can glean a few snippets about his social activities from various diaries. For instance, on 3 June 1792 Joseph Haydn recorded dining at Storace's house; also present were Nancy Storace, the singer Gertrud Mara with her husband, and Michael Kelly.[103] Kemble also gives a few brief glimpses in his diary. On 6 June 1792, three days after Haydn's visit, Kemble went to Hayes with Storace and both returned the following day; on 14 December Kemble 'fetch'd Storace out of the Country' (again presumably his house in Hayes) on the night *The Pirates* and *The*

[100] *Quarterly Musical Magazine and Review*, 4 (1822), 154; *Gazeteer*, 5 Feb. 1791.

[101] *Concert Room and Orchestra Anecdotes*, 3 vols. (London, 1825), i. 127.

[102] Cobb to the proprietors of the Theatre Royal Drury Lane, 1 Jan. 1802, 'Receipts' (BL Add. MS 25,915), no. 6. See Ch. 2 for a detailed discussion of Storace's benefits.

[103] *The Collected Correspondence and London Notebooks of Joseph Haydn*, ed. H. C. Robbins Landon (London, 1959), 254.

Doctor and the Apothecary were to be performed at Drury Lane by royal command.[104]

Again, we know only fragmentary details about Storace's professional life at this time. In 1791 both Stephen and Nancy Storace subscribed to Joseph Corfe's *Twelve Glees*. Corfe was a family friend who, after Storace's death, arranged three melodies from his operas in his *Third Set of Twelve Glees*.[105] Nancy sang songs by her brother at the Music Meetings in Oxford, 6–8 July 1791, in the presence of Haydn, who was awarded a doctorate.[106]

One of Storace's last acts before his final illness was to hire John Braham as a principal tenor at Drury Lane. He may have gone to Bath to hear him sing because Braham (a Londoner) was a pupil of Rauzzini in Bath, but Braham was already performing successfully in Salomon's London concerts by March 1796.[107] Storace was sufficiently impressed to write a major role for him in *Mahmoud*, the opera left incomplete at his death. Braham subsequently lived for about seventeen years with Nancy Storace and they had a son, Spencer Braham.

Last Works and Death

When Storace was taken ill in the spring of 1796, he had recently finished the music for George Colman junior's *The Iron Chest* and was working on *Mahmoud* to a libretto by Prince Hoare. *The Iron Chest* was in rehearsal, and stormy rehearsals they were. Colman, in his fury, wrote a long preface to the first edition of the text, blaming the whole cast and production team—not excepting Storace—for the disaster that took place at the première on 12 March:

Nay, even the composer of the music—and here let me breathe a sigh to the memory of departed worth and genius, as I write the name of Storace—even he could not preside in his department. He was preparing an early flight to that abode of

---

[104] Memoranda A, fos. 183ᵛ, 209ᵛ.

[105] Joseph Corfe, *Twelve Glees, for Three and Four Voices... Composed from Ancient Scotch Melodies* (n.p., 1791), *RISM* C 3917. Joseph Corfe, described on the title-page as 'Gentleman of his Majesty's Chapels in London', was father of the 'Mr Arthur Corfe Musician of Salisbury' to whom Nancy Storace left £100 in her will of 1797, and who is mentioned on the title-page of *Twelve Glees* as 'Mr Corfe's, Salisbury'. Another son, John, played cello or double bass in the Drury Lane orchestra in the 1790s. Joseph Corfe, *A Third Set of Twelve Glees* (London, n.d.), *RISM* C 3923, contains arrangements of 'Toll, toll the knell' (*Mahmoud*, no. 5), 'Whither my love!' (*The Haunted Tower*, no. 6), and 'From shades of night' (*Mahmoud*, no. 13).

[106] *Morning Chronicle*, 9, 11, 12 July 1791.　　[107] *Morning Chronicle*, 12 Mar. 1796.

harmony, where choirs of angels swell the note of welcome to an honest and congenial spirit.[108]

Kelly explains that Storace had been ill for some weeks before his death, and his account would explain Colman's complaints about rehearsals:

The music [of *The Iron Chest*] composed by Storace, was, I believe, the cause of his premature and lamented death. On the first rehearsal, although labouring under a severe attack of gout and fever, after having been confined to his bed for many days, he insisted upon being wrapped up in blankets, and carried in a sedan-chair to the cold stage of the playhouse. The entreaties and prayers of his family were of no avail,—go he would; he went, and remained there to the end of the rehearsal. . . . He went home to his bed, whence he never rose again.[109]

On Monday, 14 March the *True Briton* reported that 'Poor Storace is so ill with a gout and fever, that it is hardly supposed he will recover. He is principally attacked in the head; and it is said, that on Saturday his disorder was so violent, as to deprive him wholly of sight.' By the next day he was dead.[110] Kemble recorded in his diary for Tuesday, 15 March 1796: 'Poor Stephen Storace died this morning, only in his thirty fourth year!' Storace was buried on 21 March, as Kemble, in a rare outburst of emotion, wrote: 'This Day I followed Stephen Storace to his Grave—I shudder'd to hear the Earth and pebbles rattle on his Coffin!—I hope never to go .into Marybone Church again. I will endeavour to live better—He was only thirty four!—One may die tonight.—'

The first of two obituaries that appeared in the London newspaper the *Oracle* on 17 and 18 March 1796 gives us a rare glimpse into Storace's character:

His private character was sometimes mistaken—he had not the art to lower false expectation gently. He spoke his mind plainly and bluntly—his opinion might be relied on for its value and its sincerity—he had great quickness of decision, and this sometimes was mistaken for abruptness—properly attentive to his interest, and not to be diverted from its pursuit—he sometimes provoked comments, which he never deserved—we knew him to be a friendly, upright man . . .

---

[108] George Colman jun., as quoted in Richard Brinsley Peake, *Memoirs of the Colman Family*, 2 vols. (London, 1841), ii. 238–9. Peake reproduces the whole of Colman's preface on pp. 234–56.

[109] *Reminiscences*, ii. 77–8.

[110] There has been much disagreement about the actual day of Storace's death. The date of 15 Mar. is supported by various contemporary publications, including Storace's obituaries in the *Gentleman's Magazine*, 65 (Jan.–June 1796), 353, and *Morning Chronicle*, 18 Mar. 1796. Kelly (in 1826) gives 16 Mar. (*Reminiscences*, ii. 79), as does Storace's undated memorial (which gives his age inaccurately as 34). The obituaries that appeared in the *Oracle* and the *True Briton* on 17 and 18 Mar. give the lie to a date of 19 Mar., given by Fiske (*English Theatre Music*, 538) and others.

. . . His mind was strong, keen and vigorous—his habits of living uniformly temperate.

A monument was erected to Storace by his mother and sister, with an epitaph by 'his sincere and valuable friend' Prince Hoare.[111] Twenty years later, Hoare performed the same duty for Nancy Storace at her mother's request.[112]

Stephen Storace died intestate, leaving something under £5,000. In May 1797 the administration of his estate was granted to his widow by the Prerogative Court of Canterbury.[113] In 1835 the house in Hayes was put on the market with a prospectus that read: 'This Pretty Retreat was formerly the favourite Residence of that celebrated Musician, Signor Stephen Storace, who here composed many of his best Operas.'[114]

Although *The Iron Chest* was in its first (very brief) run and *Mahmoud* was left unfinished when he died, Storace had probably been composing the two operas concurrently. Kelly thought that the last music he wrote was part of *The Iron Chest*: 'The last twelve bars of music he ever wrote, were the subject of the song (and a beautiful subject it is), "When the robber his victim has noted"; which I sang in the character of Captain Armstrong.'[115] This song ends Act 2, scene 1 of *The Iron Chest*. According to the playbill for his widow's benefit night on 25 May, the finale of *The Iron Chest* was 'the last Composition of Mr. Storace'. This may mean simply that the opera was his last completed work. Common sense suggests he was working on *Mahmoud* before he became bedridden during rehearsals for *The Iron Chest* because he had composed enough of *Mahmoud* for it to be made into a makeshift version that could be performed posthumously. Nancy Storace probably completed it for its première on 30 April 1796, and the librettist Prince Hoare wrote a prologue in which he refers to its incompleteness:

> Imperfect, if you view th'intended plan,
> Accept it as we give,—'tis all we can.
> Faults will, no doubt, too evidently glare,
> And haply teach you our regrets to share.[116]

---

[111] Smith, *Nollekens*, ii. 390. The memorial is now in Marylebone parish church, 17 Marylebone Road, London NW1. See Appendix 1 for the text.

[112] Elizabeth Storace to John Soane, 23 Aug. 1817 (Sir John Soane's Museum, Correspondence Cupboard (2), Division XIII, Letters A+B, Packet 35, Item 4).

[113] Administration Act Books (London, Public Record Office, PROB 6/172, fo. 274ᵛ).

[114] William D. Hoskins, 'Stephen Storace and Eighteenth-Century Comic Opera', M.A. thesis (University College, Cardiff, University of Wales, 1974), 115.

[115] *Reminiscences*, ii. 78.   [116] Ibid. 80.

In a review in *The Times* on 2 May 1796, Hoare's prologue was strongly criticized:

The Opera was preceded by some lines intended as a lamentation on the death of the composer, Storace, and lamentable indeed they were as a composition—nor were they delivered very happily; but the best excuse for the lines themselves is the true one, they were written during the rehearsal on Saturday, and got by heart within an hour by the indefatigable Mr. Benson.

According to the *Oracle* on the same day, Benson delivered the prologue dressed as an undertaker.

Public tributes to Storace included one from Anthony Pasquin, satirist of the London theatre, in one of his more serious moments:

> Lo, the Muse demands Hope to envelope her fears!
> Lo, *Mater Orphei's* bedew'd with her tears!
> The Nine fly their symbols, and droop, and deplore,
> That STORACE, the gentle STORACE's no more.[117]

Another tribute came from the London organist and composer Stephen Rimbault, who published an elegy entitled 'A Pastoral on the Death of Stephen Storace'.[118]

Mary Storace, Widow

Storace's widow was treated considerately by Storace's friends and colleagues. Prince Hoare, for example, gave his customary author's benefits to Mrs Storace: 'Mr. Hoare, whose dramatic talents are so deservedly admired, gives the whole profits of his new Opera, if it should succed, to the family of his late friend Storace, with whom he was upon the most amicable footing, from very early life.'[119] The Drury Lane Ledger goes some way to confirming

---

[117] Eric Walter White, *A History of English Opera* (London, 1983), 224, quotes this verse as being from Anthony Pasquin, *The Pin-Basket to the Children of Thespis* (London, 1796). However, the extract does not appear in the copies of *The Pin-Basket* in the British Library.

[118] *Select Songs No. 4* (London, n.d.), not entered in *RISM*, but a copy in the British Library. Rimbault also arranged six pieces by Storace for piano duet, in *Three Duetts for Two Performers on the Piano Forte The Subjects from Storace's Popular Airs* (London [1812?]).

[119] *True Briton*, 24 Mar. 1796. The story was confirmed by *Biographia Dramatica*, comp. David E. Baker, Isaac Reed, and Stephen Jones, 3 vols. (London, 1812), iii. 7, and Kelly, *Reminiscences*, ii. 80.

Hoare's gift, with an entry 'To Cash Paid to Mrs. Storace for 5. Nights of Mahmoud by the Direction of the Author'.[120]

The benefit performance for 'the Widow of the truly estimable Composer Storace' took place on 25 May 1796, the eighth night of *Mahmoud*.[121] The playbill advertised the performance as being 'At the Request of many Friends to Worth and Genius, and In Commemoration of the late Mr. Storace. For the Benefit of His Widow and Orphan.' The night's entertainment comprised *Mahmmoud*, *A Dramatic Cento* (extracts from other operas by Storace), and *The Sultan*. The contents of *A Dramatic Cento* were:

Overture	(*The Iron Chest*)
'Five times'	(*The Iron Chest*)
'Little Taffline'	(*The Three and the Deuce*)
'Of plighted faith'	(*The Siege of Belgrade*)
'The Silver Waters'	(*The Pirates*)
'Go not, my love'	(*The Three and the Deuce*)
'Listen, listen'	(*The Iron Chest*)

The cast was impressive by any standards. Almost every singer Storace had written for at Drury Lane performed, along with dancers representing the Italian opera company, who performed the new ballet *Little Peggy's Love* to music by Casara Bossi and 'with the permission of the Proprietor of the Opera House, whose promptitude on this occasion does him infinite credit'.[122]

The evening's show concluded with the last-act finale of *The Iron Chest*, whose mood was highly appropriate for the occasion, with a text that ends:

> where fever droops his burning head,
> where sick men languish on their bed,
> around let ev'ry accent be
> Harmony, Harmony, a soft and dulcet Harmony.

As Parke recalls, 'The house, in compliment to the memory of departed genius, presented an overflowing audience.'[123] Indeed, the night's takings were excellent: £657. 12s. 0d., of which Mrs Storace was to have received £412. 18s. 3d. after the house charge was deducted.[124]

---

[120] Drury Lane Ledger, fo. 29. The total of £166. 13s. 4d., entered on 11 May 1796, would make £33. 6s. 8d. per night, or £100 for the normal three nights' author's benefits. For some reason Hoare gave Mary Storace five nights' income, but was then repaid for one night after her official benefit night on 25 May 1796.

[121] *Morning Chronicle*, 26 May 1796.   [122] *Oracle*, 27 May 1796.

[123] *Musical Memoirs*, i. 220.

[124] *London Stage*, 25 May 1796, Drury Lane. The figures in the Drury Lane Ledger, fo. 67ᵛ, are not so clear, but the amounts are close enough to indicate a very good house for the evening. The ledger seems to record a total of £631. 19s. 9d., of which the house charge was £244. 13s. 9d., leaving Mrs Storace £387. 6s. 0d.

The benefit night demonstrated the theatrical community's respect and admiration for Storace, and should have provided some financial support for his widow and child. Unfortunately, this was not immediately the case. Benjamin Robert Haydon, an artist and friend of Prince Hoare, recorded the event in his diary: 'Sheridan gave the House for a Benefit. The House was crowded of course. Sheridan went to the door keeper as manager & Friend, swept off all the receipts, and the Widow never got a shilling—so Prince Hoare told me, one of Steven Storace's intimate Friends.'[125] This cavalier treatment of Storace's family is entirely believable; Sheridan was often in wrangles over money, and regularly in debt. In fact, only two weeks later, on 9 June, another benefit performance was held for the family of Benson, who had spoken Hoare's prologue on the first night of *Mahmoud*. According to Genest, 'the house was a very good one—but it has been said, that Sheridan went to the Treasury and carried off the money, so that Benson's widow and children never got a sixpence.'[126]

The Drury Lane Ledger gives credence to the tale about Mary Storace. Sheridan's monetary responsibilities in paying off his debts to her continued at least until 1799 (when the ledger stops). Payments are recorded of £20 in 1797 in two instalments, £30 in 1798, and £273 in ten instalments in 1799.[127] Even on this generous schedule Sheridan was evidently tardy in his payments, because Mary Storace had to call in Joseph Burchell, the family solicitor. She wrote (perhaps to Richard Peake, who handled the Drury Lane accounts):

Sir

I have receiv'd of Mr Birchall [*sic*] the twelve pounds, which however acceptable, is but a poor satisfaction for the disappointments I have met with—& I wish you to inform Mr Sheridan that unless he keeps good faith with me by paying up the weekly arrears agreable to his promise, I must give immediate directions to proceed by Execution—

    M. Storace

I expect an answer
No 25 Dartmouth Street, Westminster[128]

The money Sheridan paid so reluctantly may have been from a combination of the benefit money and other money owed to Stephen Storace.

---

[125] *The Diary of Benjamin Robert Haydon*, ed. Willard B. Pope, 5 vols. (Cambridge, Mass., 1963), iii. 61.

[126] *Some Account of the English Stage, from the Restoration in 1660 to 1830*, 10 vols. (Bath, 1832), vii. 245.

[127] Drury Lane Ledger, fo. 95ᵛ.

[128] Letter from Mary Storace (BL Add. MS 29,261, fo. 54). The letter probably dates from June 1799, the only month in which payments of £12 to Mary Storace are recorded (Drury Lane Ledger, fo. 95ᵛ), and implies that payments were continued into 1800.

Sheridan did not pay all his debts to Storace because, as late as 1802, Cobb wrote what he called a 'joint Claim of the late Mr. Storace and myself, (Mr. Storace's part of this Claim being as I understand adjusted with Interest thereon, by Mr. Sheridan' for unpaid profits of authors' nights as far back as *The Doctor and the Apothecary* in 1788, and including all Cobb's and Storace's joint enterprises.[129] Cobb's share—which included one copyright claim and interest—totalled £865. 10s. 9d. Storace's would have been slightly less.

Joseph Dale, who had published Storace's operas for six years, issued *The Iron Chest* and *Mahmoud* in one volume, both as a memorial to Storace and for his family's financial benefit. The title-page reads:

The Favourite Operas of Mahmoud & the Iron Chest, composed by Stephen Storace[.] Adapted for the Piano Forte or Harpsichord by Joseph Mazzinghi. To the Public Patrons and Private Friends of Worth and Genius, These last labours of a life Devoted to the Study of Musical Science and Shortened by Unremitted Application and Anxiety in the pursuit of it are respectfully inscribed by the Widow of Stephen Storace. London, Printed for & Sold by Mrs. Storace, No. 29 Howland Street. Also Sold by J. Dale, No. 19 Cornhill and the Corner of Holles Street, Oxford Street.

The title-page includes the only known portrait of Storace, engraved anonymously and presumably from memory (Fig. 1.1). A list of subscribers follows.

Mary Storace remarried on 10 November 1801, as recorded in the *Gentleman's Magazine*: 'At Birmingham, the Rev. J. Kennedy, curate of Kimcote, co. Leicester, to Mrs. Storace, widow of the late composer.'[130] She probably kept in contact with the remaining members of the Storace family in London. In the early years of the nineteenth century, Prince Hoare wrote to Thomas Hill: 'I did not neglect to make your request to Sig[no]ra Storace, but she assures me she has no picture of herself in England—*The nearest to London* is in the possession of Mrs Stephen Storace at[?] Birmingham.'[131] Mary Storace was to be an executor, with Joseph Burchell, of Nancy Storace's will, dated 1797 and eventually executed in 1817. She was also a legatee. The will reads: 'I give and bequeath the sum of five hundred pounds and all my wearing Apparel to Mrs Mary Storace the Widow of my late Brother[.] I further bequeath unto her my Harp and all my

---

[129] Cobb to the proprietors of the Theatre Royal Drury Lane, 1 Jan. 1802, 'Receipts' (BL Add. MS 25,915), no. 6.

[130] *Gentleman's Magazine*, 90 (July–Dec. 1801), 1052.

[131] Prince Hoare to T. Hill, 18 Sept. [1805/6?] (BL Add. MS 20,081, fo. 187).

Fig. 1.1. Portrait of Storace; title-page of *Mahmoud* and *The Iron Chest* (London: Dale for Mary Storace [1797])

Music.'[132] In the event, Mary Storace must have died before her sister-in-law, because Burchell was listed as the surviving executor at the proving of the will.

Brinsley Storace, son of Stephen and Mary, would also have inherited £5,000 from his Aunt Nancy had he lived long enough.[133] In 1804 Brinsley went to work for John Soane, architect and family friend. Soane dismissed him in the autumn of 1805, thus eliciting an indignant letter from Mary Kennedy.[134] The problems were resolved, and Soane signed Brinsley's legal indentures on 25 March 1806 for five-and-a-half years.[135] Brinsley died before he completed his apprenticeship, and his death is recorded in the *Gentleman's Magazine* as taking place in March 1807.[136]

The Last of the Storaces

Nancy Storace died on 24 August 1817. She had lived for seventeen years with the tenor John Braham, by whom she had a son, William Spencer Harris Braham, in 1802. She retired from the stage on 30 May 1808, only two weeks before Michael Kelly. In 1816 she and Braham parted ways acrimoniously; they used John Soane as a 'common friend' in sorting out the division of their properties and discussing the future of their son Spencer.[137] Nancy spent the last year of her life with her mother, Elizabeth Storace, in Herne Hill. Letters from her mother to John Soane document the last days of Nancy's final illness and her own despair. Almost a month earlier, Elizabeth Storace had written that Nancy (whom she called Ann, her given name) was ill with 'a violent Fever & complaint in her Head—she is attended by doctor Hooper & the apothecary of Camberwell, the latter has attended her *twice* a day, she has undergone Cupping, Bleeding, Blistering, Leeches, *all* of which have been *repeated*—besides medicine in

---

[132] Will of Ann Selina Storace (London, Public Record Office, PROB 11/1597).

[133] Nancy's own son, Spencer, who had not been born when she made her will, would undoubtedly have disputed Brinsley's claim.

[134] Mary Kennedy to John Soane, 14 Nov. 1805 (Sir John Soane's Museum, Correspondence Cupboard (2), Division XV, Letter A, Packet 12, Item 1). The letter is transcribed in Arthur T. Bolton (ed.), *The Portrait of Sir John Soane, R. A. (1753–1837) Set Forth in Letters from his Friends (1775–1837)* (London, 1927), 127–8.

[135] Brinsley Storace's indentures (Sir John Soane's Museum, Correspondence Cupboard (2), Division XV, Letter C, Item 14).

[136] *Gentleman's Magazine*, 101 (Jan.–June 1807), 283.

[137] A large correspondence exists, most of it in Sir John Soane's Museum, Correspondence Cupboard (2), Division XIV, Letter H. Other items can be found elsewhere in the collection.

abundance.'[138] The night before Nancy died, her mother wrote: 'I'm *wretched* in the *Extreme*, all hopes are *gone*, she is alive, & that's all; I think e'er you receive this she'll be lost to us *for Ever*—oh! what will become of *me*? & her dear son?'[139]

Nancy was buried in Lambeth church; her memorial was designed by Soane with a verse by Prince Hoare.[140] Spencer, who was then at Winchester College, continued to live with his grandmother. He complained frequently to her about Winchester (where his father paid his fees) and eventually he was removed. A year later he was attending the 'Revd. Rann Kennedy's Free School' (later King Edward VI's High School) in Birmingham. Rann Kennedy, who was married to Mary Storace's sister Julia, was second master there during Spencer's stay.[141]

Elizabeth Storace outlived her daughter by four years. In 1819 she wrote to Soane: 'I grow *very* Infirm—but can expect no other *at my age.*'[142] She died two years later. James Winston recorded in his diary for 21 May 1821: 'This morning Braham went to Madame Storace's mother's funeral. She was eighty-two.'[143] In her will, made in 1817 when she was frightened by a mix-up about Nancy's will, Elizabeth Storace mentioned the same two sisters still living whom Nancy had included in her will twenty years earlier.[144] They were Sarah Trusler, spinster, and Catherine Legg (or Legge). There was no mention of her sister Mary or brother John (who died in 1820, after she wrote her will).[145] Her husband and both her children were dead, along with one of her two grandsons. Her daughter-in-law had remarried. She therefore made careful plans for her only surviving direct descendant, Spencer Braham. He was to inherit most of her money at the age of 23 if

---

[138] Elizabeth Storace to John Soane, 1 Aug. 1817 (Sir John Soane's Museum, Correspondence Cupboard (2), Division XIII, Letters A+B, Packet 35, Item 3).

[139] Elizabeth Storace to John Soane, 23 Aug. 1817 (Sir John Soane's Museum, Correspondence Cupboard (2), Division XIII, Letters A+B, Packet 35, Item 4).

[140] Prince Hoare to Elizabeth Storace, 17 Nov. 1817 (Sir John Soane's Museum, Correspondence Cupboard (1), Division IV (6), Item 65). Items 77 and 78 are copies of Hoare's text for the memorial. See also Stroud, *Sir John Soane*, 275.

[141] Spencer Braham to John Soane, 31 Mar. 1818 (Sir John Soane's Museum, Correspondence Cupboard (1), Division IV (6), Item 87). Rann Kennedy, an alumnus of the Free Grammar School as it was then called, taught there from 1799 and became Usher (second master) in 1808. Several of his sons had distinguished careers as educators and scholars, including Benjamin Hall Kennedy, the author of several Latin textbooks.

[142] Elizabeth Storace to John Soane, 5 Aug. 1819 (Sir John Soane's Museum, Correspondence Cupboard (2), Division XIII, Letters A+B, Packet 35, Item 8).

[143] James Winston, *Drury Lane Journal: Selections from James Winston's Diaries, 1819–1827*, ed. Alfred L. Nelson and Gilbert B. Cross (London, 1974), 30.

[144] Betty Matthews, 'Nancy Storace and the Royal Society of Musicians', *MT* 128 (1987), 326; Jane Girdham, 'The Last of the Storaces', *MT* 129 (1988), 17–18.

[145] Elizabeth Storace's will (London, Public Record Office, PROB 11/1686).

he had 'assumed and taken the final surname of Storace instead of or in addition to his present name of Braham unless my said trustees . . . shall deem it inexpedient for him so to do'. Thus she did her best to perpetuate the name of Storace, though Spencer seems to have taken the name only briefly, and that before his grandmother's death.

After an unsuccessful apprenticeship to an architect in Edinburgh around 1821,[146] Spencer Braham graduated from Lincoln College, Oxford, then took orders in the Church of England. He considered challenging his mother's will in 1824 on the understandable grounds that after his grandmother's life interest in his mother's shares had expired, he had more right to them than the distant cousins to whom they now passed.[147] In 1851 he changed his name to Meadows.[148] Spencer's direct line of descendants still survives.[149]

[146] John Braham to Spencer Braham, 25 Sept. 1821, in which he lectures on suitable behaviour for an apprentice, citing his own singing apprenticeship (Sir John Soane's Museum, Correspondence Cupboard (1), Division IV (6), Item 92).

[147] *Biographical Dictionary*, xiv. 302, quotes a letter from Spencer Braham to his father in which he tests his case.

[148] Matthews, 'Nancy Storace and the Royal Society', 326.

[149] Brace, *Anna . . . Susanna*, 124–5.

2

THEATRICAL LIFE IN THE
TIME OF STORACE

The role of music in the London theatres towards the end of the eighteenth century has been woefully underplayed in modern theatrical histories, which focus on spoken drama and therefore consider English operas only on the merits or otherwise of their words. This neglect extends from operas themselves to the musicians who made them possible, making it hard for us to appreciate either the importance of music in the 'whole show' or the active musical life of the theatres. Yet eighteenth-century audiences saw, heard, and enjoyed English operas, some of whose popularity continued for decades. By discussing theatrical life and procedures from a musical perspective, this chapter attempts to bring music in from the periphery of theatrical life so that it can share the central focus with spoken plays. It concentrates on Drury Lane because Stephen Storace worked there, but most of the general procedures are applicable to Covent Garden and to a lesser degree to the summer equivalent of these two, the Little Theatre in the Haymarket. Chapter 3 focuses on the theatrical musicians themselves.

The last part of the eighteenth century was one of the more settled periods of London's lively theatrical history. Legal issues such as licensing and censorship had been settled earlier in the century; by the 1780s they were accepted as irritating but permanent elements of theatrical organization and routine. Both winter and summer theatrical companies and their seasons were well established. The Drury Lane company was particularly stable between 1788 and 1796, which was coincidentally the exact tenure of both John Philip Kemble as manager and Stephen Storace as composer.[1] Kemble

---

[1] Kemble joined the Drury Lane company in 1783, became its acting manager early in the 1788/9 season, resigned as manager in Apr. 1796, but still continued to act there. After another short period as manager starting in Sept. 1800 he moved to Covent Garden.

took over the management from Thomas King, and answered to Richard Brinsley Sheridan, the active proprietor of the company.

Theatres and their Seasons

London's two theatrical seasons were well established by the last few decades of the eighteenth century. The main winter season ran roughly from September to June, and a much shorter and less important summer season lasted from June to September. Occasionally a theatre would extend its season beyond its normal end for a special show or to make up for lost shows, but seasons that overlapped by a few days caused no major upsets.

During the winter season, only the proprietors of the two Theatres Royal at Covent Garden and Drury Lane owned royal patents permitting them to perform spoken drama, including operas with spoken dialogue. The only other theatre open during the winter was the King's Theatre in the Haymarket, which was devoted exclusively to Italian opera and ballet, and geared towards a richer and more aristocratic audience than the English playhouses. The King's Theatre generally opened on Tuesdays and Saturdays, whereas Covent Garden and Drury Lane were open every night except Sunday.[2] These two, while certainly rivals, coexisted peaceably on the whole, with large enough followings to keep both institutions financially viable and with little overlap between their repertoires.

All three theatres closed during the summer. Covent Garden and Drury Lane remained shut for about three months when the Little Theatre ran its season and other social and cultural activities took precedence. Summer attractions included concerts at the various pleasure gardens, especially at Vauxhall and Ranelagh towards the end of the century. Members of the theatre companies could choose between resting for the summer, touring the provinces and Ireland, performing at the pleasure gardens, and joining the company at the Little Theatre.[3]

The Little Theatre also staged operas on a smaller scale than the two patent theatres. It was licensed by the Lord Chamberlain to stage works with spoken dialogue during the summer, solely because Samuel Foote,

---

[2] The Italian opera company sometimes started its season later than the patent theatres; their twice-weekly performances were often expanded to a third night—usually Thursday—for singers' benefit performances.

[3] Kemble, for instance, regularly took provincial tours during the summer. Representative lists of engagements were Dublin, Cork, and Limerick (1797), and York, Birmingham, Cheltenham and Gloucester (alternating nights), Margate, and Brighton (1799).

proprietor from 1747 to 1776, had been granted a patent for life in 1766 as compensation for an accident in which he lost his leg by falling from the Duke of York's horse.[4] When George Colman senior bought the Little Theatre in 1776, he was granted a summer licence by the Lord Chamberlain, renewable annually. In 1789 Colman's son George took over after his father's mental breakdown, and continued the arrangement with the Lord Chamberlain when he became proprietor after his father's death in 1794.

The Drury Lane and Covent Garden theatres were affiliated to opposing political parties towards the end of the century. Covent Garden sided with Pitt and the government; Drury Lane of course supported its owner, Richard Brinsley Sheridan, who was a leading Whig Member of Parliament. George Colman at the Little Theatre tried to be politically neutral, taking actors and audiences from both winter playhouses.[5] Newspaper reviews, like the theatres and newspapers themselves, were supposedly politically partisan;[6] even so, there is no obvious bias in either ministerial or opposition papers towards Storace's operas.

The Theatres Royal were closed on Sundays and on various annual dates including Ash Wednesday and Holy Week (or 'Passion Week' as Kemble called it).[7] In addition, Wednesdays and Fridays in Lent—eleven days in all—were devoted to oratorios and similar pieces in place of staged works. At Drury Lane Thomas Linley, who was part-owner with his son-in-law Sheridan, shared direction of the oratorio performances until he retired after the 1793/4 season; thereafter the theatre was closed on oratorio nights.

Two theatre closings in the late eighteenth century affected Storace and his company. First, on 17 June 1789 the King's Theatre burned down. Nancy Storace, who had been singing Italian opera there, then moved to Drury Lane where she took leading roles in almost all her brother's operas. Thus he gained the best comic soprano of the time. The second event was the closing of Drury Lane two years later, on 4 June 1791. The theatre was condemned as unsafe, and demolished; it remained inoperative for almost three seasons while it was rebuilt. For the 1791/2 season and part of the 1792/3 season the Drury Lane company took over the rebuilt King's

---

[4] Simon Trefman, *Sam. Foote, Comedian, 1720–1777* (New York, 1971), 148–9, 158–9.

[5] Lucyle Werkmeister, *A Newspaper History of England 1792–1793* (Lincoln, Nebr., 1967), 42.

[6] Ibid. 22, 30–1, 43. See also Jeremy Black, *The English Press in the Eighteenth Century* (London, 1987), ch. 5; A. Aspinall, *Politics and the Press c.1780–1850* (Brighton, 1973), *passim*.

[7] The regular dates the theatres closed were 'Christmas Eve, Christmas Day, 30 January (the anniversary of the execution of Charles I), Ash Wednesday, Holy Week, Whitsun Eve, on days of General Fast or Thanksgiving (as proclaimed by the crown) and in periods of mourning for members of the royal family' (*London Stage*, pt. 5, p. 1087 n. 8).

Theatre, which then had no Italian company in residence. After a new Italian company formed early in 1793, the Drury Lane company continued to use the theatre except on Tuesdays and Saturdays (Italian opera nights), when they used Colman's Little Theatre across the road. The Little Theatre was otherwise closed during the winter because Colman had only a summer licence. The following paragraph on a playbill for 5 February 1793 explained the situation to the public:

The King's Theatre having been rented to the Proprietors of Drury-Lane House, with a reserve of the Nights for the Italian Opera, to be carried on there for the Opera Trust; the Drury-Lane Patent will in future, be moved on Tuesdays and Saturdays, to the Theatre Royal: Hay-Market, where all the Old and New Renters, claiming under the Drury-Lane Patent, will be entitled to Free Admission, and to their Rents for each Night of Performance.

For most of the following season the Drury Lane company was temporarily disbanded. Colman rented Drury Lane's patent for £15 a night, hired some of the Drury Lane players along with some of his own summer company, and ran a winter season of his own.[8] Storace's contribution to Colman's season was *My Grandmother* for his sister's benefit night in December 1793.

After many delays, the new Drury Lane theatre opened on 12 March 1794 for a month of oratorio performances, then became fully operational on 21 April for the remainder of the season. The new theatre was much larger, seating over 3,600 instead of 2,000, thus making much greater demands on actors and singers. The loss of intimacy provoked many comments, including one from the Honourable John Byng:

Restore me, ye overuling powers to the drama, to the warm close, observant, seats of Old Drury where I may comfortably criticise and enjoy the delights of scenic fancy: These now are past! The nice discriminations, of the actors face, and of the actors feeling, are now all lost in the vast void of the new theatre of Drury Lane.[9]

The Drury Lane management extended the 1793/4 season some three weeks to 7 July, to make as much profit as possible. To this end they also permitted no personal benefit performances, both because of the small amount of the season remaining and because of the high cost of rebuilding. The only charity benefit staged that season was held for 'the Relief of the Widows and Orphans of the brave Men who fell in the late glorious

---

[8] *London Stage*, pt. 5, p. 1570. Because a patent was personal property rather than the theatre's, it could be sold, bequeathed, or, as in this case, rented.

[9] *The Torrington Diaries, Containing the Tours Through England and Wales of the Hon. John Byng (Later Fifth Viscount Torrington) Between the Years 1781 and 1794*, ed. C. Bruyn Andrews, 4 vols. (New York, 1938), iv. 18.

Actions under Earl Howe' on 2 July.[10] The pieces performed were David Garrick's play *The Country Girl* and *The Glorious First of June*, an occasional piece with words by James Cobb and others, and music by Storace. The night's receipts for this popular cause were an unprecedented £1,526. 11*s.* 0*d.*, the biggest takings of the entire century.[11] In subsequent seasons the routine settled back to normal.

The Evening's Entertainment: Norms and Exceptions

An evening's entertainment at a London theatre normally consisted of two substantive pieces, interspersed with various songs, dances, and other light forms of entertainment. The performance started with the biggest piece of the evening, a mainpiece play or opera, and ended with an afterpiece. The latter was both shorter and more frivolous, and Kemble usually referred to it as 'the farce'. The two pieces were advertised in many of the London newspapers on the day of the performance, often the day before, and sometimes up to a week in advance. The miscellaneous smaller items that were played in between acts and between the two pieces were seldom advertised, so our information comes from reviewers' comments and playbills of benefit performances (where they were indeed often announced).

Occasionally the usual plan of mainpiece followed by afterpiece was changed. The substitution of three 'afterpieces' (in other words, short pieces) for mainpiece and afterpiece was comparatively common at the Little Theatre but rare at the Theatres Royal, although it was occasionally necessitated by a player's indisposition. In substitutions, two short works were considered the equivalent of one long one. Thus, on 11 December 1793, *The Deaf Lover*, *The Mock Doctor*, and *No Song, No Supper* (all normally afterpieces) were substituted for *The Chapter of Accidents* and *The Prize* (a mainpiece and afterpiece), which had been announced on the previous day's bill.

This difference between managements' attitudes at Drury Lane and the Little Theatre can be illustrated by the performances of Storace's afterpiece *My Grandmother*, first performed at the Little Theatre when Drury Lane was closed for rebuilding. In 1793/4, *My Grandmother* was performed twenty-four times in the Little Theatre's special winter season, on eighteen of those occasions as one of three short works. By contrast, when

---

[10] *Times*, 2 July 1794.   [11] *London Stage*, pt. 5, p. 1570.

it was played at Drury Lane after the new theatre building was opened, *My Grandmother* was almost always the afterpiece following a normal mainpiece. It was one of three pieces only nine times out of sixty between 1794 and 1800. Three of those nine were benefit performances, which were often more varied in their contents than normal nights.[12]

The reason that benefit nights sometimes broke with the usual plan was that the beneficiary was permitted a say in the programme. There was a tendency to increase its size, both to attract a larger audience (and therefore the amount of the receipts) and to give broader scope to the beneficiary's talents.[13] The entr'acte entertainments were often especially elaborate or spectacular, and sometimes the evening's bill comprised three short works. For example, at the singer Richard Suett's benefit at Drury Lane on 4 May 1790, *The College of Physicians*, *The Heiress*, and *The Doctor and the Apothecary* were performed, and at Elizabeth Leak's benefit on 21 May 1795, *The Child of Nature*, *My Grandmother*, and *The Sultan* were staged.

Exceptional combinations of pieces occurred in other circumstances too. When the Drury Lane company moved to the King's Theatre in September 1791, James Cobb wrote an occasional prelude entitled *Poor Old Drury* on the subject of the upheavals caused by the move. This prefaced the normal two pieces for the first twelve nights of the season. However, not all such groupings are easy to understand. On two occasions in 1797, 21 February and 9 March, four pieces were performed together at Drury Lane, both times including Storace's *Lodoiska*, which was itself an unusually long afterpiece.

As well as combining long and short works, theatre managers provided variety by ensuring a careful balance between plays and operas. When the mainpiece was an opera, the afterpiece was normally entirely spoken, and vice versa. Sometimes two plays were performed on one night, but only exceptionally were two musical works heard together. Specific mainpieces and afterpieces were rarely paired deliberately for more than one performance, though sometimes two works coincided several times at the height of their popularity.[14] Naturally there were occasional exceptions. A whole

---

[12] Benefit nights were 21 May 1795 for Elizabeth Leak; 31 May 1796 for Whitfield; 14 June 1796 for the boxkeepers.

[13] St Vincent Troubridge, *The Benefit System in the British Theatre* (London, 1967), ch. 11: 'Making up the Bill'.

[14] For instance, Storace's *The Haunted Tower* was often performed with the pantomime *Harlequin's Frolicks* between 29 Dec. 1789 and the pantomime's last performance on 4 Feb. 1790, because *The Haunted Tower*'s successful opening season (première 24 Nov. 1789) coincided with the pantomime season.

evening of opera could be scheduled, more often at the Little Theatre than at the Theatres Royal. At Drury Lane whole evenings of opera were most often staged for singers' benefits. For instance, four of Nancy Storace's annual benefits consisted entirely of music, all of it by her brother.[15] Other instances include Jack Bannister's benefit at Drury Lane on 8 April 1793, when Storace's *The Pirates* and Arnold's *The Agreeable Surprise* were performed, and Kelly's benefit on 16 April 1790, when Kelly sang in two operas including the première of Storace's afterpiece *No Song, No Supper.*

When members of the royal family attended the theatre they sometimes requested particular pieces.[16] The announcement 'by Command of Their Majesties' was guaranteed to attract a large audience, and the choice of pieces was not dictated by the usual theatre policy. Thus, on 15 December 1790, Storace's two operas *The Haunted Tower* and *No Song, No Supper* were performed together at Drury Lane. Similarly, his *The Pirates* and *The Doctor and the Apothecary* were both played on 14 December 1792. On 3 February 1794 at the Little Theatre, three operatic afterpieces by Storace and Prince Hoare, *My Grandmother, No Song, No Supper,* and *The Prize,* were performed by royal command. This night turned out to be the worst theatrical disaster of the century. As Kelly describes it:

The crowd was so great, that at the opening of the doors, in going down the steps which led to the pit, three or four persons slipped and fell, and several others were hurried over them; sixteen people were trampled to death, and upwards of twenty were taken up with broken limbs. The news of this fatal accident was, very judiciously, kept from their Majesties until after the performance was over, when they evinced the deepest sorrow and regret at the event.[17]

The next day a disclaimer was attached to the playbill stating that the accident 'arose entirely from the eagerness of the croud'; nevertheless, the newspapers criticized the theatre management for weeks afterwards and made some constructive suggestions on how to improve crowd control. A few minor alterations were effected.

Variety was perhaps the most important element in the miscellaneous acts that were scattered throughout an evening's programme. In the last twenty years of the eighteenth century, singing dominated dancing; other attractions included virtuoso instrumental performances, monologues, and mimicry. Two singers' benefits will serve as illustrations of the most

---

[15] See *London Stage* for 5 Feb. 1791, 11 Mar. 1793, 16 Dec. 1793, and 9 May 1796.

[16] Harry W. Pedicord, *'By Their Majesties' Command': The House of Hanover at the London Theatres, 1714–1800* (London, 1991), 35–6.

[17] *Reminiscences*, ii. 56.

typical acts, though on normal nights there would have been fewer. It is important to realize that music was prominent in all entr'acte entertainments, not just at the singers' benefits which are used here as examples.

When Margaret Martyr, a singer at Covent Garden, held her benefit on 9 May 1794, four complete works were performed: *Hartford Bridge*, *The Follies of a Day*, *Love and Honour* (a pastiche arranged specially for that night, with music by Shield, Reeve, Storace, and Parke), and *The Prisoner at Large*. This already long programme was expanded by several shorter items. The ballet *The Lucky Escape* was danced in *Hartford Bridge*, presumably between acts; Charles Incledon sang 'Water parted from the sea' (which came from Arne's Italianate opera, *Artaxerxes*) 'after the manner of a celebrated Italian Opera Singer', and after Act 1 of *The Prisoner at Large* he sang the well-known 'Sally in our alley'.

The benefit performance for Storace's widow, held on 25 May 1796, which was naturally dominated by Storace's music, included several extra items. Its three main works were Storace's last (unfinished) opera, *Mahmoud*, *A Dramatic Cento* (with music compiled for the occasion from works by Storace), and *The Sultan*. Entr'acte entertainments were the ballet *Little Peggy's Love* (performed by dancers from the Italian opera company at the King's Theatre) and, at the end of the entire evening, the finale from Storace's *The Iron Chest*. In *The Sultan*, Nancy Storace (who did not usually perform in the piece) inserted two of Stephen's most popular songs.

THE AUDIENCE

Each evening's show was designed to draw a big audience to the theatre. All London audiences had a powerful influence on productions at the playhouses, not just members of the royal family who could demand a favourite show, but also the regular middle-class theatregoer who had other ways of expressing his or her opinion. The audiences at the Theatres Royal were made up of people from virtually every social sphere:

The upper classes still sat in the front and side boxes; the 'critics' and professional men, civil servants, tradesmen and a general cross-section of the middle class in the pit and lower gallery; the working class, including servants, journeymen, apprentices, sailors and the women-folk, in the upper gallery.[18]

Such seating arrangements were naturally reflected in ticket prices. Prices for the Drury Lane company from 1791 onwards were as follows (not

[18] Michael R. Booth *et al.*, *The 'Revels' History of Drama in English*, vi: *1750–1880* (London, 1975), 4.

taking into account the annual subscriptions paid by some patrons at both theatres):

Seating	Price	'Half Price'
Boxes	6s. 0d.	3s. 0d.
Pit [orchestra]	3s. 6d.	2s. 0d.
First gallery	2s. 0d.	1s. 0d.
Second gallery	1s. 0d.	6d.

Compare these figures with a 2-guinea ticket for a box at the Italian opera and it becomes clear how the Italian opera audience retained its exclusivity. To give some perspective to the value of these prices, a careful family 'could hope to keep itself out of debt on a pound a week', according to Roy Porter.[19] At the Theatres Royal, which catered to working people, a person was charged 'half price' for admission after the end of Act 3 of the mainpiece (in a five-act piece). On occasional special nights no discounts were allowed.

The only seats that could be booked in advance were the boxes—for which purpose the 'box office' was available. Other patrons bought 'tickets', which were reusable metal tokens, at the door. Benefit nights were exceptional, with the beneficiaries selling tickets in advance. The seats the audience then took were benches running the width of the auditorium without any central aisle. Chairs were only used as the front seats of some boxes. Servants often kept places for their employers in the boxes, because many members of the audience considered any empty place their prerogative, booked or not.[20]

The management took audience response seriously, and adjusted their schedules accordingly. At certain times of year, they also planned in accordance with particular traditions. Christmas was pantomime season; at Easter the theatres tended to cater to the lower classes and children by putting on boisterous comedies.[21] Towards the end of the season, often starting on Easter Monday but more frequently in May, they sometimes deferred to their own performers, who chose the programmes for their benefit nights.

Audiences were vociferous in their reactions. Their behaviour could be unmannerly; they were persistent in their demands for explanations of changes in the cast or programme, and they expressed their disapproval freely and often enough to make diversionary tactics necessary on occasion.

[19] *English Society in the Eighteenth Century* (Harmondsworth, 1982), 13.
[20] *London* Stage, pt. 5, pp. xxvi–xxvii, xxxi.
[21] Leo Hughes, *The Drama's Patrons* (Austin, Tex., 1971), 159–62.

As Kemble wrote in a note to himself: 'Whenever there is Danger of a Riot, always act an Opera; for Musick drowns the Noise of opposition.'[22] Kemble demonstrated his acumen on the occasion of the Drury Lane company's opening night at the King's Theatre in 1791, when the doors were not opened on time and chaos ensued. As Kelly reports:

The doors were not opened at the hour announced in the bills of the day; the crowd was immense, and when they entered the house, they could not find their way to the different places; all was hurry, bustle, and confusion. The prelude [*Poor Old Drury*] began with Palmer and Parsons, who attempted to address the infuriated audience in vain; they were obliged to retire; the manager was called for, and Kemble came forward; a paper was given to him from the pit, stating, that the cause of their disapprobation was the delay in opening the doors, and the great inconvenience of the passages. Kemble stood the fire well, and assured them, those inconveniences should be remedied on the next evening's performances.

The storm then ceased; the handing up the paper (which was done by a friend of the management) was a lucky *ruse*, and did great credit to the projector, General John Kemble himself.[23]

The real cause of the protest was the rise in ticket prices that had just taken place. However, a few days later Kemble was able to comment: 'The Opposition to the raised Prices so completely over, that not one voice complained of them.'[24] A year later, Covent Garden had a similar problem. As Kemble described, 'Great Riot at Covt. Garden on account of raised Prices, & taking away the Upper Gallery—The Town was promised an Upper Gallery.'[25] Two days later he wrote, 'We acted to-night to divide the Covt. Garden Rioters, if possible. The Riot was totally quell'd to-night.'

The audience at the King's Theatre was generally polite, but factions could be unruly. In 1795 Michael Kelly (who was a regular performer at Drury Lane and an occasional one with the Italian opera company) took the brunt of some Italian prejudice:

It was not without great indignation that we saw a *miserable Italian Cabal* in the Pit for the purpose of opposing the appearance of this favourite Performer upon the Italian Stage. . . . We trust, that the readiness which he has manifested upon this occasion to oblige, will not be damped by the malevolence of a few miscreants, who are probably hired to support the hopeless cause of some discarded Performer. Mr. Kelly ought to think alone on the liberal and just applause of the elegant part of the Audience, nor cast away a single thought on the miserable though malignant efforts of a pitiful cabal.[26]

---

[22] Memoranda A, fo. 139. [23] *Reminiscences*, ii. 16. [24] Memoranda A, 24 Sept. 1791.
[25] Memoranda A, 17 and 19 Sept. 1792. [26] *True Briton*, 9 Feb. 1795.

Audience behaviour was normally reasonable as long as its members thought they were being treated fairly. If an actor they expected to see was not going to perform, they wanted an explanation. The following paragraph in *The Times* refers to such a situation at Covent Garden:

Bannister was so ill on Saturday night that he could not perform *Giles*, in the Maid of the Mill. *Reeve* had never studied the part, and there not being any other person in the house who could undertake the part, necessity borrowed *Williames* from Drury-lane, for whose appearance an apology was made to the audience.[27]

Audience members expected value for money, but could be understanding as long as they were treated to an explanation or apology for any alterations. One of the most common reasons for altering a programme was when singers' voices were not up to par. This could mean changing an entire work, or making a minor alteration such as in the incident described below:

Kelly omitted his *bravura* in the last act—but the audience were unwilling to lose it—the performance was therefore interrupted till Kelly appeased the discontented party, by assuring them his exertions on that and the previous evening had rendered him so hoarse, that he was unable to go through so difficult a song; his apology was accepted—and the omission allowed—.[28]

Kelly's breaking out of character was clearly more acceptable to the audience than his silently omitting the song it was waiting for.

Audience reaction occasionally had a real effect on the action on stage. An accident involving Anna Crouch and Kelly in a performance of Storace's *Lodoiska* proved ultimately successful when (in Kelly's version at least) he rescued her from flames and a fall, then,

catching her in my arms, scarcely knowing what I was doing, I carried her to the front of the stage, a considerable distance from the place where we fell. The applause was loud and continued. . . . I always afterwards carried her to the front of the stage, in a similar manner, and it never failed to produce great applause.—Such are, at times, the effects of accident.[29]

Finally, the audience always expressed its collective opinion at the end of a work, and its degree of enthusiasm was often reported in the newspapers. At the première of a new work, this took on extra significance because the audience not only applauded the show it had just seen but also responded to the promise of its repeat performance. Normally an announcement of the next's night's show was made at the end of the mainpiece, but when

---

[27] *Times*, 19 Apr. 1790.   [28] *Thespian Magazine*, 1 (1792), 126.
[29] Kelly, *Reminiscences*, ii. 60. Anna Crouch's account differs in detail.

the afterpiece was new it was held back until the end of the evening. Thus, two days after the première of Storace's first English opera, the *Times* critic reported that 'the *Doctor* and the *Apothecary* was given out for this evening without a dissenting voice; and will have, no doubt, a very great run.'[30] When *The Siege of Belgrade* was given its first performance two years later, it 'was announced for a second representation amidst the most flattering marks of approbation, in which their Royal Highnesses the Prince of Wales and Duke of Clarence took the lead'.[31] Lest it should be thought that audiences reacted favourably out of mere politeness, the following remark was made about *The Iron Chest* after its première: 'The Piece was given out by Bannister Jun. for a second representation, when Mr. Kemble should be well enough to appear, amidst a mixture of disapprobation and applause.'[32]

Lack of enthusiasm was more often left unmentioned.

The Progress of a Production

Preparations for the staging of plays and operas were roughly the same, except for music rehearsals, usually taking a month or more. Rehearsals took place, the Lord Chamberlain's office had to approve the text, publicity was distributed, and, in the case of an opera, song texts were prepared for sale on the opening night.

We know a few details about rehearsal procedures from a short series of records kept on the backs of playbills by William Powell, the Drury Lane prompter, between April 1794 and March 1795.[33] Rehearsals almost always took place in the mornings and lasted for one or two hours. Thus a player would have time to be ready for a performance in the evening, leaving the stage hands time to set up the scenery. Readings were held in the green room, full rehearsals on the stage. A new work was given a substantial number of rehearsals before its première and a few more after the first night. A play already in the repertoire usually needed one or two run-throughs before its first performance each season.

Three operas by Storace were first performed during the period Powell

---

[30] *Times*, 27 Oct. 1788.   [31] *Times*, 3 Jan. 1791.   [32] *True Briton*, 14 Mar. 1796.

[33] Drury Lane playbills, owned by William Powell (BL, 'Drury Lane, vols. 4 and 5'), as recorded in *The London Stage*, pt. 5, p. cxlv n. 192, p. 1675, and as incorporated into the calendar. See also Charles Beecher Hogan, 'An Eighteenth-Century Prompter's Notes', *Theatre Notebook*, 10 (1955–6), 37–44. Powell was working at Drury Lane by 1784, was assistant prompter by 1791, and became prompter, thus effectively assistant manager, from Apr. 1793 until his death in 1812 (*Biographical Dictionary*, xii. 140–3).

kept records: *Lodoiska*, *The Glorious First of June*, and *The Cherokee*. *Lodoiska* and *The Cherokee* followed similar patterns, and are probably typical for operas. *Lodoiska* had a month's rehearsals before its première on 9 June 1794, with music rehearsals scheduled early on. Two further rehearsals were held after 9 June, to smooth over cuts made after the première and for other minor improvements. A few more rehearsals preceded the first performance of the following season. Powell's records for *The Cherokee* cover only its first season. As a mainpiece, it was given slightly more rehearsal time than *Lodoiska*. Again, music rehearsals started early in the five weeks of preparation. Two days after the première, on 22 December 1794, a rehearsal was held, no doubt necessitated by an alteration announced on that night's playbill, in which 'The Public are respectfully informed that the War-Whoop Chorus, which was so much honoured with their Approbation, is now removed to the End of the First Act.'[34]

There was no time for the usual series of rehearsals for *The Glorious First of June*. It was an occasional piece designed as a fund-raiser for the families of men killed on 1 June 1794 under Earl Howe against the French, and written, rehearsed, and performed all in a few days. First came three dance rehearsals, before the text was completed. Then followed a mere two full rehearsals. Time was so short that the theatre had to be closed for an evening. As the playbill for 30 June explained: 'On Account of the Preparations for the New Entertainment on Wednesday, there will be no Play at this Theatre To-morrow Evening.' Even so, the piece was under-rehearsed, as implied by a review in *The Times* on 2 July: 'The new Piece . . . may be fairly exempted from passing the ordeal of criticism, as having been written so much on the spur of the occasion, that the copy, we understand, was not delivered to the Prompter till Monday morning.' The closure of the theatre for rehearsals was rare but not unique. On 9 February 1795 the Drury Lane playbill read: '*On account of the indispensable necessity of having an Evening's Rehearsal of [Alexander the Great], Ladies and Gentlemen will please take notice there can be No Play at this Theatre on Wednesday Evening* [11 February].'

While rehearsals were in progress, the theatre manager was responsible for submitting the text of a new play or opera to the Lord Chamberlain's office for licensing and censorship. John Larpent was appointed Examiner of Plays in 1778, and held the office until his death in 1824. Many of the copies sent to Larpent now form the Larpent Collection in the Huntington Library in San Marino, California. Although not every manuscript survives,

---

[34] Printed slip attached to Kemble's playbill, as quoted in the *London Stage*, 22 Dec. 1794.

the collection is a remarkable source of theatrical works, many of which were never printed.

Normal procedure was as follows. A fair manuscript copy of every staged work (whether or not it contained spoken dialogue), prefaced by a dated letter of application from the theatre manager, was sent to the Lord Chamberlain's office at some time prior to the first performance. By law the text had to arrive a fortnight before the première, but, to judge from Storace's operas, that deadline was entirely ignored. Texts were sent anywhere from thirteen days in advance (once only) to a single day before (for *The Glorious First of June*). Tardiness did not seem to incur any penalty. The Examiner of Plays then read the play, censored any passages he considered unsuitable for public performance, and informed the theatre of any alterations he required. It is not entirely clear how Larpent conveyed his alterations to the theatre managers. He may have returned the edited manuscripts on the understanding they would be sent back to him again.[35] If so, he must have been particularly insistent, given the large collection he amassed. The manager then had to pay 2 guineas for a licence. Again, promptness was not an issue. Entries in the Drury Lane Paybook indicate that some fees were paid just before the première and others several months later.[36]

Most of the Examiner's censorship involved short cuts in the text, often of derogatory allusions to the political system or to the upper classes. Two cuts made to Act 2, scene 2 of James Cobb's libretto for *The Haunted Tower* are typical. They are shown below in italics:

LORD WILLIAM (in disguise). Ha! ha! ha! You mistake us, my Lord, we Jesters are privileged, *for we dare speak truth to Princes without the danger of losing our place.*

BARON. That's a slap at me now I dare say, tho' I don't understand it.

LORD WILLIAM. We anatomize Vice and Folly.

[Immediately after the song 'Tho' time has from your Lordship's face':]

BARON. Sir, let me tell you Jesters may be impertinent[.]

LORD WILLIAM. Impertinent!

BARON. Nay I only speak my opinion, what say you my pretty Lass[?]

LADY ELINOR (in disguise). I believe, my Lord, we are seldom angry at a jest, Except we feel the satire to be true.

BARON. That's another slap.[37]

---

[35] Leonard W. Conolly, *The Censorship of English Drama 1737–1824* (San Marino, Ca., 1976), 19. See also Vincent J. Liesenfeld, *The Licensing Act of 1737* (Madison, Wis., 1984), *passim*.

[36] Drury Lane Paybook B, fo. 35ᵛ. The list covers the period from 1 Jan. 1791 to the end of the 1794/5 season. No fee is recorded for *The Cave of Trophonius*.

[37] *The Haunted Tower* (Larpent MS 850), Act 2, scene 2.

After the cuts were made, the last sentence reads as a response to the song, which is indeed barbed.

Occasionally the Examiner required alterations of an extent that made rewriting necessary, such as those made to Colman's text for *The Iron Chest*, based on William Godwin's recent novel *Caleb Williams*. The original version sent to Larpent is lost, but some emendations survive that were sent to him the day before the première with the following note from William Powell: 'The inclosed Speeches intended to be introduced in the *Iron Chest*—They are meant merely to connect, where omissions have been made according to your directions.'[38] Larpent hardly ever refused a licence outright. Even on the few occasions he did, the piece could be reworked, resubmitted, and accepted.[39]

To judge from the manuscripts of Storace's operas, the Examiner was not concerned with song texts.[40] In fact he did not always read them, because some manuscript librettos were left incomplete. Sometimes, as in *The Glorious First of June*, spaces are left for songs; sometimes they are written in another hand or obviously added later. Larpent seems to have made no attempt to see the missing verses, and all of Storace's operas were approved.

Quite obviously, time constraints did not allow a theatre manager to wait for the Lord Chamberlain's approval before preparing a work for performance. Since experience showed that major adjustments were rarely required, he went ahead in good faith. Thus, when Kemble sent *Lodoiska* to the Lord Chamberlain's office on 30 May 1794, rehearsals had already been in progress for three weeks; similarly, when he sent *The Cherokee* on 18 December 1794, rehearsals had been running for a month and the première was only two days away.

While the theatre was preparing a new work for production, the author was often preparing the text for publication. As a result of the different interests and responsibilities involved, printed texts sometimes differ considerably from Larpent's manuscripts and do not always incorporate his emendations.[41] Song texts, on the other hand, were the responsibility of the theatre management, who had them printed for sale at the door.

[38] *The Iron Chest* ['Speeches to be Introduced in'], Larpent MS 1116.

[39] Only seven works were refused licences between 1776 and 1800. Three of these were accepted after rewriting (*London Stage*, pt. 5, p. clxxi).

[40] Only one of the cuts made to song texts of Storace's operas was possibly by the censor, although it does not fit any of the criteria usually used for censorship. The line drawn through a stanza of 'The pleasures of life are in madness' (*The Cave of Trophonius*, Larpent MS 899, p. 51) could equally well have been made by a member of the theatre company in rehearsal.

[41] Dougald MacMillan (comp.), *Catalogue of the Larpent Plays in the Huntington Library* (San Marino, Ca., 1939), p. viii.

Advance publicity was essential to the theatres. Both Drury Lane and Covent Garden made regular arrangements with certain newspapers to print advertisements for upcoming programmes. From the late 1760s to 1782 the *Gazeteer* and the *Public Advertiser* had actually paid the theatres for the privilege; by Storace's time the theatres paid the papers, but only the advertising stamp duty rather than the much larger real cost.[42]

Advertisements appeared in the first column of the front page on the day of performance and often in advance. The body of an advertisement usually contained the titles of the pieces, principal actors, ticket prices, times of performance, and names of composers (but not authors). Male performers were listed first, though exceptions were made. Nancy Storace, for instance, headed the cast list for her debut at Drury Lane on 24 November 1789. Another form of advertising was the puff, paid for at the full advertising price.[43]

Single-sheet playbills, large and small, included the same information as the newspaper advertisements. Drury Lane's playbills were printed by Charles Lowndes, whose premises were 'next the Stage-Door' at 66 Drury Lane. Each day's bill contained the following day's programme at the bottom and, towards the end of the century, an outline of the following week's pieces. Often a performance was described at the top of the playbill as, for instance, 'the thirty-third night'. In 1794 Tate Wilkinson described this numbering system as 'the new-fangled manner of advertising', though in fact it had been going on for several years.[44] The 'big bills' were posted outside the theatre and in other locations by 'billstickers' employed by the theatres.[45]

Small bills were sold by the 'book women' or 'orange-sellers', so called because they sold fruit for refreshment, but who also sold play and song texts (which, having cast lists at the front, also acted as programmes), and playbills. These women were not employed by the theatre management but worked on concession. At Drury Lane in the 1790s they were organized by a Miss Giles. Kemble described the system in his diary:

Miss Giles allows them no Profit whatever on the Sale of the Books,—so they think themselves entitled to extort what they can from the Audience. . . .

Each woman in the Boxes and Pit pays Miss Giles one Guinea at the beginning of the Season, another the week before Lent, and half a Crown at Xmas,

[42] Robert L. Haig, *The Gazeteer 1735–1797: A Study in the Eighteenth-Century English Newspaper* (Carbondale, Ill., 1960), 222–3.

[43] Ibid. 223. See also *The History of* The Times, i: *'The Thunderer' in the Making 1785–1841* (London, 1935), 47–8.

[44] *The Wandering Patentee*, 4 vols. (York, 1795), iv. 62.

[45] An unspecified number of billstickers at Drury Lane were paid a total of £1. 16s. 0d. per week in the early 1790s (Drury Lane Paybook B, fos. 51, 75 ff.).

besides eight pence halfpenny every Saturday for her six nightly Play-bills and the Paper that lines her Fruit-basket.[46]

Their charging had obviously got out of hand, because the following message appeared on the Drury Lane playbill for 2 January 1795:

The Public are respectfully informed, that, a sufficient Profit being allowed to the Persons who sell Plays and Books of Songs in the Theatre; those Persons are forbidden to demand for such Plays, or Books of Songs, more than the Price marked thereon, upon pain of dismission from their employ.

Song texts were always available on opening nights, advertised on playbills as 'books of the Songs to be had at the Theatre'. Play texts became available between a week and a month later, a situation that provoked the critic Thomas Dutton to express his chagrin: 'Why *prose-dialogue* should not be entitled to the same privileges and advantages as *sing-song*, we must confess ourselves utterly at a loss to ascertain.'[47] The print run for song texts of *The Haunted Tower* was 3,000 copies, for which the theatre charged Miss Giles £54.[48]

Opening Night and Beyond

Opening night brought reviewers from the daily press out in force. Reviews also appeared in a variety of monthly magazines, ranging from the *European Magazine*, which routinely culled large excerpts from reviews printed in the daily papers, to the *Thespian Magazine*, a short-lived journal with the worthy intention of providing an alternative to the unsatisfactory situation in which

the accounts of new plays, &c. are frequently sent by the authors themselves to the papers, and that *Puffs* being now accepted as *advertisements*, managers and performers have many opportunities of being extolled for their *active attention* and *wonderful abilities*. . . . It is therefore evident that no credit can be given to the theatrical reports of daily papers.[49]

Commentary in the magazine was indeed refreshingly interesting.

Critics generally wrote anonymously, though some signed themselves with pseudonyms such as 'Dramaticus', 'One of the Boxes', or even 'Philo-

---

[46] Memoranda B, fo. 34.
[47] *Dramatic Censor*, 3 vols. (1800–1), ii. 114–15, as quoted in *London Stage*, pt. 5, p. cxxxvii.
[48] Drury Lane Paybook B, fo. 30.   [49] *Thespian Magazine*, 1 (1792), p. iii.

Thespis'. Pretentious as some of the names are, they gave the critics some identity, and some of their real names are known.[50] Critics occasionally resorted to writing a review of a work they had not seen, but few were as foolish as the writer in 1805, whose outrageous review provoked the Drury Lane management into printing a strong rejoinder entitled 'Premature criticism!!!'. The opening paragraph, prefacing a copy of the vituperative review itself, reads:

The following *liberal* critique being *ready manufactured* on Saturday, was inserted on Sunday last, in a Newspaper called The British Neptune. It is only necessary to add that the Play, in which the Performers are so severely handled, was not performed; the Comedy of She Stoops to Conquer having been substituted in consequence of the indisposition of Mr. Elliston.[51]

A moderately successful opera was typically performed frequently in its first season, then staged gradually less often until finally it was only revived—if at all—for an occasional singer's benefit. Storace's *The Pirates* is a good example. It was performed thirty times in its first season (1792/3), then a few times in each of the next three seasons. Between 1796 and 1800, individual songs from the opera were performed on four different benefit nights.[52] Finally, the whole opera was revived for three performances between 1800 and 1802. His more popular *The Siege of Belgrade* was staged forty-seven times in its first season, then at least once and up to eight times each season from 1791/2 to 1802/3. Thereafter it continued to be performed sporadically, at least until 1829/30.

Revivals were not uncommon several seasons after a work's first run. *Lodoiska*, for instance, was originally in the Drury Lane repertoire from the 1793/4 season to the 1796/7 season, then was not seen again until a revival in 1799/1800. The first performance, on 1 January 1800, was publicized on the playbill as having been 'not acted these Three Years'. *Lodoiska* continued to be revived occasionally until at least 1831/2.

Some pieces, such as *Poor Old Drury* and *The Glorious First of June*, were never designed to last more than one season; others were simply not popular enough to survive. *Dido, Queen of Carthage* was performed only five times, all in the 1791/2 season. It was never enthusiastically received. *The Cave of Trophonius* was performed once at the end of the 1790/1

---

[50] Theodore Fenner, *Opera in London: Views of the Press, 1785–1830* (Carbondale and Edwardsville, Ill., 1994), app. 1; Charles H. Gray, *Theatrical Criticism in London to 1795* (New York, 1931), 250–307 *passim.*

[51] Printed sheet, following playbill for 5 Oct. 1805.

[52] On 25 May 1796 for Storace's widow; 6 June 1797 for Sedgwick; 23 May 1798 for Barrymore and Sedgwick; 19 Apr. 1799 for Suett.

season on Anna Crouch's benefit night, then four times in the next two seasons. *The Cherokee* was played sixteen times in its first season of 1794/5, then proved difficult to revive at the beginning of the following season and was played only once.

New stage works only gradually took on something like stable forms. Alterations were made at almost every step in their production, starting with rehearsals and continuing through the season in response to audience reaction. Newspaper reviews sometimes comment on cuts made after the première; other modifications can be identified by comparing the various written and printed forms of the texts and music, which were generated at different stages of their production. Manuscript librettos sent to the Examiner of Plays are our earliest sources, followed by printed song texts (available on the first night), then later printed scores and librettos (when these exist). Differences between these versions underline the flexibility of theatrical performances and emphasize the point that there is no single correct version of a work.

Newspaper reviewers commonly remarked that new works were too lengthy; sometimes later reviews would reveal that cuts had since been made, though they were rarely specific. One of the problems for the librettist, composer, and director was that, in the words of a reviewer, 'in popular music great allowance should be made for encores'.[53] The number of encores could not, of course, be estimated until the audience reaction was known, so that successful operas were often too long at first. The reverse situation could also occur. In the case of *Dido, Queen of Carthage*, Storace's only English all-sung opera and an almost instant failure, two reviews in *The Times* a few days apart give an indication of the problem:

The piece is infinitely too long for representation. Much of the unaccompanied recitative should be omitted, and perhaps an Air or two might be dispensed with, as at present we really have too much of a good thing.

The Queen of Carthage yesterday evening tripped much more lightly over the Haymarket boards, for having discarded nearly half her train of Recitative.[54]

The Siege of Belgrade, one of Storace's most popular works, was clearly too long, and, in the opinion of one critic, 'allowing for the encores, and there

[53] *Times*, 27 Oct. 1788, writing about Storace's *The Doctor and the Apothecary*.
[54] *Times*, 24 and 26 May 1792.

were not less than Seven; the piece will require a reduction of near an hour'.[55]
Drastic measures were taken, and three descriptions of the cuts made after
the first night are unusually detailed:

The *mausoleum* scene, with the *sepulchral* music, are very properly omitted.[56]

The house is not filled with smoke by the firing in the second act, and the tomb
scene in the third act is totally omitted.[57]

Since the first evening the part of Krohnfeldt has been omitted, and some other
alterations made, which have improved the Opera.[58]

Storace's tomb music is, of course, lost. Only one piece of Storace's cut operatic music has survived, from his afterpiece *The Prize*. The last piece in
the score includes a note that 'this Song is left out in the representation'.[59]
It was probably published because the score was very short, containing only
seven other pieces.

Attempts by reviewers to convey their distress at excessive length sometimes brought out their own metaphorical excesses. Two comments on *The
Pirates* appeared on consecutive days in the *Diary*:

The Pirates cannot but make a prosperous voyage on the sea of public favour; the
success, however, will be considerably forwarded by a judicious curtailment of the
vessel. She is much too long in the keel, and will sail swifter when considerably
shortened, and lightened of her ballast.

Mr. Cobb has judiciously profited by the observations made in yesterday's paper,
lightened his vessel considerably, thrown much ballast overboard, and enabled
her to make for port more safely and swiftly.[60]

The removal of an entire character in *The Siege of Belgrade* was most
unusual, although sometimes playbills mislead us into thinking that major
alterations were made by omitting information. For instance, the cast list
for *My Grandmother* at Drury Lane on 23 November 1795 excludes the
names of four of the nine characters: Sir Matthew Medley, Woodly, Sou-
france, and Charlotte. Such omissions in practice would have ruined the
plot. Playbills with big cast lists were particularly prone to pruning. As the
season progressed space on the playbill would be needed for other information, so the printer would remove a suitable section of the text. A
striking example is the gradual 'depletion' of the chorus in *The Cherokee*,
where the printer gradually removed lines of names of chorus members

---

[55] *Times*, 3 Jan. 1791.   [56] *Gazeteer*, 4 Jan. 1791.   [57] *Morning Chronicle*, 4 Jan. 1791.
[58] *European Magazine* (Jan. 1791), 70.
[59] Storace, 'Ah ne'er ungrateful', *The Prize* (London [1793]), 15.
[60] *Diary*, 22 and 23 Nov. 1792.

from the playbill over the course of its first season, working up from the bottom line. On the opening night, 20 December 1794, the playbill listed the names of thirteen Indian warriors and forty-four other chorus members. On 23 December the chorus dropped to thirty-five (plus thirteen Indians); after another nine performances only six Indians and twenty-two chorus members were included. By 9 February the Indians were omitted and the chorus apparently totalled only thirteen; on 19 February it was omitted entirely. It was, of course, present at the actual performances.

Careful planning on the management's part could be thwarted for several reasons. A work could have proved more or less popular than anticipated, requiring either an extended season or an abbreviated one. Changes made at the last minute were unpredictable, and usually made because an important player was 'indisposed' or a show was not ready for public view; then a piece would be substituted that was easy to perform at short notice. An opera might then be substituted for a play if that was most convenient, possibly resulting in two operas being performed together. Such a programme was tiring on the singers' voices, so that even more complications sometimes ensued. On one evening, an entire night's bill was changed because of Kemble's illness, even though he was only cast in the first piece. A newspaper report explained why:

The performances at this Theatre were changed last night on account of the indisposition of Mr. Kemble.—Henry the Fifth gave way on this occasion to the Siege of Belgrade, and the *Cave* of *Trophonius* was also superseded, as it was impossible for the Vocal Performers to sustain the whole effort of the Night.[61]

'Indisposed' did not necessarily mean ill, as the following comment from Thomas Dutton makes clear: 'Mrs. Jordan *happening*, like other great performers, to be taken ill (it is wonderful how much great actors and actresses are subject to *sudden* indisposition!) Trueman was under the necessity of substituting The Prize for the afterpiece.'[62] An extreme example, also involving the troublesome Mrs Jordan, involved complications worthy of a farce:

The representation announced for last night at this Theatre was *Twelfth Night*; but as Mrs. Jordan *found herself too ill* to perform, new bills were issued, and the substitute was to be *The Siege of Belgrade*. About the middle of the day, however, Mrs. Jordan *found herself well enough* to perform, and the other bills were circulated, importing that the Play was to be *Twelfth Night*. But, in the afternoon,

---

[61] *Morning Post*, 18 Oct. 1791.
[62] *Dramatic Censor*, ii. 244, as quoted in *London Stage*, 5 June 1800, Drury Lane. The comment refers to the fact that *The Prize* replaced *Three Weeks after Marriage*.

Mrs. Jordan *found herself too ill* to perform, and a message was sent again to the Theatre, signifying the melancholy disappointment. It was then too late to make any other change, and *Twelfth Night* was represented, Mrs. Goodall reading the part of *Viola*.

There was considerable difficulty in collecting the Performers, after these repeated changes. Barrymore could not be found, and Caulfield dressed for *Orsino*; but when he was ready to appear, Barrymore arrived, and took the part. It was then discovered that Phillimore was absent, and Caulfield was doomed to dress once more, for Phillimore's character; but soon after Phillimore came to the House. Mrs. Kemble being indisposed, Miss Mellon took her part of *Maria*. However, as Dodd and Palmer retained their parts, and supported them with their usual spirit and humour, the Play went off with effect. The audience (a large one) indeed grumbled a little at this kind of dramatic *hocus pocus*, but, on the whole, were not churlish in their testimonies of satisfaction.[63]

Small wonder Mrs Jordan's fellow actors became irritated, even to the extent of trying to embarrass her in public. Kemble recorded one such attempt as 'Kelly's asking me to put [on] a bad Farce to mortify Mrs. Jordan'.[64] Kemble himself was sorely tried by her temperament, remarking as early as 1788: 'Mrs. Jordan again fancied herself ill. I spent above two Hours in coaxing her to act—N.B. She was as well as ever she was in her Life, and stayed when she has [*sic*] done her Part to see the whole Pantomime.'[65]

Of course genuine mishaps did occur, and details were often reported in the newspapers. On 8 February 1800 the *Morning Herald* recorded an accident in a performance of *Lodoiska* two nights earlier: 'Towards the conclusion [Maria De Camp] fell with Kelly, while in the act of running down the stage; her head striking with so much violence against the boards that she fainted away.'[66] The day after the accident, a printed slip was added to the playbill announcing that 'the Publick are most respectfully informed that in consequence of the accident Miss De Camp met with in Lodoiska yesterday evening, the New Musical Entertainment called Of Age Tomorrow, is unavoidably deferred.' Sometimes a last-minute emergency required not a change of programme but an alteration to the work about to be staged. Thus, 'Sedgwick not coming to the Theatre, his 1st Scene in My Grandmother was oblig'd to be omitted. The above Neglect Mr Sedgwick is too often guilty of.'[67]

Works were sometimes postponed because they were not yet ready for public performance. This may be why the première of *The Three and the*

---

[63] *True Briton*, 13 Jan. 1796.   [64] Memoranda A, 22 Oct. 1794.
[65] Memoranda A, 22 Dec. 1788.   [66] As quoted in *London Stage*, 6 Feb. 1800, Drury Lane.
[67] Powell's notes, as quoted in *London Stage*, 7 Feb. 1795, Drury Lane.

Deuce was 'unavoidably postponed' for several days in 1795.[68] In the case of *The Iron Chest* a postponement occurred after its disastrous première on 12 March 1796. On 19 March the following notice appeared in the *True Briton*, indicating that alterations had been made to the work:

The second performance of *The Iron Chest* was to have taken place on Thursday; but not being quite ready, the intended substitute was *First Love*. The absence, however, of some Performers, occasioned another change, and the substitute was *The Trip to Scarborough*. The return being *non est inventus*, with respect to Barrymore, the character of *Colonel Townly* was wholly *omitted*, but not *missed*.

When the Drury Lane company first moved into the King's Theatre in September 1791, alterations to the announced programmes had to be made because modifications to the sets had allowed only limited rehearsal time. On 24 September, their second performance there, the playbill read: 'The Comedy of The School for Scandal, Intended for This Evening's Representation, is deferred till Tuesday; the Stage having been so constantly occupied by the Workmen preparing and adapting the various Scenes for this Theatre, that the usual course of Rehearsals has been necessarily impeded.' On another occasion, 14 February 1795, some of the performers seem to have double-booked themselves. The Drury Lane playbill announced:

On account of the Engagements of some of the principal Performers at the Opera House it is absolutely impossible to give the Grand Heroic Pantomime of Alexander the Great this Evening: the third night will be on Monday next, and every Accommodation is making for an Arrangement that will prevent any future interruptions of this Representation.

Semiramide, by Francesco Bianchi, was performed at the King's Theatre that night, with Kelly as Arsace.

'BY PERMISSION': PERFORMANCES AT OTHER THEATRES

Drury Lane and Covent Garden rarely intruded on each other's ground. Each theatre had a separate repertoire of both plays and operas, except for plays by Shakespeare and other dead authors. However, pieces owned by one theatre could be performed by the other for special occasions after suitable permission had been granted. Storace's operas were sometimes given at Covent Garden 'by permission of the Proprietors of the Theatre-Royal, Drury Lane', usually at a singer's benefit performance.[69] Permission needed

---

[68] *London Stage*, 31 Aug. 1795, Little Theatre in the Haymarket.
[69] See e.g. Miss Waters's benefit performance, quoted in *London Stage*, 24 May 1799, Covent Garden, at which *No Song, No Supper* was performed.

to be given only once in a season; thus *No Song, No Supper* was given four times at the Little Theatre in the summer of 1798, only the first time 'by permission'.

George Colman's *The Iron Chest*, with music by Storace, seems to have passed through at least two owners.[70] After its initial failure at Drury Lane, Colman removed the work and produced it at his own theatre. At its first performance at the Little Theatre, on 29 August 1796, it was billed as 'by Permission', even though Colman already owned the copyright, which he registered at Stationers' Hall on 21 July. He must have obtained the performing rights some time later, for it was performed on 23 April 1799 for H. Johnson's benefit at Covent Garden with the note on the playbill: '(First time at this Theatre) by permission of Mr. Colman.'

On very rare occasions the two Theatres Royal did set up as rivals. On Saturday, 7 November 1789 Kemble wrote in his diary that 'we performed [William Hayley's play *Marcella*] at two Days notice to teach Covent Garden good manners. Mrs. Powell was not perfect, otherwise we played it better than the other House who had been a fortnight preparing it— N.B. The Piece is so dull that nothing could be made of it.' The first performance at Covent Garden took place three days later. Opinion about the relative quality of performances did not support Kemble, but his judgement of the quality of the play was probably right: it was played once only at Drury Lane (to make a point) and twice at Covent Garden.

Running a theatre company in the late eighteenth century was certainly never easy. Even so, the routines of theatrical production were well established, and survived upheavals such as moving a company from one theatrical building to another. Music had a firmly established and valuable role in the form of operas, entr'acte entertainments, and other incidental music. The effect of music on theatrical life should not therefore be minimized; without music the institutions would have been markedly less successful.

---

[70] Drury Lane paid Colman a total of £300 in two instalments in Jan. and May 1796 for 'his Play', undoubtedly *The Iron Chest* (Drury Lane Ledger, fo. 50). If the estimate of £1,000 made in the *Oracle*, 14 Mar. 1796, is correct, he did not receive his full fee.

3

MUSICIANS AT DRURY LANE

Operas were clearly integral to the London theatre world in the 1790s, many of them popular and profitable. Music was not confined to operas, however, as many staged works combined speech and music in varying proportions, ranging from plays with occasional stage songs to operas which had spoken dialogue. Many actors could perform a simple song adequately, and all singers had to deliver spoken lines convincingly, although a few actors never sang in public (Mrs Siddons is a case in point, and her brother John Philip Kemble rarely sang), and some singers (such as Nancy Storace) never performed in entirely spoken works. Theatrical musicians included singers, instrumentalists, and support personnel who were employed on a regular basis. Orchestral players in particular were present on virtually every night the theatre was open, to provide opening music, accompaniments, and incidental music, because no evening's show was complete without some music.

Our knowledge of theatrical instrumentalists is very limited because eighteenth-century critics almost always confined their commentary to soloists. Contemporary reviews do give us a rounded view of individual singers' performances and abilities, while memoirs and anecdotes provide intimate and often exaggerated glimpses into their personal lives. Instrumentalists, however, were rarely mentioned in the press, so we know little about the quality of their performances, their working lives, or the personalities involved. The oboist William T. Parke's memoirs give us some insight into the professional activities of a soloist, but he too concentrates on his more prestigious performances, even though he was also a member of the Drury Lane orchestra in the 1790s.[1]

Two important sets of manuscripts shed some light on musicians'

---

[1] Parke, *Musical Memoirs.*

working lives: Kemble's theatrical diaries and the Drury Lane account books.[2]
While they give only a partial picture of personnel and activities, they do
give us some idea of the life of a theatrical musician. From the account
books, which list salaries and other payments, we can weigh the relative
importance of various musical positions within the company. From Kemble's
diaries we can identify orchestral players by name, and learn about the organization of their various instrumental groups.

Kemble wrote his diaries on printed date books, and when he was manager of Drury Lane between 1788 and 1796 he entered the titles of the
works performed each evening. During the theatrical seasons the books are
little more than calendars of performances with a few personal opinions
about new pieces and other theatrical matters. However, he used the space
left in the summer (when the theatre was closed) to summarize the year's
activities. He recorded the names of the company members, the chorus, and
on two occasions the surnames of the individual band members. These are
the only surviving membership lists for the Drury Lane orchestra in the
late eighteenth century; even more importantly, Kemble grouped the
names in such a way as to indicate a complex system of orchestral organization. Although many questions remain unanswered, we can now begin
to understand the musical workings of the theatre.

The singers and dancers were obviously better known to the public than
the less visible instrumentalists or backstage personnel. Dancers were of
little importance to operas, as their main role was to perform in pantomimes and provide entr'acte entertainments. Only on rare occasions did
Storace's operas involve dances, and even then most were marches. Singers,
however, spent the vast majority of their time on stage singing works by
Storace in the 1790s. Few changes of personnel took place from one season to the next, either of soloists or of chorus members, with the latter only
rarely being promoted to solo roles. The chorus itself was divided into the
regular house chorus and a smaller group of extras. None of the chorus singers
can have been full-time, as they were only needed for some of the more
substantial operas.

The orchestra comprised about thirty players, not all of whom were needed
every night. Extra players were sometimes hired for particular pieces, occasionally even an entire band. Instruments were occasionally rented,
presumably to be played by regular members of the orchestra. A number

---

[2] Kemble, Memoranda A and Memoranda B; Drury Lane Paybook B, Drury Lane Ledger, Drury
Lane Paybook A, Drury Lane Journal. Note that the paybooks run concurrently. Paybook B is organized with a page (or more) per person or activity, while Paybook A is a daybook. The ledger is the
chronological continuation of Paybook B.

of backstage personnel belonged to the permanent company to support all the musical performers. We are not sure of all those involved at Drury Lane (or indeed any other London theatre), but we do know that the theatre employed a composer, director (often the same person), music copyists, a chorus master, a music porter, and a 'music caller'. The theatre would not have been able to function musically without all of these people. On different levels the orchestral players and backstage personnel were important underpinning for the public display of the 'whole show'.

Singers

The singers were of course the best-known group of musicians in the theatre. Chorus members apart, nobody was exclusively a singer, as all the operas produced at Drury Lane had spoken dialogue. However, some performers were hired primarily for their singing abilities rather than any notable acting skill; some performed exclusively in operas. Most other actors could take on a small singing role when necessary and play minor roles in operas; some played regularly in Storace's works.

In the 1790s three singers dominated the main operatic roles at Drury Lane: Nancy Storace, Michael Kelly, and Anna Maria Crouch (née Phillips). First to join the company in 1780/1 was Anna Crouch, who had been articled to Thomas Linley.[5] Kelly joined her on his return from Vienna in the spring of 1787, and finally Nancy Storace came to Drury Lane early in the 1789/90 season from the King's Theatre.

For almost ten years the relative status of these three singers remained fairly stable, as did the types of roles they performed. They first came together in November 1789 in Storace's *The Haunted Tower* (Nancy Storace's first role at Drury Lane). Kelly and Anna Crouch were cast as the upper-class hero and heroine in the persons of Lord William and Lady Elinor; Nancy, as Adela, was the servant heroine and main plotter. She was joined in her machinations by John (Jack) Bannister as Edward, her lover. Although he was not primarily a singer, Jack Bannister (whose father Charles was a bass singer at Drury Lane and elsewhere) was quite capable of holding a tune if it was not too demanding, and he was a character actor of some distinction. He partnered Nancy Storace for many years.

The full-length 'comic' play or opera of the time, whether English or

---

[5] Fiske, *English Theatre Music*, 626–7; *Biographical Dictionary*, iv. 81.

Continental, usually involved two pairs of lovers—the serious, aristocratic couple and the comic peasants or servants. The casting in Storace's operas was absolutely stereotyped: Kelly and Anna Crouch played the upper-class pair, Nancy Storace and Bannister the lower-class. The latter were always given the more interesting roles: they plotted, played tricks, and manipulated the other characters towards a happy ending. Only occasionally were the two pairs of equal social status, as in *The Cave of Trophonius*, where Nancy Storace and Anna Crouch played two sisters, paired with their usual partners.

Even in those of Storace's later works that broke with the traditional division of roles, the singers remained typecast. For instance, the only woman's singing role in *The Iron Chest* is a peasant, and the main aristocratic role is a non-singing villain (originally played by Kemble). Nancy was therefore cast as the peasant girl Barbara, and Anna Crouch did not perform. Bannister was Nancy's partner as the secretary Wilford (a much more important acting role than hers), while Kelly was given a cameo role as the robber chief. Conversely, the only female role in the afterpiece *Lodoiska* was Princess Lodoiska, the rescued heroine. This was Anna Crouch's role and Nancy Storace did not play.

Afterpieces had less complex plots than mainpieces, and often called for only a single pair of singers. Usually they were comic and thus vehicles for Nancy and Bannister; *Lodoiska* was exceptional. In *The Prize*, Nancy Storace was the heroine in a work created for her; her lover had a non-singing part, so Bannister played the rejected lover, for which his acting skill was essential. In *The Three and the Deuce*, on the other hand, Bannister was the star of the show, playing three triplets with contrasting characters. In this virtuoso showpiece, none of the other main singers appeared, as they were not playing the summer season at the Little Theatre, where it was first performed.

The singers' status as soloists was just as firmly established as the types of roles they performed. Their relative importance can be gauged by comparing the amount of music given to each one, because most of the operas performed at Drury Lane between 1788 and 1796 were composed by Storace specifically for his best singers. Nancy Storace almost always had the largest singing role, even though she was usually the servant to Anna Crouch's and Kelly's aristocrats. Kelly usually had the next biggest singing part, followed by Anna Crouch. Bannister, who was not a professional singer, always had the smallest musical role of the four. He had been trained to some extent by his wife, the former Elizabeth Harper, who had been the leading soprano at Covent Garden before the advent of Elizabeth

Billington in 1786. He and Anna Crouch also performed regularly in plays, whereas Nancy Storace and Kelly (both of whom still sang Italian opera on occasion) were designated singers and confined themselves entirely to operas.

The singers' pay also reflects their musical status. Nancy, a lively actress as well as a singer with a successful *opera buffa* career behind her in Vienna and elsewhere, transferred her abilities successfully to the English stage and was paid accordingly. The Drury Lane account books record payments of £10 per performance in 1789, rising to 10 guineas in 1792/3.[4] This was less than she had earned at the King's Theatre,[5] but it put her on a par with the leading Drury Lane actress Dorothy Jordan. She was the only singer among the group of top performers whose contracts committed them to a set number of performances per season, plus benefit, for a set fee per performance. Less highly ranked players and singers were paid weekly, an amount varying according to the number of days the theatre was open. For a six-day week in 1789/90, Kelly earned £11, Anna Crouch £12, and Bannister £10. By the 1792/3 season, Kelly was earning £15 to Anna Crouch's £14; from the reopening of the new Drury Lane theatre in April 1794, Kelly and Anna Crouch were listed together and paid a joint sum in accordance with their intimate domestic arrangements. Bannister's salary is not recorded individually each week because he belonged to Dale's list.[6] All four soloists made comfortable livings, and Nancy Storace had a high income. According to Porter, £50 to £100 a year was a normal income for a member of the petty bourgeoisie, while £300 would keep a gentleman in style.[7] Porter's estimates may be a little low, at least according to Storace's uncle John Trusler, but even by his standards these singers were well off.[8]

In 1796 a new soloist joined the Drury Lane company at Storace's invitation, the young tenor John Braham. Like Nancy Storace, he had been taught by Rauzzini, a castrato then living in Bath. Early in the year he performed in London at Salomon's concerts and elsewhere, and by March he had agreed to join the Drury Lane company. The playbill for 10 March 1796 announced that 'Mr. Braham is engaged at this Theatre, and will very

---

[4] Drury Lane Paybook B, fo. 55.

[5] Judith Milhous and Robert D. Hume, 'Opera Salaries in Eighteenth-Century London', *JAMS* 46 (1993), 50–2.

[6] Drury Lane Paybook A, fo. 2ᵛ and 6 Apr. 1793. On 26 Apr. 1794 the first regular payment of £29 is recorded to Kelly and Anna Crouch jointly. Alec Hyatt King ('Kelly, Michael', *New Grove Opera*, ii. 974) writes that, contrary to popular belief, their relationship may have been platonic.

[7] *English Society in the Eighteenth Century*, 13.

[8] 'Memoirs', vol. ii (Bath Central Library, typescript of MS, late 18th cent.), 110–12. Trusler gives detailed accounts to prove that a clergyman with a wife and two children cannot live on £150 a year.

shortly make his First Appearance in A New Comick Opera.' The opera in question was *Mahmoud*, a work obviously designed to include tenor roles for both Kelly and Braham, which Storace left unfinished at his death. Braham therefore made his Drury Lane debut after Storace's death. As it turned out, Braham and Nancy Storace left Drury Lane together soon afterwards to tour continental Europe, making Braham's early career on the English stage successful but brief, and breaking up Storace's long-established group of soloists. By the end of the 1796/7 season, Braham and Nancy Storace had returned to England but not to Drury Lane.

Other solo singers who appeared more or less regularly on the Drury Lane stage in the 1790s included Ida Bland (née Romanzini), Charles Dignum, Thomas Sedgwick, and Richard (Dicky) Suett. Some were young singers of as yet unproven abilities; others were actors who, though untrained, were more or less competent singers. Most of them were close in age. Storace's four principals (Nancy Storace, Kelly, Anna Crouch, and Bannister) were all born in the 1760s, as was Dignum; Suett was only slightly older. Ida Bland was born in 1770, and Sedgwick too was probably somewhat younger than the principals. Two even younger singers, John Braham and Maria Theresa de Camp (later Mrs Charles Kemble), who were both born in the 1770s, joined the company later. Maria de Camp took over some of Nancy Storace's roles after she left Drury Lane. Also notable was young Master Thomas Welsh, a boy soprano born in about 1781 who was for several years prominent in Storace's operas, appearing first in the masque *Neptune's Prophecy* which concluded Storace's *Dido, Queen of Carthage* (23 May 1792). Welsh's vocal technique must have been outstanding, to judge from the song 'Sweet bird' that Storace composed for him in *Lodoiska* (no. 12), as well as his music in *The Cherokee*. He also created the main character in Thomas Attwood's *The Adopted Child* in the 1794/5 season. He was still singing treble parts in *The Iron Chest* in March 1796.

Like the principals, the other soloists were cast in fairly well defined types of role. Suett, for instance, was assigned character roles, often professional men, and through the 1790s the amount of singing he was given increased gradually from opera to opera. Sedgwick performed a mixture of sub-sidiary roles, always with a small amount of singing. He was not only a weak actor, but, according to Kelly, he stuttered.[9] Dignum was even less important than Sedgwick, both in his roles and in the amount of singing he was assigned. Ida Bland was usually the third-ranked woman after Nancy Storace and Anna Crouch, with somewhat less singing than Anna

---

[9] *Reminiscences*, i. 258 n.

Crouch and roles of a slightly lower social status and much smaller size than Nancy's.

The soloists' voice types were standard for the period. Hero and heroine were tenor and soprano (Storace, like his contemporaries, wrote no solo parts for low female voices). Anna Crouch and Nancy Storace were both coloratura sopranos, with Anna Crouch specializing in sentimental roles while Nancy Storace excelled in the comic. Ida Bland and Maria de Camp were generally given simpler airs in a mezzo-soprano range. Michael Kelly was the only tenor of any strength at Drury Lane until John Braham joined the company in 1796. Kelly was famous for his top notes because, unlike anyone in living memory (including Braham), he sang them in full voice instead of the usual falsetto. Dignum was also a tenor; Jack Bannister and Suett were baritones.[10] There was no regular bass soloist, despite Kemble's comment in his diary on the importance of a bass: 'Always take Care to have a Singer of the deepest Bass, no matter how he speaks; the Gallery loves a Rumble—The elder Mr. Banister [*sic*] no Actor—great Favourite.'[11] Indeed, Charles Bannister did take the bass line in Storace's glee 'Around the old oak' in *The Three and the Deuce* (no. 1), a show in which his own son was the undoubted star. On other occasions, Sedgwick, unreliable and bad actor as he was, had his uses. Kelly called him a bass, as he sang the lowest part in ensembles, but Storace never wrote really low parts for him, usually only going down to B flat.[12]

Soloists' salaries varied according to their importance. Ida Romanzini (later Mrs Bland) earned £5 for a six-day week in 1789/90, Dignum and Sedgwick earned £4. In 1791/2, Sedgwick's salary was raised to £6, while Dignum still earned £4. For the short season in the spring of 1794 (when Kelly and Crouch were earning £15 and £14 respectively), Thomas Walsh earned £9, Ida Bland £8, and Dignum was still at £4.[13]

Solo singers were all entitled to at least one personal benefit night per season. The higher the status of the performer, the better choice of date he or she was given. Some of the minor performers shared benefit nights, in an arrangement that saved the theatre a night's profit, guaranteed the recipients a larger audience than they could have attracted alone, and allowed them to share the house charge. The venture could be financially risky because the beneficiaries were responsible for selling their own tickets and paying the substantial house charge, which could result in little or

[10] Mollie Sands, 'Some Haymarket and Drury Lane Singers in the Last Decade of the 18th Century', *MMR* 89 (1959), 178–9.
[11] Memoranda A, fo. 139.   [12] Kelly, *Reminiscences*, i. 258 n.
[13] Drury Lane Paybook A, fos. 4ᵛ–5, 82, 158ᵛ–159ᵛ.

no profit to the player unless he or she made sure of a large audience.[14] Some players preferred to adopt the safer alternative of accepting a lump sum in lieu of benefit profits. In 1791, 1792, and 1793 Kelly made this choice, taking £100, £200, and £200 respectively. In later years he changed the pattern of his benefits. Instead of the usual two or even three pieces, he cut down the programme to one mainpiece (usually an opera by Storace), to which he added many ballets and other sundry items.[15]

One important characteristic of a benefit night was that the singer sometimes performed a role he or she did not normally play. For instance, at Anna Crouch's benefit on 3 May 1791, which was the première of Storace's *The Cave of Trophonius*, she also performed Miss Neville in the mainpiece *Know Your Own Mind*, 'being her First Appearance in that Character' as the playbill put it. Similarly, on 25 May 1796, at the benefit for Storace's widow, Nancy Storace played Ismene in *The Sultan*, again '*for that Night Only*'.

On at least one very special occasion, some Drury Lane soloists formed part of the chorus. The first play performed after the opening of the new Drury Lane Theatre, on 21 April 1794, was Shakespeare's *Macbeth*, in which Anna Crouch, Kelly, and some minor soloists appeared on the playbill as members of the chorus of witches and spirits, singing 'the Original Music of Matthew Lock, and Accompaniments by Dr Arne, and Mr Linley'.[16]

The house chorus at Drury Lane performed almost exclusively in operatic mainpieces and would certainly have needed other employment to supplement their income. Storace wrote chorus parts for all his mainpieces and for one afterpiece, *Lodoiska*. Kemble listed the size of the chorus for 1790/1 as fifteen with ten extras. The house chorus was divided into seven sopranos, one countertenor, five tenors, and two basses; the extras were four boys (treble), two countertenors, one tenor, and three basses. Added together, say for an opera by Storace, they would have made a fairly well balanced, if slightly top-heavy, group. The numbers increased greatly the following season, probably because they had to sing in the larger King's Theatre and match an expanded orchestra. The house chorus of thirty-five was made up of ten women, four boys, four countertenors, nine tenors, and eight basses. By 1794/5 it was reduced to eleven men and twelve women, with eighteen

[14] Troubridge, *The Benefit System in the British Theatre*, 45–50. The account books indicate that beneficiaries regularly owed money to the theatre after expenses had been deducted. See for instance Drury Lane Paybook B, fos. 59–62.

[15] Drury Lane Paybook B, fo. 63ᵛ. Later benefits took place on 8 May 1799, 14 May 1800, 6 May 1801, and 2 May 1803.

[16] The original music was really by Richard Leveridge. See Roger Fiske, 'The "Macbeth" Music', *ML* 45 (1964), 114–25; Robert E. Moore, 'The Music to *Macbeth*', *MQ* 47 (1961), 28–40.

extra men (probably to play the Tartars in *Lodoiska*). The orchestra too had been reduced.[17]

The Drury Lane account books also register payments to 'Dr. Cook's boys'. If Dr Cook was Benjamin Cooke, Master of the Choristers at Westminster Abbey from 1757 and organist from 1762 until his death in 1793, then those boys were certainly part of his church choir and possibly 'the boys' listed in Kemble's lists for 1790/1 and 1793/4. They were replaced by women in the regular chorus in 1794/5.[18] Thereafter the account books mention boys from St Paul's Cathedral and Westminster Abbey only occasionally. Other unidentified chorus members participated in big works. They tend to be described as 'with the Assistance of additional Voices' on playbills, as at the première of *Dido, Queen of Carthage* on 23 May 1792.

The membership of the chorus was a little less stable than that of the other groups of musicians in the 1790s. Even so, at least two-thirds of the names appear regularly in Kemble's annual lists. We know almost nothing about them except their names, but these indicate that there was something of a family tradition in belonging to the chorus. For instance, at the première of *The Cherokee* on 20 December 1794 the playbill lists both Dorion and Dorion junior, and Mr and Mrs Maddocks. Master de Camp (probably a relation of Ida de Camp, the soprano soloist) and Welsh (who may have been Master Thomas Welsh's brother or father) were also named.

The chorus master was, at least for his own operas, Storace. A few passing remarks in newspaper reviews tell us a little about both the chorus and their director. One review of *The Cherokee* included unusual praise for the chorus:

Few things are more fatiguing to the spirits than the drilling of choruses for the stage; and we never heard, on a first night, choruses that, upon the whole, were better performed; neither do the singers, as formerly, stand motionless, with their hands clasped, their bodies stiff, and nothing moving but the contortions of their countenance. At present the chorus has assumed animation, and even passion; and we are essentially indebted to the Pygmalion who has found the art of animating such blocks.[19]

This Pygmalion may well have been Storace, if we can believe the writers of two reviews of *Mahmoud*, Storace's posthumous opera, two years later:

[17] Kemble, Memoranda A, fos. 91, 141[V].

[18] The last mention of Cook's singing boys is a record of their pay up to 14 Dec. 1792 (Drury Lane Paybook B, fo. 115). They were paid 1 guinea per performance, and paid separately for various benefit performances.

[19] *Morning Chronicle*, 22 Dec. 1794.

The choruses wanted that charming spirit and effect which they used to produce under the direction of Storace.[20]

Mr. Attwood kindly superintended the Musical Rehearsals—those of the dialogue were left, we believe,

'To the joiner Prompter, or old Grub'.[21]

Instrumentalists

Storace sometimes directed the orchestra from the keyboard, at least for operas, while Thomas Shaw led from the violin. Their division of labour is not entirely clear, but we do know that operas all over eighteenth-century Europe had dual orchestral direction of this kind. The oboist William T. Parke once remarked that 'Mr. Shaw led the band, and Mr. Linley presided at the organ' at the 1791 oratorios.[22] This was a normal arrangement, and it seems likely that the keyboard player was more concerned with the singers, the violinist with the orchestra.[23] Various newspaper reviews mention Storace playing at the premières of his operas, and one noted that, at the second performance of *The Three and the Deuce*, 'Storace left the Orchestra to Shaw last night'.[24] Here we can draw a direct parallel with the Italian opera houses, where the composer presided over the first three performances from the first harpsichord, then left the principal first violinist in charge.[25] Shaw also controlled the Drury Lane ensemble in rehearsal, as a famous anecdote about Kemble's lack of musical ability reveals:

Kemble, who had got the tune of [a song] tolerably well, being very deficient in keeping the time, Mr. Shaw, the leader of the band, impatiently exclaimed, 'Mr. Kemble, that won't do at all!—you *murder* time abominably!'—'Well, Mr. Shaw', replied Kemble, 'it is better to *murder* it, than to be continually *beating* it as you are.'[26]

---

[20] *Morning Chronicle*, 2 May 1796.

[21] *Oracle*, 2 May 1796. John Grubb was part-owner of Drury Lane, who took over as acting manager from Apr. 1796 until the end of the season, after Kemble resigned.

[22] *Musical Memoirs*, i. 141.

[23] Daniel J. Koury, *Orchestral Performance Practices in the Nineteenth Century: Size, Proportions, and Seating* (Ann Arbor, Mich., 1986), 52–4; Robin Stowell, ' "Good Execution and Other Necessary Skills": The Role of the Concertmaster in the Late 18th Century', *Early Music*, 16 (1988), 22.

[24] *Oracle*, 4 Sept. 1795. See also *Times*, 10 June 1794; *World*, 25 Nov. 1789.

[25] Jack Westrup, Neal Zaslaw, and Eleanor Selfridge-Field, 'Orchestra', *New Grove Instruments*, ii. 827.

[26] Parke, *Musical Memoirs*, i. 72. The story is also reported in Frances Ann Kemble, *Records of a Girlhood* (2nd edn., New York, 1883), 60.

Shaw was leader of the Drury Lane orchestra from 1786 into the early nineteenth century. His importance is clear, both in Kemble's orchestra lists—where he heads the otherwise alphabetical list of names of instrumentalists—and in the account books, where his pay is listed separately from that of the rest of the orchestra. The other instrumentalist with some status at Drury Lane was a harpsichordist called Costollo, who is also listed separately in Kemble's lists for 1794/5. He may have had a special role in direction (perhaps when Storace was not present), or he may have been the equivalent of a rehearsal pianist. He certainly would also have been a continuo player, as was normal in an opera orchestra in the 1790s.[27]

Newspaper critics were quite uninterested in instrumental performers at the theatres, so our knowledge of orchestral music suffers by comparison with vocal. We know the players were remarkably versatile, providing opening music, accompaniments for songs and dances, and incidental music for operas, no doubt often with little rehearsal.

Unfortunately, we are unable to study the orchestra's repertoire in any detail, because very little survives in orchestral parts or full scores. Certainly much theatre music was destroyed when both Drury Lane and Covent Garden burned down early in the nineteenth century, but several operas by Storace continued to be performed into the 1830s, and they were also performed in provincial towns, Dublin, and in America. The possibility exists that some scores still await discovery.

No record survives of the many miscellaneous pieces the pit orchestras must have played in the late eighteenth century. For instance, we know the orchestra was expected to play two or three 'musics' to quieten the audience before the prologue to a play and in effect act as a supplement to the warning bell, but we do not know what that music was on a particular evening.[28] In an opera, the overture took the place of the prologue; whether or not the orchestra played other music before the overture is not clear. Entr'acte entertainments, especially songs and ballets, also called for participation from the orchestra, but again, little of that music survives. Incidental music was normally not published; librettos give stage directions for music, but only one piece by Storace is extant: the 'Symphony Play'd During the Sun Sett' in Act 1 of *The Doctor and the Apothecary* (no. 3).

Even when the music survives, we have little real idea of the music the band played or its level of difficulty, because the published versions of operas

---

[27] In London continuo playing also survived in purely instrumental performances. See Neal Zaslaw, 'Toward the Revival of the Classical Orchestra', *PRMA* 103 (1976–7), 178–9.

[28] *London Stage*, pt. 5, p. lxxiii.

by Storace and other late-eighteenth-century composers provide only skeletal keyboard accompaniments. In the published scores, many vocal numbers begin with orchestral introductions or 'symphonies'; in other cases the singer seems to have started without any instrumental prelude. Kelly explains that, in such a case, 'a full chord was given from the orchestra to pitch the key'.[29] Such small pieces of information help us understand the minutiae of musical performance.

Kemble recorded surnames of the Drury Lane instrumentalists twice in his diary, for the seasons 1791/2 and 1794/5. Because he wrote them in three groupings, we can now both name the players and understand some of the musical and administrative strategies employed by the theatre. Taken with information from the files of the Royal Society of Musicians and Doane's *Musical Directory* of 1794, the orchestra begins to take on a distinct form.[30]

At the beginning of the 1791/2 season, when the Drury Lane company opened at the King's Theatre, a reviewer in the *Diary* wrote that 'the Orchestra of this theatre is larger than it was at Drury-lane, and the band is much strengthened and increased'.[31] Kemble lists a total of thirty players in three different combinations: the first list is headed by Shaw but otherwise includes the entire band in alphabetical order; the second gives the names divided into two equal 'half bands'; the third groups the players in six 'day bands' with a few names omitted. Grouping into 'day bands' is most unusual, and raises the question of what function those groups fulfilled. References elsewhere to groups similar to day bands or half bands are rare. Something similar to a half band was used at the Comédie-Italienne in Paris on vaudeville nights in the late eighteenth century.[32] Earlier in the century, some European orchestras had employed two identical groups of players on alternate nights.[33] Drury Lane's half bands may have operated similarly, but Kemble's lists do suggest strongly that the entire group played together sometimes. A more likely division may have been between the entire group playing for operas and the half bands for nights needing only small amounts of music.

[29] *Reminiscences*, i. 312.

[30] Kemble, Memoranda A, fos. 192, 272; J. Doane, *A Musical Directory for the Year 1794* (London [1794]); Matthews, *The Royal Society of Musicians of Great Britain*; Deborah Rohr's private research files. The *London Stage* does not list the regular orchestra members. It gives only names listed on playbills (soloists), and individually in account books (extras).

[31] *Diary*, 23 Sept. 1791.

[32] David Charlton, 'Orchestra and Chorus at the Comédie-Italienne (Opéra-Comique), 1755–99', in Malcolm H. Brown and Roland J. Wiley (eds.), *Slavonic and Western Music: Essays for Gerald Abraham* (Ann Arbor, Mich., 1985), 91.

[33] Westrup *et al.*, 'Orchestra', *New Grove Instruments*, ii. 825.

When then were the day bands used? Kemble listed one for every day of the week except Sunday (when the theatre was closed). Table 3.1 gives Kemble's information in capitals, with additional information (by no means definitive or complete) in lower case. Because Kemble listed only surnames, we often cannot distinguish one family member from another. Identifying their instruments is also problematic, first because it was usual for orchestral musicians to play more than one instrument, and secondly because they commonly exaggerated their skills when applying for membership of the Royal Society of Musicians. The lists indicate that all day bands contain between three and five players with a preponderance of strings, and most include at least one bass instrument and a wind or brass player. Four members of the full band are not included in the day bands: Parke, Flack Senior, Foster, and Schutze. The same players are omitted in the 1794/5 lists, where Kemble queries their absence.

The role of the day bands is open to at least two reasonable interpretations. The first is that 'day' should be taken literally, that the small groups provided sketch orchestras for musical rehearsals, when called. The assignment of set days would mean that players could commit themselves to other employment such as teaching on days when they were not scheduled to be at the theatre. Although the Thursday and Friday bands probably lacked any bass instruments, a bass could have been provided (however inadequately) by the harpsichordist. On the other hand, if a harpsichordist was present, there seems little need for such a skimpy ensemble for rehearsing the singers. Again, there are few precedents for such a rehearsal practice in other theatres. At the Comédie-Italienne in Paris in 1774, two violins and a cello provided accompaniment for some rehearsals.[34] This ensemble would certainly have been equivalent in size to the day bands, but there is no indication that the French players rotated according to the day of the week.

A second interpretation is that 'day bands' were the ordinary bands for the days (or, more accurately, evenings) when only a small amount of music was performed because no opera was on the programme. This presupposes that 'half bands' did not fulfil that function but instead, perhaps, played for operatic afterpieces. By today's standards, there is a real problem with the variegated composition of the day bands, which seems unlikely to have produced satisfactorily balanced ensembles, but lack of contemporaneous comment makes the point moot. Whether or not any of these scenarios is accurate, we do know that half bands and day bands were part of

[34] David Charlton, *Grétry and the Growth of Opéra-Comique* (Cambridge, 1986), 15.

Table 3.1. Drury Lane orchestral players 1791/2: Expanded from Kemble's diaries[a]

Day	First name	SURNAME	Instruments[b]
Mon.	Thomas	SHAW	Principal violin
	Elisha	ARCHER	Violin
	John	COLES	Violin
	Jeremiah	PARKINSON	Bassoon
	Robert	MASON	Cello
Tues.	William	HOWARD [jun.]	Violin
	Henry	COOPER	Violin, viola
	Christopher *or* S. or Martin	SCHRAM	Cello, violin *or* Violin (both)
	Stephen *or* Walter	JONES	Violin *or* Bassoon
	Michael *or* William	SHARP JUN.	Oboe, flute, violin, viola, flageolet *or* Cello, viola
Weds.	Charles	EVANS	Violin, viola, harpsichord, organ
	James *or* Richard	OLIVER	Violin, viola, clarinet, oboe *or* Violin, bassoon, cello, clarinet, oboe, viola
	John	FLACK JUN.	Violin, trombone, trumpet, horn
	John	DRESSLER	Trombone, double bass
	Hezekiah	CANTELO	Bassoon, trumpet
Thurs.	?	HOLLES	[Violin?]
	William	WARREN	Violin
	George	FOX	Violin
	C.	PARKINSON	?
Fri.	?	WHYMAN	[Violin?]
	?	BEILBY [or Bielby]	Violin, cello
	Michael *or* Richard	SHARP SEN.	Oboe *or* Double bass
Sat.	Samuel	TATTNAL	Violin, clarinet
	John	CROUCH	Violin, viola, harpsichord
	James	HEWITT	Cello, violin
	John	CORFE	Double bass, cello

The following players appear in the band, but not in any of the day bands:

	John Casper	FLACK SEN.	Trombone, horn, viola
	William	FOSTER	Oboe
	William	PARKE	Oboe, viola
	Daniel	SCHUTZE	'He plays all instruments'

[a] Kemble, Memoranda A, fo. 192. Kemble gives only the day and the players' surnames, here in capitals.

[b] J. Doane, *A Musical Directory for the Year 1794* (London [1794]); Betty Matthews (comp.), *The Royal Society of Musicians of Great Britain: List of Members 1728–1984* (London, 1985). Both sources are unreliable because Doane dates from some three years after the 1791/2 season, and performers listed their instruments (the number of which they sometimes exaggerated) on the dates they joined the society. The information in these files was first made available to me through Deborah Rohr's extensive notes. Added information comes from *Biographical Dictionary*.

Drury Lane's regular orchestral routine, listed by Kemble for two non-consecutive years.

From Kemble's lists we have the names of over thirty instrumentalists who performed at Drury Lane between 1791 and 1795. Table 3.2, a comparison of the personnel for the two seasons, shows that the orchestra, like other departments of the Drury Lane company, was remarkably stable in the early 1790s. Over a four-year period, six players out of a total of thirty left the band, and five were added in replacement.[55] Doane's *Directory* of 1794 names nine other players as instrumentalists at Drury Lane. They may have been extras; two of them worked at Drury Lane in other capacities.[56]

Pay records tell us little about the regular instrumentalists, though they do identify some extra players. Only the total amount paid per week is recorded for the regular orchestra. For a six-day week in 1789 the band's total pay was £45. 15s. 0d.; by 1794 it had risen to £57. 15s. 0d.[57] In 1789/90 and 1790/1 John Crouch was paymaster as well as a member of the band. Later Pilsbury took over, but is not listed as consistently as Crouch. The allocation of paymasters for specific groups of employees was normal theatre procedure. Occasionally players' names are specified in the account books in relation to pay rises. The normal rise was 10d. or a multiple of 10d.[58] Like other members of the company, instrumentalists were charged forfeits when they did not turn up or were late. Items such as 'music Forfeits of this Season £15. 19s. 1d.' are listed at the ends of seasons in the account books.[59]

Extra musicians were often hired by the theatre. Payments were made to the Duke of York's Band fairly often between 1791 and 1793, and the Duke of Gloster's Band starting in 1798. In 1789 four individuals were paid at the end of the season: Cornish, tabor and pipe; Asbridge (or Ashbridge), kettledrums; Hogg and Thompson, trumpets. Asbridge, Hogg, Thompson, and Hyde (also trumpet) frequently appear in the early 1790s, and by 1794/5 Hyde had become a regular member of the orchestra. Asbridge was still playing in 1798. A trombonist called Marriotti was paid £18. 15s. 0d. for playing in *The Pirates* for twenty-five nights.[40]

---

[55] The direct comparison may mask other changes, because the band was reduced in size in the short 1793/4 season (Kemble, Memoranda A, fo. 241ᵛ).

[56] D'Egville, Thomas Dorion jun., Gallot, Gibson, R. Harris, John Howles, James Henry Leffler, David Richards, and James Welsh are all listed in Doane's *Directory* as playing instruments at Drury Lane. D'Egville was a dancer, Dorion a copyist.

[57] Drury Lane Paybook A, fos. 11ᵛ–12, 170.

[58] e.g. Jones was given a 10d. rise on 26 Nov. 1791, Jeremiah Parkinson the same on 17 Dec. Mason and Archer were given a rise of 1s. 8d. each on 19 Feb. 1791.

[59] Drury Lane Journal, fo. 104ᵛ.   [40] Drury Lane Paybook B, fo. 115.

Table 3.2. Drury Lane orchestra, 1791/2 and 1794/5[a]

Day	1791/2	1794/5	Changes
Mon.	Shaw	Shaw	
	Archer	Archer	
	Coles	Warren	Moved from Thursday
	Parkinson	Parkinson	
	Mason	Mason	
Tues.	Howard	Howard	
	Cooper	Cooper	
	Schram	Schram	
	Jones		No replacement
	Sharp jun.	Sharp jun.	
Weds.	Evans	Evans	
	Oliver	Oliver	
	Flack jun.	Flack jun.	
	Dressler	Dressler	
	Cantelo	Cantelo	
Thurs.	Holles	Holles	
	Warren	Slezak	(violin). Warren to Monday
	Fox	Hyde	John (trumpet, violin)
	C. Parkinson	Atwood jun.	Thomas (piano)
Fri.	Whyman	Whyman	
	Beilby	Beilby	
	Sharp sen.	Sharp sen.	
Sat.	Tattnal	Tattnal	
	Crouch	Cornish	James (oboe), Thomas (oboe), or James John (oboe, violin, clarinet)
	Hewitt	Atwood sen.	Thomas (viola, horn/trumpet)
	Corfe	Corfe	

[a] Kemble, Memoranda A, fos. 192, 272.

The theatre sometimes rented instruments as well as hiring extra musicians. For instance, in 1789 the journal records a payment of 5 guineas to 'Longman & Broadrip [*sic*] for Use of Harp &c.'[41] We have to assume that one of the regular instrumentalists was able to perform the harp part; certainly, to judge from their applications to the Royal Society of Musicians, most musicians were remarkably versatile.

Perhaps the main reason we know so little about the professional orchestral players at the theatres is that their status in the company was so dismal. As Dougald MacMillan wrote in 1938, 'Only the very lowly members

[41] Drury Lane Journal, fo. 108.

of the staff—the stage-hands, the dressers, the musicians in the orchestra, the sweepers, and the wardrobe women—failed to receive in addition to their regular remuneration part of the proceeds of a benefit performance.'[42] The fact that these skilled, musically literate individuals are grouped with such company indicates that status was not a matter of talent and skill but rather of individuality and visibility in the theatre. Though physically visible in front of the stage, the orchestra was ignored in newspaper reviews and memoirs. Even Parke, a member of the Drury Lane orchestra, avoided describing his performances as a member of the band. There is little doubt that, despite their competence, the orchestral members were considered the lowliest of the musical performers in the London theatres.

Other Musical Personnel

Lowlier still were the backstage employees associated with music. Here our information is very sparse indeed. Music copyists were obviously essential in an establishment that put on new musical works regularly. In the early 1790s Foulis was the main music copyist, helped on occasion by Dorion, Tatnall, Lewis, Schuchart, and Forster. By the late 1790s the names in the account books had changed to Wyber, Buckholtz, and William Lion.[43] They were obviously skilled musicians and fast workers, to judge from Charles Dibdin's treatment of Foulis: 'I came to the Theatre, before the rehearsal, and in Foules's room, I made some trifling alteration in the accompaniments, and marked a tune to be played a tone higher.'[44] Presumably the copyist had to transpose the instrumental parts immediately for the rehearsal about to begin. The copyists were paid piece work, but we can rarely tell how much they received for a particular job. We do know that Thomas Attwood was paid £28. 15s. 10d. for copying his own opera *The Prisoner*, a price roughly the equivalent of the copyists' pay at the King's Theatre.[45]

Music rehearsals were regularly attended by a music copyist or librarian. From 1788 (if not earlier) Samuel Tattnall was paid between £11 and £12 a year to attend rehearsals; in 1794 Dorion was paid similarly,

---

[42] Introduction to *Drury Lane Calendar 1747–1776* (Oxford, 1938), p. xxi.
[43] Drury Lane Paybook B, fos. 56ᵛ, 78; Drury Lane Ledger, fo. 131.
[44] *The Musical Tour of Mr. Dibdin* (Sheffield, 1788), 254.
[45] Drury Lane Paybook B, fo. 115; Curtis Price, 'Opera and Arson', 90.

including 2 guineas a night for twelve nights for attending the oratorios.[46] Their jobs were conceivably a combination of emergency copyist and music librarian to distribute and collect parts. The theatre's orchestral parts must have been numerous. When the company moved to the King's Theatre in 1791 they paid a separate sum for 'use of a Room to hold Music'. This would have been different from the 'music room', a term used for their performance space in front of the stage.[47] That same season Thomas Daglish was paid £3 'for care of [music] Books'. Daglish is listed as a music copyist by Doane and as a 'music-caller' by Kemble.[48] The theatre also employed music porters: Thomas Stevenson was paid 9s. a week in 1793; Appleby and William Dupee were music porters in 1794.[49]

Tuners for the keyboard instruments were also essential. Either the harpsichord-maker Jacob Kirckman or a member of his family took care of the harpsichord from 1791 to 1794 at 18 guineas a season; in 1791 he was paid separately the sum of £15 for tuning the organ for the oratorios. The following year the company had moved home, and the organ-builder Samuel Green was paid the substantial sum of £33. 15s. 0d. for moving and tuning the organ for the oratorios at the King's Theatre.[50]

Composers

When David Garrick ran the Theatre Royal, Drury Lane, between 1747 and 1776 he did not employ a regular house composer; instead he commissioned individual works from various composers. However, when Sheridan took over ownership from Garrick, he persuaded his father-in-law Thomas Linley to join him in the enterprise, and Linley reluctantly became 'composer to the theatre'. His last opera, *Love in the East*, was produced in February 1788, after which he confined his activities to some arranging and the composition of a few individual songs.[51] Although in practice Storace took over from Linley in 1788, Linley retained his title until his death in 1795. The other theatres also had house composers: William Shield worked at Covent Garden in the last decades of the century, and

---

[46] Drury Lane Journal, fo. 105; Drury Lane Paybook B, fos. 21, 78, 141.

[47] Drury Lane Paybook B, fo. 87ᵛ; John Orrell, 'The Lincoln's Inn Fields Playhouse in 1731', *Theatre Notebook*, 46 (1992), 149.

[48] Drury Lane Paybook B, fos. 78, 87ᵛ; Doane, *Directory*, 17; Kemble, Memoranda A, fo. 45.

[49] Drury Lane Paybook B, fo. 117; Doane, *Directory*, 2, 20.

[50] Drury Lane Paybook B, fo. 89, 103.

[51] Gwilym Beechey, 'Thomas Linley (i)', *New Grove*, xi. 8–9.

Samuel Arnold wrote the majority of new musical works for the Little Theatre in the 1790s.

Even though Linley stopped writing operas in 1788, he continued to act as director of oratorios until 1794. He shared this responsibility with Samuel Arnold from 1788 to 1793, then in 1794 he was joined instead by Storace. In one performance that season, we are told, 'Shaw led the band, Mr. Linley presided at the organ, and Storace played the *Carillons*.'[52] After Linley stopped directing oratorios Storace did not continue the tradition, and the theatre was closed on oratorio nights for the rest of the century.

At the end of the 1794/5 season, Linley sold his share of the theatre and ceased all activities connected with it, but still retained his title of composer to the theatre, with a salary and nominal duties. He died early in the following season, so no 'composer to the theatre' was listed at the end of that season. Unfortunately, Storace too was dead by then. Had he not died so inopportunely, he would undoubtedly have become officially what he had long been in practice—house composer. As it was, William Linley (Thomas's son) was listed as house composer starting in the 1796/7 season. William Linley was at best unproven as a theatrical composer when he was appointed: born in 1771, he had been a civil servant in India from 1790 to 1795, and he composed only two unsuccessful operas for Drury Lane during his short tenure.[53]

Because of Thomas Linley's continuing hold on Drury Lane, Storace was treated as a freelance composer. Instead of a salary he shared the proceeds of the authors' benefit nights with his librettists. Traditionally the author of a new piece received the profits (minus the usual house charge) of the third, sixth, and ninth nights of a mainpiece, and of one night of a new afterpiece.[54] In fact many works did not run for nine nights, although all of Storace's mainpieces except *Dido, Queen of Carthage* did so. The author also received a bonus payment if the work lasted twenty nights in its first season, though this practice was less firmly established.[55] Charles Dibdin described the origin of the tradition:

It has been some times a private compact from *managers* to *authors* to give an extra benefit on the twentieth night of a piece. Mr. Rich introduced this custom in a very handsome way. On the twentieth performance of *Miss in her Teens*, Garrick, when he received the bills in the morning found the farce advertised,

---

[52] *Thespian Magazine*, 3 (1794), 128.

[53] Gwilym Beechey, 'William Linley', *New Grove*, xi. 10.

[54] George Winchester Stone, introduction to *London Stage*, pt. 4, p. cviii.

[55] James Cobb to the proprietors of the Theatre Royal Drury Lane, 1 Jan. 1802, 'Receipts and Letters of Jas. Cobb, 1787–1809' (BL Add. MS 25,915), no. 6.

without any previous notice, for the benefit of its author, which was himself. In the instance of the *Padlock*, he gave Mr. Bickerstaff his choice of an extra benefit or an hundred pounds.[56]

Authors' benefits were organized differently from those of performers. The author did not sell his or her own tickets but simply relied on the income from a normal evening's attendance. An author's income was therefore a true reflection of a work's popularity. According to the *Oracle*, there was also an alternative whereby 'authors submit to the chance of benefit nights, or accept the equivalent of [£]300'.[57]

Kemble sometimes mentioned authors' benefit nights in his diary, but he did not record whether payments were actually made. Storace was certainly owed a great deal of money by the theatre when he died. The account books list only two unspecified payments to him: £200 in 1792 and £210 (200 guineas) in 1794, both to 'cash on account'.[58] These payments were apparently not profits from benefit nights, which are sometimes listed elsewhere, though, as his librettist James Cobb indicated, the theatre was often years behind in paying its debts. For instance, in December 1790, Cobb and Storace each signed for receipt of £14. 7s. 6d. as their shares of the sixth night of *The Doctor and the Apothecary*, which had taken place over two years earlier.[59] Payment for their next collaboration, *The Haunted Tower*, was considerably more prompt, being paid less than two months after its première. Cobb received £150. 8s. 0d., Storace £100, plus 5 guineas for earrings for his sister Nancy.[60] Later Cobb protested that 'although the Opera was performed Sixty nights the first Season, no further remuneration was received by the Author either for a Twentieth Night or for the further Success of the Piece'.[61]

In the early 1790s Cobb and Storace probably felt they were achieving suitable financial reward for their labours. Their next collaboration, *The Siege of Belgrade*, for instance, netted each man £220. They were paid promptly, in February 1791.[62] However, the theatre's laxity surfaced again, because Cobb later declared that a balance of £79, for the three original benefit nights and the twentieth night, remained due to each of them.[63] In 1802 Cobb was so provoked by the theatre's non-payment that he addressed

---

[56] *Musical Tour*, 287–8 n.   [57] *Oracle*, 14 Mar. 1796.

[58] Drury Lane Paybook B, fo. 98ᵛ.

[59] Cobb, receipt dated 11 Dec. 1790, 'Receipts' (BL Add. MS 25,915), no. 5.

[60] Cobb, receipt dated 1 Jan. 1790, 'Receipts' (BL Add. MS 25,915), no. 3.

[61] Cobb to the proprietors of the Theatre Royal Drury Lane, 1 Jan. 1802, 'Receipts' (BL Add. MS 25,915), no. 6.

[62] Drury Lane Paybook B, fo. 57ᵛ. The full amount owed to each man was £238. 9s. 6d.

[63] Cobb to the proprietors, 'Receipts' (BL Add. MS 25,915), no. 6.

the proprietors with 'a joint Claim of the late Mr Storace and myself', in which he asserted that he had received only partial payment of £122. 17s. 6d. for *The Pirates* and nothing for *The Cherokee*. Storace had received nothing for either opera.

Payments for Storace's collaborations with Prince Hoare are less well documented. Hoare alone is recorded as having received payment (£78. 3s. 0d.) for *No Song, No Supper*, though Kemble listed the benefit as being for both men.[64] Hoare and Storace took the alternative payment plan for *The Prize*. In Kemble's words, 'there was no Benefit for the Prize, the Proprietors giving Mr. Storace and Mr. Hoare 150 Pounds in lieu of it'.[65]

Payments for successful performances were not the only profits made by authors and composers. An author's other source of income was the fee paid by the theatre for the copyright, from which the composer (and music) was excluded. In 1790, Hoare received £63 'by the Copy right of No Song No Supper exclusive of the right of selling the Songs'; in 1793 he was paid 200 guineas for *The Prize* '& other Peices'.[66] Again, Cobb listed payment from the theatre of £52. 10s. 0d. for the copyright of *The Haunted Tower* and a debt of 200 guineas for *The Pirates*.[67] Composers (at least at Drury Lane) were luckier in this regard, as they dealt with music publishers, to whom they sold their music copyrights, and who probably paid more promptly. Storace must have derived his income in large part from sales of music from the operas, discussed in Chapter 4.

Theatres in late eighteenth-century London employed full complements of musical personnel, whose importance has been consistently undervalued. The musicians ranged from very prominent members of the company to the most lowly. The singers shared the same backstage support as the actors—director, prompter, set designers, carpenters, 'mantua makers' (dressmakers), and so on. The orchestral players, each of whom earned perhaps a tenth the salary of Anna Crouch or Kelly, held an ambiguous position. On the one hand, they were salaried performers and professionals, many of them belonging to the Royal Society of Musicians; they had their own hierarchy, and their own copyists and porters. On the other hand their performance was virtually ignored as long as it was competently executed. For many instrumentalists, playing in a theatre orchestra must have been a secure (though not well-paying) career, with an income which they could supplement by teaching, performing in other groups, and—for some—trying to realize their ambitions as composers. They had one of the most regular

[64] Drury Lane Paybook B, fo. 57^v; Kemble, Memoranda A, 12 Oct. 1790.
[65] Memoranda A, fo. 224^v.   [66] Drury Lane Paybook B, fo. 47.
[67] Cobb, 'Receipts' (BL Add. MS 25,915), nos. 4, 6.

and stable jobs for an eighteenth-century instrumentalist, yet they belonged to an almost invisible profession, virtually ignored by the public. Composers, who certainly held greater responsibilities and appropriately higher status than orchestral musicians, were better known, but they were financially insecure if they worked on a freelance basis. Storace was particularly unfortunate in this regard, because not only did the theatre often fail to pay him, but by rights he should have been the salaried house composer, and therefore paid more reliably and regularly.

All of these musicians, from the star singers to the music porters, represent a face of the eighteenth-century London stage that must be included in any balanced view of London theatrical life. Without them, the shape of late eighteenth-century theatre would have been vastly different.

4

MUSIC PUBLISHING IN THE
LATE EIGHTEENTH CENTURY

In *A Letter to the Musicians of Great Britain* of 1833, Herbert Rodwell wrote that 'in England, the composer, by being rewarded by the publisher only, must study what will be most likely to *sell*.'[1] His words were certainly applicable to the latter part of the eighteenth century, when publication fees were a major source of a composer's income.

The Sequence of Publication

The typical sequence to publishing operas in the eighteenth century is complicated by the number of different versions printed for various audiences. The words were published without music, both the complete libretto and the song texts alone, with different editors and publishers taking responsibility for the two versions. The music was published complete in a two-stave reduction for voice and keyboard, and various numbers were also printed individually. English operas were never published with spoken dialogue and music together, nor as orchestral scores or parts.

The timing of the publication of an opera was initially related to its theatrical production. Song texts were the first part to appear, entitled 'Songs, Duets, Trios and Chorusses' and sold at the the theatre to patrons attending the performances. They included complete cast lists and were normally available at the première. Playbills often stated that 'Books of the Songs [are] to be had at the Theatre'. The theatre management took responsibility for their publication, passing them on to the orange-sellers to sell

[1] *A Letter to the Musicians of Great Britain* (London, 1833), 6.

on commission. They were often published anonymously and never copy-righted.[2]

Complete texts were published by literary publishers under the super-vision of the author. Sometimes a libretto was published soon after the pre-mière, though the theatre might buy its copyright from the author and keep the work unpublished while it remained in its repertoire. Librettos were bought by theatrical enthusiasts, and no doubt by a few unscrupulous the-atre managers outside London who intended to stage the work without per-mission. The same was true of complete scores, which were almost always the first version of the music to appear in print.

All forms of musical publication were directed at amateur musicians. A two-stave reduction of the complete music was normally published between one and two months after the première; other versions of the music fol-lowed at varying intervals, depending on what the publisher thought the market could sustain. Such editions often included an instrumental arrange-ment of the complete opera (most often for flute), along with a selection of separate numbers (mostly solo songs). These were printed primarily by the original music publisher, but some appeared in unauthorized editions and new arrangements put out by rival firms both in London and abroad. Occasionally individual numbers were published several years after a work's first season, probably stimulated by a revival of the opera. The various musi-cal publications were designed for the most popular forms of amateur music-making: singing and playing with keyboard accompaniment at home. Their purchasers were therefore from the middle and upper end of the social scale.

The complete opera was always published in an oblong quarto volume suitable for placing on a keyboard music-rest, from which singers could be accompanied or could accompany themselves at the piano or harpsichord. Since the music was normally printed on only two staves, an amateur key-board-player could perform both the vocal part and its simplified accom-paniment with ease. One-stave arrangements of the entire opera for flute or guitar appeared in octavo volumes. These included the words so that a singer could use them unaccompanied, but were transposed to keys suit-able for the amateur instrumentalist. Finally, and most lucratively to judge from the number of prints surviving, selected pieces were published indi-vidually. These were mostly solo songs but included some vocal ensembles and an occasional overture or other instrumental piece. Extracts usually

---

[2] The publisher of the song texts at Drury Lane was probably Charles Lowndes, who regularly printed playbills and whose premises were next to the theatre.

appeared in the same two-stave arrangement as the complete score, but newly set by the printer in an upright quarto format. Only overtures were reissued as offprints from the original oblong plates, perhaps because the title already appeared at the top. Most London editions of individual numbers took up two or more pages of paper, with the last page often filled by a one-stave instrumental arrangement. Lastly, the official publisher and others occasionally made arrangements of the most popular songs, usually as glees for unaccompanied voices. All of these individual extracts were selected for their popularity, and were therefore also the targets for most of the pirated editions that followed.

One other form of publication that reflected a piece's popularity was the set of variations. Song melodies were often used by other composers as themes for variations, in which case the new composer took the credit on the title-page, sometimes mentioning the composer whose melody he used, or the song's title. Melodies used in this way were treated as common property and not covered by the original composer's copyright registration, at least in the eighteenth century. Like pirated editions, they helped disseminate the music and added to a composer's reputation, even though he gained no direct financial benefit.

Copyright

Storace must have developed a particularly lively interest in the various aspects of publishing after one of his early works became the subject of a court case against a music publisher. The procedures followed by Storace's publishers are typical of the generation that pioneered the regular use of music copyright in Britain.

The various degrees of legal and illegal publication require some explanation because unauthorized publication of both literary and musical works occurred with monotonous regularity in the eighteenth century. Yet the the various terms used for publication with and without the composer's approval and for legal and illegal publication are often used inaccurately. The terms 'authorized', 'authentic', and 'official' all imply the permission of the composer to publish.[3] Naturally, authorized publications can be registered as copyright, either to the composer or to a publisher who has bought the copyright from the composer. The usual term for any unauthorized

---

[3] *The Authentic English Editions of Beethoven* (London, 1963), 22.

publication, 'pirated', masks a distinction between two kinds of unauthorized edition, one legal and the other not. An unauthorized but legal publication in eighteenth-century England was one that lacked the author's explicit permission but which had not already been published in a copyrighted edition, whereas a pirated copy was an illegal publication, where a copyright edition already existed.[4] The term 'unauthorized' would then cover both English editions copied from authorized but not copyrighted editions and foreign publications sold abroad for local consumption. 'Pirated' applies specifically to editions produced and sold in England in direct contravention of the copyright law.

Pirated editions meant a loss of sales to the copyright-holder, whereas the activities of foreign publishers interfered only minimally with an English publisher's profits. Storace emphasized this point in his affidavit when he sued Longman & Broderip.[5] From a musical point of view the distinction between authorized and unauthorized (including pirated) editions is significant because the authority of the composer suggests—though by no means guarantees—reasonable accuracy in an edition. Many unauthorized editions, on the other hand, abound in mistakes, misprints, and even deliberate alterations.

By the late eighteenth century, composers and music publishers had begun to appreciate the benefits of copyright registration. For them, of course, it meant some protection against duplicate editions of music and therefore lost income. For us, it often provides the most accurate means available of dating music prints. In the earlier part of the century, musical publications were seldom registered as copyright; by the last two decades many were.

In 1709 the 'Act for the Encouragement of Learning, by Vesting the Copies of Printed Books in the Authors or Purchasers of such Copies, during the Times therein mentioned' was passed by the British parliament.[6] The Act of Anne, as it was known, clarified a confused situation and answered the petitions of many publishers for an enforceable copyright law.[7] In brief, the Act gave copyright protection to the owner (usually the publisher) of a printed work for fourteen years, after which ownership reverted to the author for the following fourteen years if he or she was still living. In order to acquire the protection afforded by law, the copyright-owner had to enter the work in the register of the Worshipful Company of Stationers before

---

[4] 'Music Copyright in Britain to 1800', *ML* 67 (1986), 272.

[5] London, Public Record Office, C31/247/39. The affidavits of both plaintiff and defendants are transcribed in Jane C. Girdham, 'Stephen Storace and the English Opera Tradition of the Late Eighteenth Century', Ph.D. diss. (University of Pennsylvania, 1988), app. 4.

[6] The text is reproduced in Harry Ransom, *The First Copyright Statute: An Essay on 'An Act for the Encouragement of Learning'* (Austin, Tex., 1956), 109–17.

[7] Ibid., chs. 6–7, see esp. p. 85.

its official publication, pay 6*d.* per entry, and within ten days of entry supply nine copies of the work to the Stationers' Company. These copies were then distributed to nine 'copyright libraries' on request.[8]

An amendment to the Act of Anne in 1801 required that, among other minor adjustments, eleven copies should be provided, because the number of copyright libraries now included two in Ireland following the Act of Union in 1800. The Act of Union, by which the 'United Kingdom of Great Britain and Ireland' was formed and Ireland lost its legislature in Dublin and thus the partial autonomy of its legal system, had a widespread effect on the Irish publishing industry. Whereas music publishers in Dublin had previously subsisted mainly on producing cheap unauthorized editions of English music, they now fell under the jurisdiction of British copyright law. This change meant that what had been merely unauthorized publications in the eighteenth century, irritating to some but legal, became clearly illegal in the nineteenth.

Because the Irish publishing trade was not bound by English copyright law until the nineteenth century, the activities of eighteenth-century Dublin publishers were legal as long as their editions were sold only locally and not where the works were covered by copyright. In other words, a Dublin publisher could legally sell his or her wares to the Irish public, but as soon as those works were exported to Britain they became illegal. Even so, the ethics of publishing British works without permission were frequently dubious. Dublin booksellers conducted a large export trade, both to American cities and across the Irish Sea.[9] In 1791 the London bookseller James Lackington wrote:

As to Ireland, I shall only observe, that if the booksellers in that part of the empire do not shine in the possession of valuable books, they must certainly be allowed to possess superior industry in reprinting the works of every english author of merit, as soon as published, and very liberally endeavouring to disseminate them, in a surreptitious manner through every part of our Island, though the attempt frequently proves abortive, to the great loss and injury of the projectors.[10]

Some literary publications were condoned and encouraged by London publishers, who sold the rights for Irish publication to Dublin publishers.[11] However, there is no evidence that Irish music publishers either bought

---

[8] Tyson, *Authentic English Editions*, app. I: 'Entry at Stationers Hall'.

[9] James W. Phillips, 'A Bibliographical Inquiry into Printing and Bookselling in Dublin from 1670 to 1800', Ph.D. diss. (Trinity College, Dublin, 1952), 186–7, table opposite 208.

[10] *Memoirs of the First Forty-Five Years of the Life of James Lackington, the Present Bookseller in Chiswell-street, Moorfields, London. Written by Himself. In a Series of Letters to a Friend* (London [1791]), 279.

[11] Phillips, 'Bibliographical Inquiry', 189.

rights to their prints or exported the prints to England, so that Irish editions, along with the multitude of American ones, should be considered merely unauthorized.

Other countries had their own national copyright laws, none of which protected a foreign publisher against unauthorized publication. A solution used by some publishers was to publish and copyright a new work simultaneously in all the countries in which it was to be distributed.[12] In the late eighteenth century, English theatrical music was performed and published in Britain, Ireland, and America, but almost never in continental Europe. Music was not mentioned in American copyright law until 1831, and British publishers therefore seem to have been unconcerned about registering their operatic works as copyright anywhere except Britain. In London, rival music publishers did not always obey the letter of the law, but they were chary of publishing a work registered as copyright by another British publisher. Irish and American publishers on the other hand, who were out of the reach of English law and not constrained by duplicate registration in their own countries, produced numerous editions of English stage songs as soon as they were available. As a result, a profusion of unauthorized foreign editions exists, and a large number of published extracts from Storace's operas were published by several Irish and American publishers as well as their English copyright-holders.[13]

Authorized British publications entered in the Stationers' Hall register usually included the copyright notice 'Entered at Stationers' Hall' on the title-page. However, just as publishers were not obliged to register new works, so there was nothing to stop them including that notice on publications that were not registered. It saved them the price of registration while providing some deterrent to other publishers.

The copyright law as it applied to music was not entirely clear until the late 1770s, and few musical editions before that date were registered as copyright.[14] However, in 1773 Johann Christian Bach brought a lawsuit against the publisher James Longman for the unauthorized publication of two of his compositions. Judgment was eventually given for Bach in 1777, when Lord Chief Justice Mansfield declared that music fell within the definition

---

[12] Joel Sachs, 'Hummel and the Pirates: The Struggle for Musical Copyright', *MQ* 59 (1973), 32. For information on foreign copyright laws that affected music, see Joel Sachs, 'English and French Editions of Hummel', *JAMS* 25 (1972), 215; Richard J. Wolfe, *Early American Music Engraving and Printing* (Urbana, Ill., 1980), 192–3.

[13] Wolfe, *American Music Engraving*, 190. For the most complete list of Storace's publications available, see Girdham, 'Stephen Storace', app. 6.

[14] For a description of the problems faced by music publishers before 1775, see John A. Parkinson, 'Pirates and Publishers . . .', *Performing Right*, 58 (1972), 20–2.

of literary property and therefore came under the Copyright Act.[15] Thereafter entries of musical publications in the Stationers' Hall register increased steadily.

Another court case in London, brought by Stephen Storace against Longman & Broderip in 1788, raised the question of a composer's ownership, this time against the unwritten rights of theatrical copyists. Storace had Bach's case as a precedent, and probably encouragement from his uncle John Trusler, who had once sued a publisher for breach of copyright.[16] In a production of Paisiello's *Il re Teodoro* at the King's Theatre that opened on 8 December 1787, Nancy Storace performed an aria by her brother, 'Care donne che bramate'. The number was well liked and Storace, who was not paid by the theatre for his aria, published it at his own expense.[17] He entered it at Stationers' Hall on 21 December 1787, the second work he had ever copyrighted. Meanwhile, a copyist employed by the theatre sold the whole opera, including Storace's aria, to Longman & Broderip, who then published the aria alone shortly afterwards, entering it as copyright on 31 December.[18]

Storace sued Longman & Broderip in the Court of Chancery in January 1788, and final judgment was given in July 1789. Meanwhile he used 'Care donne' in two adaptations, perhaps to fortify his claim to his own music.[19] The copyist claimed that at the King's Theatre he had 'absolute and exclusive power of disposing of the Copy right thereof it being part of his salary'.[20] The defence contended that the copyist had the right to sell the music and that Storace had no rights in Badini's words. Storace conceded the latter point, as the modified copyright entries allocate the rights in the words to Longman & Broderip. Their argument that the music of their edition differed from Storace's was soon dropped; they admitted that the variants were trivial. After many hearings and a counterclaim by Longman & Broderip, Storace eventually won his case in July 1789. He was awarded a token 1s., plus legal costs and an injunction against Longman & Broderip

---

[15] Hunter, 'Music Copyright', 278–9; John Small, 'J. C. Bach Goes to Law', *MT* 126 (1985), 526–9.

[16] Trusler, *Memoirs*, 155–6.   [17] Price, Milhous, and Hume, *Italian Opera*, i. 389–93.

[18] In their original copyright entries, Storace claimed the whole of the rights in his edition, Longman & Broderip the whole of theirs. The entries were updated so that they both credited Storace with the rights in the music and Longman & Broderip with the rights in the words. The amendments were probably made as part of the final settlement in July 1789, a month after Longman & Broderip's lawyer was given copies of them.

[19] Storace adapted 'Care donne' as 'How mistaken is the lover' (*The Doctor and the Apothecary*, no. 14) and used the melody as the rondo theme in the finale of his Sonata no. 2 in C for piano, violin, and cello. Both works date from 1788.

[20] The defendants' affidavit (London, Public Record Office, C31/247/81); Storace's affidavit (London, Public Record Office, C31/247/39).

publishing his aria. The judge thus established that a composer retained ownership of his composition until he chose to dispose of it himself, and affirmed that sheet music was covered by the Act.[21] Thus, in the last decade of the eighteenth century, any London publisher who printed a pirated edition did so in the knowledge that he was breaking the law and leaving himself open to prosecution.

The increasing number of musical publications entered in the Stationers' Hall register demonstrates that music publishers and composers recognized the significance of the court cases fought over musical copyright. A count of musical and non-musical entries (including the few books on music) for 1790 and 1798 illustrates the trend clearly. In 1790 the ratio of music to other publications was 1 : 3 (97 musical entries and 301 other); in 1798 music had more than doubled to 210 entries while non-musical publications barely changed at 315, making the ratio a striking 2 : 3.

The increasing use of copyright for musical publications in the 1790s reflects a change in policy by music publishers including Dale, Storace's main publisher. In his first publication for Storace in 1791, *The Siege of Belgrade*, he copyrighted only the complete score (plus one extract much later, in 1798), even though he published many separate extracts soon after the complete score. However, when he published Storace's subsequent works, he registered first the complete edition, then almost all the single extracts, plus a number of new arrangements of pieces from the operas.

Usually a composer sold the rights of a new work to his publisher for a lump sum, after which any profit from sales belonged entirely to the publisher. Our knowledge of the prices paid for operatic works comes from a variety of roughly contemporaneous publications, none of which are necessarily reliable. According to *The Quarterly Musical Magazine and Review* in 1822, Storace was paid £400 for *The Haunted Tower*; William T. Parke in 1830 named £500 for the same opera.[22] Figures for *The Siege of Belgrade* are more divergent. A few days before its publication the *Gazeteer* reported that Storace was paid 500 guineas (£525); Parke later claimed he was paid £1,000.[23] To judge from some of the sums paid to authors earlier in the century, even the latter figure would not have been inordinately large.[24] Further, Thomas Busby stated in 1825 that 'Longman and Broderip gave

---

[21] London, Public Record Office, recordings of proceedings in Chancery (C33), fourteen entries in 1788 and 1789.

[22] C. C. T., letter to the editor, *The Quarterly Musical Magazine and Review*, 4 (1822): 154; Parke, *Musical Memoirs*, i. 123–4.

[23] *Gazeteer*, 5 Feb. 1791; Parke, *Musical Memoirs*, i. 135.

[24] See e.g. Philip Gaskell, *A New Introduction to Bibliography* (New York, 1972), 184–5.

Mr. Shield one thousand guineas for his opera *The Woodman*; and to Stephen Storace more than five hundred guineas, for most of his musical dramas; and often paid fifty or a hundred guineas for a single vocal composition.'[25] Some recent writers have taken Busby's word literally;[26] however, his statement should be treated cautiously as it derives from a basic fallacy. In fact only Storace's first three operas were published by Longman & Broderip; starting with *The Siege of Belgrade* they were published by Joseph Dale.

Storace's compositions, like those of other popular composers of the time, were sometimes pirated by London publishers. Dale, obviously aware that other publishers were taking some of his business, put the following notice at the bottom of a catalogue of Storace's music:

NB. The above Works are the sole Property of J. Dale & Entered at Stationers Hall. The Public are respectfully entreated to take Notice that to each Piece in future will be added this Catalogue, with his address as above,—to prevent spurious Copies, as many of the Airs have been Imitated & with other words Sold as if Sung in the above Operas.[27]

Dale was not entirely law-abiding himself. On 20 December 1794 the Edinburgh publisher George Thomson placed an advertisement in *The Times* stating that

J. Dale, of London, has published some spurious Sonatas, under the name of Pleyel, similar in form, and with a Title-Page so closely imitating that of the real Work, as may at first sight deceive the unsuspecting Purchaser; a proceeding which Mr. Thomson is compelled thus to expose, to prevent injury to his property.

Dale's and Thomson's statements describe—and condemn—two strategies used by publishers when printing pirated editions. Some kept barely on the right side of the copyright law by setting familiar music to new words; others risked legal action from the copyright-holder by copying the original almost exactly. As well as relying on statements such as these to alert the public to copyright offences, publishers do seem to have used the Stationers' Hall ledger to uphold their rights. Entries sometimes include a later inscription 'certificate given' and the date, suggesting its owner was demonstrating his rights to a work.

The issue of who owned the rights to song texts was raised in Storace's

---

[25] *Concert Room and Orchestra Anecdotes*, i. 127.

[26] Fiske, *English Theatre Music*, 300; Hunter, 'Music Copyright', 281.

[27] Dale's catalogue, as it appears in his edition of the overture to *Mahmoud* (entered at Stationers' Hall on 27 Dec. 1797) and other contemporary publications.

suit against Longman & Broderip, but it remained unresolved well into the nineteenth century, as James Robinson Planché, an early nineteenth-century dramatist and the librettist of Weber's *Oberon*, wrote in his reminiscences for 1829:

It had been a custom of long standing for an author to allow the composer of his opera to publish the words with the music. They were not considered of any value, and in a literary point of view there might, in too many instances, have been some truth in the assertion. Still, without the words, however poor they might be, the music of a new opera could not be published. The fact never appeared to have occurred to any one, or, if it had, no author had thought it worth his while to moot the question.[28]

Planché was not entirely correct, though his point should be taken in essence. There is one other mention of song texts related to Storace, this time in the Drury Lane account books. In 1790 a payment of £63 was made to Prince Hoare, librettist of Storace's *No Song, No Supper*, 'by the Copy right of No Song No Supper exclusion of the right of selling the Songs'.[29] In other words, Hoare was giving Storace the rights to the words so that Storace could sell the copyright to the songs (words and music) to a music publisher. No later entries for copyright include such addenda, probably because Storace's librettists made it known that they would not disturb the *status quo*.

DATES

Exact dating of musical editions from the late eighteenth century would allow us to study trends of popularity, but such precision is not always possible. English music publishers rarely included imprinted dates on their editions; indeed, only two out of several hundred English editions of Storace are dated. We must date Storace's editions through a combination of information from premières, advertisements and printed catalogues, copyright entries, watermark dates, and any facts known about the composers and publishers themselves.

Some approaches to dating are less useful than others. For instance, plate numbers were rarely used in English music before the nineteenth century; none of Storace's London editions contains one.[30] Watermarks are

---

[28] *Recollections and Reflections: A Professional Autobiography* (London, 1901), 106.

[29] Drury Lane Paybook B, fo. 47.

[30] Alec Hyatt King, Oliver W. Neighbour, and Alan Tyson, 'Great Britain', in Donald W. Krummel (comp.), *Guide for Dating Early Published Music: A Manual of Bibliographical Practices* (Hackensack, NJ, 1974), 132. See also O. W. Neighbour and Alan Tyson, *English Music Publishers' Plate Numbers in the First Half of the Nineteenth Century* (London, 1965), 10–11.

equally unhelpful, although paper after 1794 generally includes a water-mark date. An Act was passed in 1794 requiring British paper to contain a watermark date in order that booksellers could claim back part of the paper duty when books were exported. The law was rescinded in 1811, but many paper-makers continued to include watermark dates.[31] Paper was normally used within five years of the date when it was made, but in most cases a five-year margin is too wide to provide dates any more precise than we can achieve by other methods.[32]

The date of a première certainly provides the earliest publication date for a staged work, because no work is known to have been published in advance of this. Newspaper advertisements are some help, though the phrase 'published this day' should not always be taken literally. Catalogues (where these can be dated) should provide a latest date for the works included there. However, Dale's catalogues should be used with caution, because he left Storace's works in them long after they were first published. Also, he sometimes reissued works years after the original publication date, using the old plates. For instance, *Lodoiska* was originally published in 1794, yet a copy of Dale's edition exists in the British Library on paper with an 1805 watermark.[33] Finally, Dale seems to have included speculative pieces in his catalogues, which means that the catalogues only give us the date he offered a work for sale, whereas the piece may actually have been published considerably later, if at all.

Copyright entries in the Stationers' Hall ledgers provide by far the most accurate information about publication dates for authorized editions. Copyright editions were required to be registered before publication, and the fact that most entries, including those for Storace's pieces, are copied exactly from the engraved plates ready for publication indicates that entries were made in the register only a short time before the actual publication dates, sometimes only days before.[34] Copyright dates are therefore the most precise we have.

The entries in the Stationers' Hall register routinely include the date, the name of the copyright-owner, the proportions of ownership if the copyright is shared, and a full entry of the title-page, including full subtitles. Each entry records the receipt of the obligatory nine copies and the signature of the clerk. Also noted in the ledger entries are the dates of any

---

[31] C. B. Oldman, 'Watermark Dates in English Paper', *Library*, 4/25 (1944–5), 70–1.

[32] Jan LaRue, 'British Music Paper 1770–1820: Some Distinctive Characteristics', *MMR* 87 (1957), 178.

[33] Some watermark dates are given in Laureen Baillie (ed.), *The Catalogue of Printed Music in the British Library to 1980*, 62 vols. (London, 1981–7).

[34] Tyson, *Authentic English Editions*, 139–41.

certificates of ownership given, and to whom. The submitted copies are some-times signed at the bottom of the title-page by the copyright-owner.

Appendix 3 lists all the works by Storace or incorporated by him in his operas that were entered at Stationers' Hall before 1800. It therefore pro-vides precise dates for over a hundred editions and confirms the dramatic increase in copyright entries for music that began in the 1780s. The entries also allow us to deduce something of Joseph Dale's general publishing pro-cedures. Dale owned the rights to all of Storace's published operas from *The Siege of Belgrade* up to the memorial volume of *The Iron Chest* and *Mahmoud*, which he printed for Storace's widow Mary in 1797. She owned the copyright of the memorial volume; Dale kept the rights in the extracts from both works. He almost always published the complete edition of each opera first, usually between one and two months after its première. The slightly longer gap that occurred between the premières of *Lodoiska* and *The Glorious First of June* in June and July 1794 and their publication the following September is probably due to the intervention of the summer season. The only real exception to the short time-lag is the joint volume of *The Iron Chest* and *Mahmoud*, published a year after Storace's death. The complete edition of each opera was followed by a series of extracts, sometimes published over a period of several years. Only one extract was published before the opera: Storace's adaptation of Kreutzer's overture to *Lodoiska*.

Dale was fairly careful to copyright his publication of Storace's works, but he was not entirely consistent. If we consider only publications after 1791—that is, those for which Dale usually copyrighted all versions in their first editions—two particular groups of extracts are noteworthy. Twenty-three pieces listed in his various catalogues were neither entered as copy-right nor are extant; five others—'Ah tell me softly' (*The Prize*); Overture and Grand March, Overture and Symphonies, and 'Sweet bird' (*Lodoiska*); 'Full many a lad' (*The Three and the Deuce*)—survive but were not reg-istered, at least before 1804. The two editions involving the overture to *Lodoiska* may perhaps be excluded from further discussion on the grounds that Dale did copyright his first edition of the overture.[35] It is highly unlikely that the editions of the other three pieces date from the nineteenth century, even though their operas were all still in the Drury Lane reper-toire early in the century. 'Sweet bird' was issued as an offprint from the

---

[35] This did not stop at least two other contemporary publishers pirating the work. Preston re-named it *Dodolska*; Goulding left it as *Lodoiska*. Many later publishers also produced editions and arrangements.

original plates of *Lodoiska* and will be discussed later. The other two pieces are anomalies. Perhaps he simply forgot to register them as copyright.

The twenty-three pieces that only exist as titles in Dale's catalogues are more puzzling. The catalogues, which he attached to many of his editions, sometimes include works by a number of composers, though two at least (which differ only slightly in content) are devoted entirely to Storace. The first is included in the various separate extracts from *The Iron Chest* and *Mahmoud* published at the end of 1797; the second, appearing in an edition of 'Ye streams' (*Lodoiska*, no. 8) dates from about 1800 'and is slightly fuller. It includes all the pieces by Storace that Dale ever published, except the ballet *Venus and Adonis* and glee arrangements of airs.

Some of the twenty-three 'lost' editions that were never copyrighted continued to be listed in Dale's catalogues for years. The most obvious explanation for their continued presence is that Dale was enacting a deliberate if obscure policy of including in his catalogues pieces that he was prepared to publish on request, but that had not been (and never were) actually published. He may have listed all the operatic extracts he thought might be of interest to the public, then prepared new editions of only those whose popularity was already established in the theatre. If he then waited to print the others until somebody requested them, he was bound to be left with some pieces in his catalogues that were never republished as individual pieces or, in consequence, registered as copyright. Those that were later requested would be copyrighted upon preparation of the new plates, just before publication. Such a policy would explain the existence of a few airs with late copyright dates, such as 'Oh dear delightful skill' (*The Prize*, no. 3), which was first performed in March 1793 but not entered at Stationers' Hall until February 1798. Unfortunately we are unable to tell when Dale first offered the piece for sale, as there are no complete catalogues of Storace's music before late 1797; however, the song was included in the 1797 catalogues.

'Sweet bird', the song that was issued separately as an offprint from the plates of the complete opera but not copyrighted, belongs to a different group of prints. It was one of only three vocal numbers issued as offprints; the other two were registered at Stationers' Hall. The ledger entries for 'We the veil of fate undraw' (*The Pirates*, no. 28) and 'Five times by the taper light' (*The Iron Chest*, no. 1) are taken word for word from the tops of the pages in their respective complete scores. All three would have been cumbersome and complicated to re-engrave, as 'Five times by the taper light' is a vocal quartet with accompaniment, 'We the veil' is a trio, and 'Sweet bird' is a virtuoso air with complex notation on three staves. Unlike the two ensembles, 'Sweet bird' was not a likely seller, being one of Storace's most difficult songs. It may originally have belonged to Dale's speculative list then been reissued at a (surely rare) patron's request. It would not have been worth re-engraving, and perhaps was not even worth the 6*d*. copyright fee.

A comparison between Dale's various catalogues leads to one further conclusion. His earliest catalogue to include pieces by Storace appears in the front of *The Pirates* (registered at Stationers' Hall on 24 December 1792) and the last in 'Ye streams' from *Lodoiska*, dating from about 1800. All Storace's pieces in the first catalogue continue to be listed in the last one seven or eight years later, which suggests that Dale kept the works in print, or at least kept the engraved plates in store and available for reissue, over a number of years. The 1794 edition of *Lodoiska* on paper watermarked with an 1805 date must have been just such a reissue, and should serve as a warning not to date editions by their watermarks.

Sometimes a publisher's changes of address or partners can provide useful dating information. From this point of view, it is unfortunate that Dale's publishing house was very stable in the 1790s, when he was publishing Storace's works. He did, however, use a variety of wordings for his addresses. As D. W. Krummel mentions, the actual wording of an address can often be pinned down to a particular period of a publisher's career.[36] In fact, Dale was so conscientious in copyrighting Storace's works after 1791 that a study of the variations in his address usually just provides confirmation of information we already know. He owned two shops in London, one at 19 Cornhill, the other at 132 Oxford Street. He often included extra directions in his prints, probably to help prospective clients find the shops. The following versions of his addresses exist, all starting with 'No. 19 Cornhill':

. . . and No. 132 Oxford Street
. . . and No. 132 Oxford Street opposite Hanover Square
. . . and No. 132 Oxford Street facing Hanover Square
. . . and No. 132 Oxford Street at the corner of Holles Street
. . . and the corner of Holles Street No. 132 Oxford Street

Dale used the shortest form, 'No. 19 Cornhill and No. 132 Oxford Street', throughout his relationship with Storace, on extracts from almost all his operas. He generally used it when he had the least space available. All the complete operas, with their full title-pages, use longer forms. Some were used over a narrower range of dates but only 'No. 19 Cornhill and the

---

[36] *Guide for Dating Early Published Music: A Manual of Bibliographical Practices* (Hackensack, NJ, 1974), 65.

corner of Holles Street No. 132 Oxford Street' does not overlap any other long version. Beginning in 1797 all the pieces registered as copyright show this form of address, until at least 1798, the last of Dale's entries for pieces by Storace. He may have used the same form until about 1802, when he added a shop in New Bond Street. We can use this information to distinguish early from late prints. As far as the authorized editions of Storace's works are concerned, we are lucky that Dale was such a conscientious publisher; his puzzling editions are few and far between.

Music Publishers

Eighteenth-century music publishers were specialists.[37] They catered to a variety of musical tastes, and they formed working relationships with composers that often lasted for years. They also provided for a broad range of other musical needs, often combining music publishing with activities such as making and selling instruments. Joseph Dale's announcement of his activities is fairly typical:

Joseph Dale, Importer and Publisher of Music, and Manufacturer of Musical Instruments at his Warehouses No. 19 Cornhill, and No. 132 Oxford Street, London: Where Music and Instruments are sold or let out by the Month, Quarter, or Year, and if Purchased and payment made within Eight Months, the hire will be returned. Musical Instruments conveyed in an easy Machine to any part of the Town or Country—also—Tuned on the shortest Notice. Pedal Harps Imported from Paris. Merchants, Captains, & others, supplied for Exportation.[38]

He also patented 'improvements on the tambourine' in 1799, which involved a new method of tightening the skin.[39] Dale was also a composer, with numerous piano works (including two concertos) and songs to his credit.

Longman & Broderip, one of Dale's major competitors, engaged in similar activities, including renting instruments, selling concert tickets, and patenting improvements in instrumental design. An announcement for one novelty reads:

---

[37] Charles Humphries and William C. Smith, *Music Publishing in the British Isles from the Beginning until the Middle of the Nineteenth Century: A Dictionary of Engravers, Printers, Publishers and Music Sellers, with a Historical Introduction* (2nd edn., Oxford, 1970), 1–42 *passim*.

[38] Dale's announcement appears on the back of the title-page of his edition of Storace's *The Pirates*, arranged for flute, entered at Stationers' Hall on 7 Feb. 1793.

[39] *Patents for Inventions, Abridgments of Specifications Relating to Music and Musical Instruments. A.D. 1694–1866* (London, 1871), 33–4.

Patent Piano Forte Guitars.

Longman and Broderip, at their Grand Musical Magazines, No. 26, Cheapside, and No. 13, Haymarket, respectfully acquaint the Nobility, Gentry, and Publick in general, that they have obtained his Majesty's Royal Letters Patent for their great improvement of those instruments, being made to play with keys; an invention which gives them a decided superiority over every instrument of the kind, as it not only renders the fingering remarkably easy and graceful, but also adds a superior degree of brilliancy to the tone. They have also this singular advantage, that the machinery is so curiously contrived, that on the least accident happening to the movement, it can be drawn out with the greatest ease, and immediately rectified.[40]

In the late eighteenth century, a number of music publishers, including Dale, owned circulating music libraries. Dale's contained over 100,000 volumes, many of which he bought from Samuel Babbs in 1786.[41]

On a more casual note, Thomas Busby reports that Longman & Broderip not only paid their composers well but also 'conferred a nearly equal service by keeping an open table, at which professors and amateurs, from every part of the world, had the opportunity of meeting, and of eliciting from each other information of mutual and considerable advantage'.[42]

Storace's Published Music

COMPLETE EDITIONS

Storace was associated with the firms of Longman & Broderip and Birchall & Andrews between 1782 and 1791, the year he established his relationship with Dale. He also once used Andrews as his publisher after Robert Birchall and Hugh Andrews had parted ways in 1789. In addition, Storace published several of his early works himself, probably under an arrangement also used for literary publications, where a book was published for its author on commission, with the publisher keeping a percentage of each copy printed or sold but the author owning the engraved plates.

---

[40] *Morning Chronicle*, 5 Mar. 1787. No patent for Longman & Broderip is listed in *Patents for Inventions*. However, the descriptions of Christian Clauss's patent for a keyboard attachment to a guitar (p. 14, no. 1394) and John Goldsworth's for a repair mechanism and other additions (pp. 15–16, no. 1491) taken together agree with the description given in the *Morning Chronicle*. Longman & Broderip probably built an instrument that incorporated one or both of these 'improvements'.

[41] Alec Hyatt King, 'Music Circulating Libraries in Britain', *MT* 119 (1978), 134–48; Ian Maxted, *The London Book Trades, 1775–1800*, 59.

[42] *Concert Room Anecdotes*, i. 127.

Larger projects, such as *Storace's Collection of Original Harpsichord Music*, were generally financed by subscription.

As an unestablished figure in the musical world, Storace bore the financial burden of publishing his largest early ventures himself, namely *Storace's Collection* and his first two operas, *The Doctor and the Apothecary* and *The Haunted Tower*. When he became successful, publishers were willing to take on the risk. Thus the last volume of *Storace's Collection* was published by Andrews, and both operas were subsequently printed by publishers under their own names using Storace's original plates. The only pieces he later published himself were three short vocal works not associated with operas: 'Captivity', 'The Lamentation of Marie Antoinette', and 'Io non era'. These were all printed by Dale for Storace and listed in Dale's catalogues.[43]

Storace's earliest publications include songs and chamber works, his first operas, and *Six Easy and Progressive Sonatinas* in 1791. Some were published by professional publishers; others were his own publications. He began his exclusive relationship with Dale in 1791 with *The Siege of Belgrade*. Dale, some twelve years older than Storace, had opened his business in 1783. He published few operas by other composers, all of whom had their own regular publishers.[44] Storace was his main operatic composer in the 1790s.

The complete music of thirteen of Storace's sixteen English stage works was published in reduced scores, which served as a basis for all later editions and arrangements. Two operas were never published: *The Cave of Trophonius* (1791) and *Dido, Queen of Carthage* (1792). *Dido* was Storace's only all-sung English opera and his only serious work; *The Cave of Trophonius* was set in the world of faery. Both were almost immediate failures on stage and therefore not considered worth publishing.

If we accept Tyson's thesis that dates of entry at Stationers' Hall were very close to publication dates, then copyright dates establish that publishers waited at least a month before making the music of a new opera available to the public. While the delay must have been needed in part to prepare and engrave a keyboard reduction, it also allowed the publisher to ensure that the opera was a success before he began such a major production as a

---

[43] Strangely, Dale owned the copyright of 'Captivity'.

[44] Most of Shield's works were published by Napier from 1778 to 1784, when he moved to Longman & Broderip. Napier seems to have been in financial difficulties around that time, as Dale acquired some of his plates around 1785 (Humphries and Smith, *Music Publishing*, 241). Dale seems to have taken over the entire publishing rights of William Shield's *Rosina*; he also published Michael Kelly's music for *The Castle Spectre* and *A Friend in Need* (both 1797), but no other theatrical music by Shield, Thomas Attwood, or Samuel Arnold, who were some of Storace's most prominent contemporaries.

complete opera score. Music cut from stage productions shortly after the première is not usually included in the complete scores.

As far as we can tell, the complete editions of Storace's works contain all the vocal music from each opera, even one number that was not performed on stage.[45] They include the overtures, airs, ensembles, and occasional incidental music. Each individual piece is headed by the name of its original singer; there is no other title, though the character's name sometimes appears within the score at the first vocal entry. In his earliest operas, Storace consistently labelled borrowed pieces at the top right-hand corner; later he acknowledged his debts to other composers only on the title-pages. Spoken dialogue is never included in the scores; the beginnings and ends of acts are sometimes indicated, but scenes are never specified.

The arranger of Storace's complete scores is almost always anonymous, but was probably Storace himself, except for the memorial volume of *The Iron Chest* and *Mahmoud*, which credits Storace's former colleague Joseph Mazzinghi with the arrangement. The standard format for operas is a two-stave reduction for voice and keyboard in which the vocal line and bass dominate a simplified texture, but with a flexibility that allows for an additional stave for particularly important instrumental parts. Vocal ensembles usually include a stave for each voice, or, in some larger ones, one stave for every two voices. Small notes are sometimes used for brief indications of instrumental parts, to fill in harmonies on the upper stave, and occasionally to provide the amateur singer with notes of a suitable range. Figured bass is included in Storace's earliest operas, though only in *The Siege of Belgrade* with any consistency. Figure 4.1, the first page of 'Blithe as the hours of May' in Dale's complete score of *The Siege of Belgrade*, illustrates many of these features: the singer's name, the composer from whom music was borrowed (Martin y Soler), the character's name above bar 12, small notes, figured bass, and a few other instrumental indications.

Four of Storace's operas survive in complete editions by more than one publisher: his first three, as he was establishing himself in London, and *The Iron Chest* from the end of his life. In the early works, a proper exchange of copyright took place between the first and second publisher. Storace's first English opera, *The Doctor and the Apothecary* (1788), went through two editions, the first by Birchall & Andrews for Storace (who owned the copyright), the second by Longman & Broderip, who simply took over the earlier plates but substituted their own firm's name and address on the

---

[45] 'Ah ne'er ungrateful', *The Prize*, pp. 14–15, is marked 'N.B. This Song is left out in the representation.' The only omitted number is an overture to *The Glorious First of June*, which was, however, published separately. It was probably not composed by Storace.

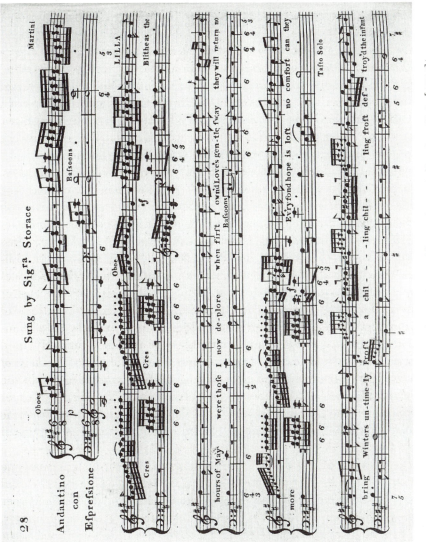

Fig. 4.1. 'Blithe as the hours of May', *The Siege of Belgrade*, no. 9 (London: Dale [1791])

otherwise original title-page. They probably took over the rights in 1789 when Birchall & Andrews disbanded. Evidently Hugh Andrews, who published Storace's three sonatas the following year, had no interest in operatic editions, whereas Longman & Broderip made operas a large portion of their business.

The Haunted Tower (1789) appeared in no less than six editions, the first for the author, then two by Longman & Broderip, and finally three dating from the early nineteenth century: one by Dale, and two by Clementi and partners. Storace's and Longman & Broderip's first editions are dated 1789, though neither was entered at Stationers' Hall until January 1790. Storace's edition was copyrighted on 16 January; a signed and witnessed superscription was added on 18 January to the effect that he had sold his rights to Longman & Broderip. Apparently neither party held a grudge after their court case, settled only six months earlier. All the later editions are based on the original engraved plates, with an increasing number of substitutions as the originals wore out or were damaged. Charles Dibdin describes a similar situation in bragging about his afterpiece *The Padlock* of 1768: '*Comus* is known to have sold very extensively, but after upwards of thirty years, three fourths of the original plates are still in use. What then will be said when I assure the public the *Padlock* had, seven years ago, nearly worn out three entire sets!'[46] The later editions of *The Haunted Tower* also use modified versions of Longman & Broderip's pictorial title-page.

Both Longman & Broderip and Dale published *No Song, No Supper* (1790). Longman & Broderip owned the copyright; they also published the customary flute arrangement and individual songs. Dale probably republished the work to coincide with a new stage production after 1791, when he became Storace's publisher. An exact date is unavailable, because the work was performed regularly into the nineteenth century and Dale did not copyright his edition.

The situation as regards *The Iron Chest* is different. Dale entered his edition for Mary Storace at Stationers' Hall in March 1797; George Walker then published an edition between 1812 and 1820, after the fourteen-year copyright had expired in 1811. He designed his edition in the new manner, with an upright format. Certain numbers have titles that would allow them to stand alone, including two sets of page numbers, one related to their position in the complete score, the other for the individual number only. Thus Walker prepared the overture along with numbers 1, 5, 7, and 11 with the dual aim of collective and individual publication. Walker's

---

[46] *The Musical Tour of Mr. Dibdin*, 287.

edition was probably unauthorized but not actually illegal because of the time that had elapsed since the 1797 copyright date.

Instrumental arrangements of operas were popular in England towards the end of the eighteenth century. Most were for 'German' or transverse flute, some for guitar. The catalogue in Longman & Broderip's edition of *The Haunted Tower* (1789), for instance, includes thirty such arrangements by various composers. They were designed for unaccompanied amateur players; they could also be used (sometimes transposed) by singers because they resemble melody-line song books with the complete text underlaid. A few of the numbers less suitable for solo arrangement were usually omitted, but some duets and trios were included.

Twelve of Storace's thirteen published operas (all but *The Doctor and the Apothecary*) were arranged anonymously for flute by their original professional publishers. *The Pirates* and *The Prize* were also arranged for guitar. Dale lists a third guitar arrangement for *The Siege of Belgrade* in his catalogues, but no copies survive and it may never have been published. There are no unauthorized editions, probably because of the limited market for instrumental arrangements.

All of Storace's instrumental arrangements have a reduced number of staves, many are transposed, some instrumental sections of vocal pieces are cut, and a few entire numbers are omitted. Transpositions take into consideration suitable ranges and easy keys for the instrument; cuts depend on the amount of space on a page and the number of pages available in the volume.

In Storace's flute arrangements, by both Longman & Broderip and Dale, transpositions balance ease of playing in a particular key against the range of each melody, fitting it to a range between d' and d'''. Storace's original keys range (in major) from E flat to A; transpositions range from C to A, with most in G or D.[47] The most common keys in the guitar arrangement of *The Prize* are F, C, and G major, one degree flatter than keys for the flute. A single stave is used throughout the guitar arrangements; occasional chord and bass notes are added to the melody line, notably in the overture.

In the flute arrangements, editorial policy regarding the adaptation of

---

[47] Only one number in Storace's entire output is transposed into a flat key: 'Where jealous misers starve' (*Mahmoud*, no. 3) starts in D minor, because the middle section is in the tonic major.

ensembles is inconsistent, and not always musically appropriate. Sometimes a vocal line is omitted; on at least one occasion a tenor line is transposed up an octave, so that in the instrumental version it sometimes rises above the original soprano line.[48]

Orchestral 'symphonies' are sometimes cut (most often introductions), leaving the vocal sections intact. Such cuts seldom alter pieces significantly, since introductions are often instrumental versions of the first vocal section. However, editorial policy was not always guided by musical considerations, because equal numbers of such introductions are included and excluded in the arrangements.

Overtures and larger ensembles are omitted fairly consistently. However, a lack of foresight sometimes results in an overall imbalance. In *The Pirates*, for instance, ensembles are included towards the end of the opera that would normally have been left out; in *Mahmoud* the reverse procedure occurs, as four out of six numbers in Act 3 are omitted. These two examples suggest that in the first case the arranger found himself with too much space left, in the second case with too little. We can conclude that the arranger (or printer perhaps) was more concerned with the practical aspects of publishing than with musical integrity.

Instrumental arrangements were also included at the end of eighteenth-century editions of individual songs. They are more varied than the arrangements of complete operas because they were printed by many different publishers both in England and abroad. Their transpositions make it clear that they were intended for independent performance, not to accompany the preceding song. A few prints even append entirely different pieces. For instance, Rhames's Dublin edition of 'Sweet little Barbara' (*The Iron Chest*, no. 5) is followed by 'Miss Duval's Hornpipe or Lawyer's Quick Step'. Often such arrangements were printed to fill an otherwise blank page, but prints can also be found in which a publisher had to cramp both the song and the instrumental arrangement in order to fit them both on to one page.

Instrumental addenda are normally for flute, guitar, or violin, or sometimes a combination. A few editions even contain separate arrangements for flute and guitar in different transpositions. Most of the transpositions match those of the complete arrangements, and differ mainly by sometimes being textless and therefore having beamed notes. Figure 4.2 gives Dale's edition of 'Peaceful slumb'ring' (*The Pirates*, no. 9), which includes

---

[48] In 'Love's sweet voice to Hymen' (*The Haunted Tower*, no. 17), the arranger used the top chorus stave from the complete edition (originally labelled 'Trebles & Tenors') but ignored the alto line on the stave below. He then allocated the two a stave each, with the tenor now sounding in the flute's range, an octave higher than it originally did.

Fig. 4.2. 'Peaceful slumb'ring on the ocean' (London: Dale [1793]), from *The Pirates*

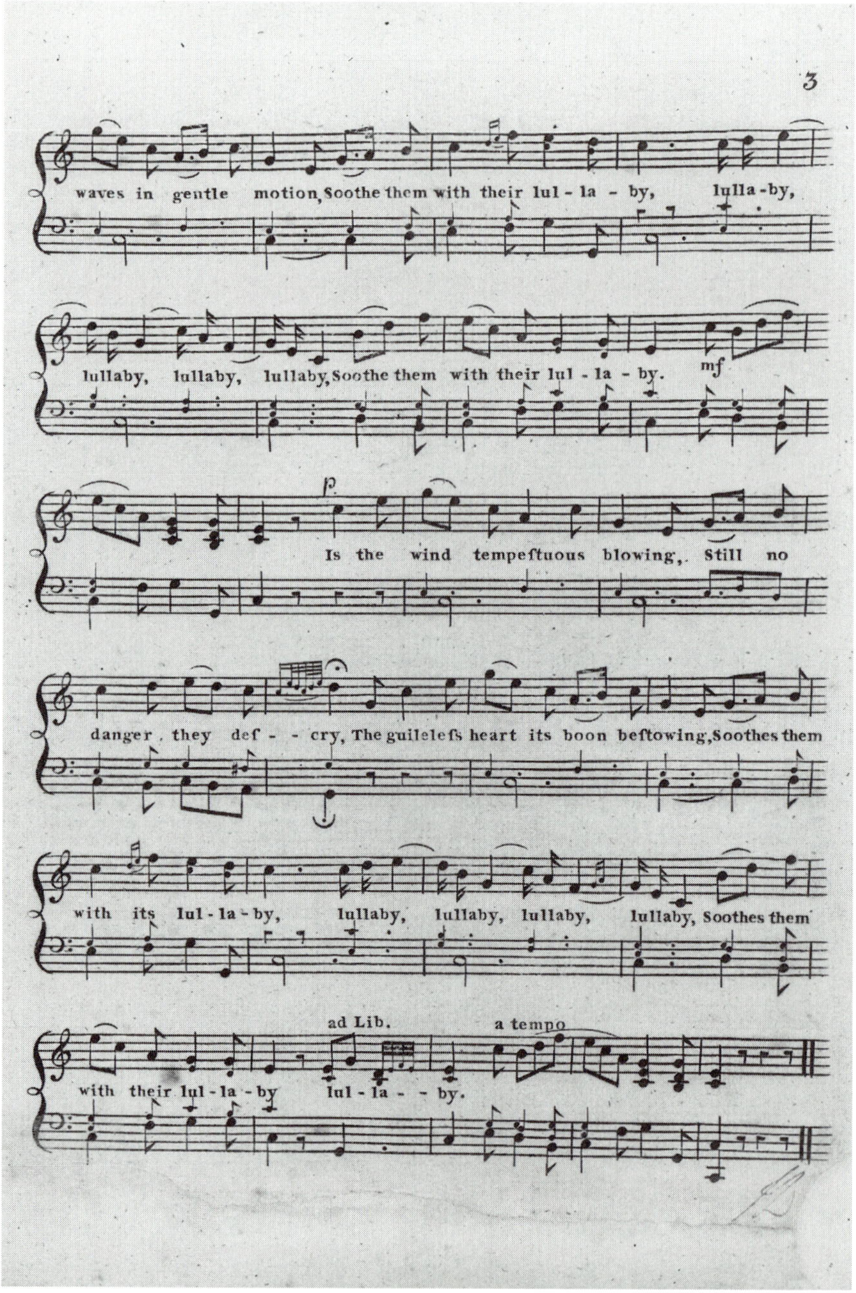

Fig. 4.2. *continued*

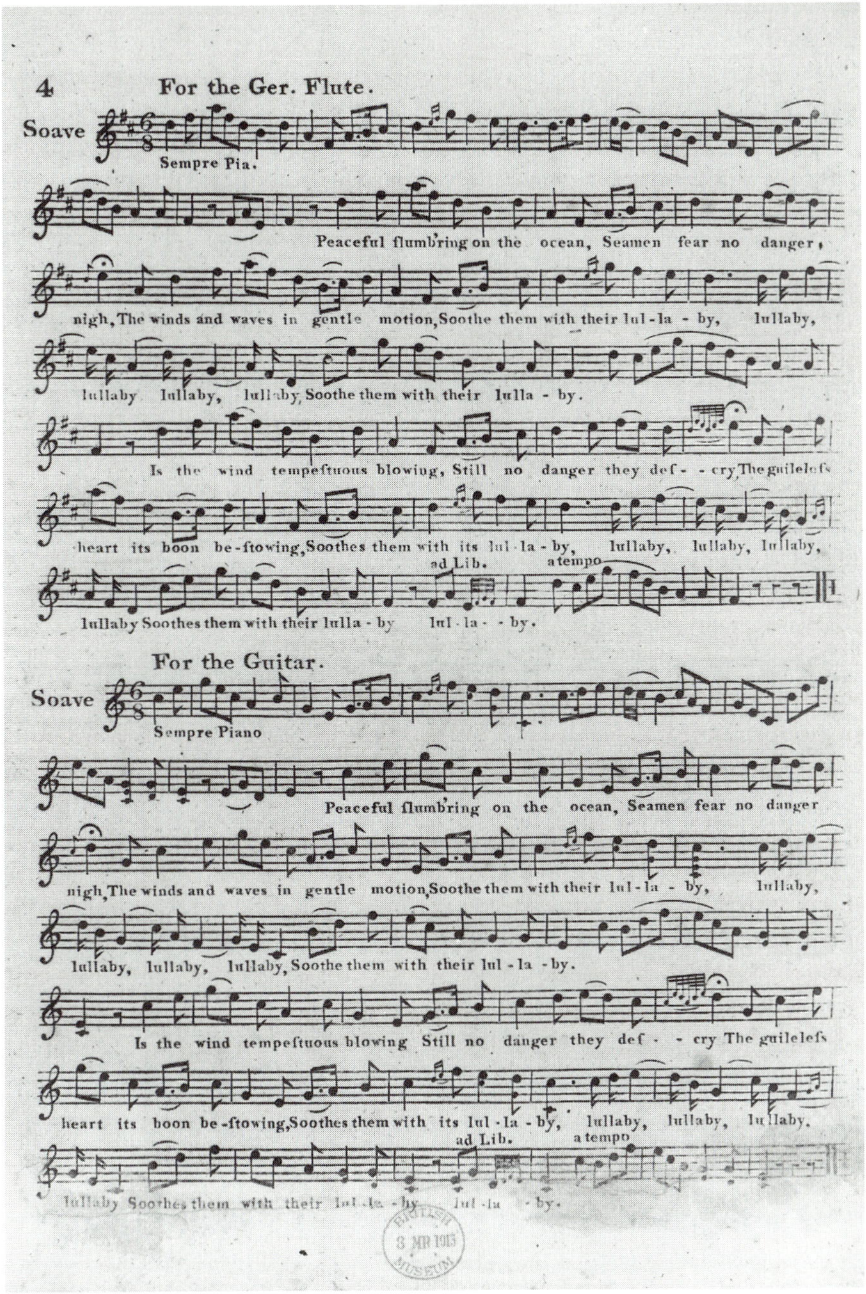

Fig. 4.2. *continued*

arrangements for flute and guitar, one transposed to D, the other suitable in the original C major.

Not all arrangements fit the typical pattern. Dale's most unusual arrangement of a piece by Storace is 'A shepherd once had lost his love' (*The Cherokee*, no. 15), an extremely popular song. The three-stave arrangement that follows the song is headed 'for the Harp or Piano Forte with an accompaniment', has a vocal accompaniment, and is transposed from A to B flat.

SINGLE SONGS

The history of the song sheet dates back to the end of the seventeenth century, when it was a peculiarly British phenomenon.[49] By the late eighteenth century, editions of individual songs had often grown into several pages of music, and the repertoire had been expanded by John Walsh, who in mid-century initiated the idea of publishing instrumental overtures and dances from stage works.[50] Unfortunately, our information about sheet music is often not reliable, sometimes because of misleading and inadequate cataloguing in libraries, and sometimes because many individuals still own copies of prints whose editions are not recorded.[51]

By Storace's time songsheets were commonplace, and included large numbers of both operatic extracts and songs performed at the pleasure gardens in the summer. Just as all but two of Storace's English operas were published in complete editions, so songs from all but those same two—*The Cave of Trophonius* and *Dido, Queen of Carthage*—were published individually by both their authorized publishers and others.

Prints of individual numbers give us a good idea of public taste in theatrical music, because some pieces were not published singly at all, while others survive in a myriad versions, many of which were unauthorized or pirated. The majority were taken directly from the complete editions of the operas and merely re-engraved in an upright format with new titles; a few numbers were also published in new arrangements.

The publication of individual songs was intended for the amateur singer,

[49] Douald W. Krummel, *English Music Printing 1553–1700* (London, 1975), 166–70.
[50] Ibid. 170.
[51] C. B. Oldman, introduction to *BUCEM*, vol. i. p. xii. Many of Storace's prints are not to be found in the standard reference books, and several are misleadingly listed. For instance, the use of titles by some publishers and first lines by others has resulted in some confusion in *RISM*, where a single piece occasionally appears as two separate entries. References to 19th-cent. editions are rarer than to those before 1800, except for individual library catalogues and those editions included in Richard J. Wolfe's *Secular Music in America 1801–1825: A Bibliography*, 3 vols. (New York, 1964). Yet Storace died only four years before the turn of the century, and his songs continued to be published into the 19th cent., both in England and abroad.

keyboard player, and sometimes flautist or guitarist. Duets as well as songs were published, but rarely large ensembles, except for glees. Like the complete opera scores, the extracts are suitable to be played by a keyboard player alone, as the top stave gives the vocal part, and the two staves together need no great keyboard technique.

The only single songs that can be dated precisely are copyrighted editions, plus some that appeared in dated journals such as *Walker's Hibernian Magazine* from Dublin and similar American ones. As a result, we can tell which were the most popular pieces, but not precisely when they became fashionable, nor whether their popularity was stimulated by a season of local performances or a revival, or how long interest in them lasted.

Individual extracts were always printed in upright format, apart from overtures and the few vocal offprints from the original oblong plates already discussed. Each piece was completely re-engraved, both to take account of the upright layout and to create up to half a page of space for a title and other preliminary information. A title typically included either the first line of text or a newly created title, which was followed by the names of the opera, composer, and its original singer. New titles sometimes describe the character, sometimes the song's function in the opera, or sometimes, for example 'The Ballad-Singer's Petition', both.[52] Similarly, 'Peaceful slumb'ring on the ocean' (*The Pirates*, no. 9) became known as 'Lullaby' in most of its numerous independent editions. Other titles take words from the refrain or a particularly catchy part of the text, such as 'Well-a-day! Lack-a-day!' for 'Ah me! I am lost and forlorn' (*My Grandmother*, no. 4). Irish and American publishers often gave shorter titles than did English ones; they sometimes included the name of a local singer and often omitted the name of the composer.

London publishers pirated only the most popular individual numbers, taking advantage of the large buying public for stage music. For that reason it is unlikely that a pirated edition ever appeared before an authorized one. Irish and American publishers, on the other hand, were catering for different audiences, and several of Storace's songs not published at home were indeed published abroad. Most unauthorized editions follow the official ones closely, differing only in the choice of title and in the instrumental arrangements that sometimes followed the song. Foreign publishers evidently did not find sufficient demand for complete editions to produce their own, as none of any of Storace's operas survives in a complete foreign edition.

---

[52] 'With lowly suit and plaintive ditty': *No Song, No Supper*, no. 5.

When an authorized publisher issued a selection of individual songs after the complete edition of the opera, he followed the original closely, making only the few changes necessitated by a new upright format and the creation of additional space for a title, and minor corrections to the music or text. Storace's are all substantially the same as the complete editions, though sometimes small differences allow us to identify which version was the source for an unauthorized edition. Such alterations include additional slurs and omission of instrumental indications, neither of which would affect performance by a singer or keyboard player. Of course a few new errors were created, most of them as trivial as those corrected. A few changes such as omitted tempo markings have a real effect on performance, and the omission of characters' names in duets can make undifferentiated dialogue read unintelligibly. Dale regularly omitted characters' names in individual editions.

Dale issued a few offprints from the original oblong plates, mainly overtures. He left the original heading (not a title) and page numbers unaltered, but added his name and address and the price at the bottom of the first page.

Dale's print of the air 'My plaint in no one pity moves' (*The Siege of Belgrade*, no. 12) is unusual. It was entered at Stationers' Hall on 7 February 1798, seven years after the complete edition. Clearly in that time Dale's editorial policy had changed in small ways, as is demonstrated by the alterations found in the new edition. He added slurs over beamed quavers, in line with his other posthumous editions of Storace's music, notably extracts from *Mahmoud* published in late 1797. Not surprisingly, he omitted the figured bass of the original version. He also took the unusual step of transposing the air down a minor third to G, probably because of the high tessitura of the original (up to *b flat'''*).

The quality of Dale's work is consistently good: clear, well spaced, accurate, and complete. Figure 4.2 is a typical example of his work. Only once does the quality of a print belie his reputation, in 'Tho' pleasure swell the jovial cry' (*Mahmoud*, no. 4), where considerations of space on the page seem to have dictated the omission of the postlude, many half-bars left open at ends of lines, and little space for the heading.

Unauthorized publishers had no obligations to the composer or the copyright-holder when they printed extracts from Storace's operas. They inevitably introduced new variants, both deliberate and accidental. They often had a choice of editions on which to base their own, including the complete edition, authorized extracts, and sometimes other unauthorized editions of the extracts. Ultimately, of course, almost all unauthorized editions derive from the copyright editions of the complete operas.

Table 4.1. Pirated editions of Storace's works

First line	Opera	Publisher	New Text
Tho' pity I cannot deny	*The Haunted Tower*	Preston	Attune the pipe
Blithe as the hours of May	*The Siege of Belgrade*	Goulding	Blest was the vernal day
Peaceful slumb'ring	*The Pirates*	Ding	Would you taste joys
Adieu my Floreski	*Lodoiska*	Goulding	Adieu my Lorenzo
		Birchall	Adieu my Fernando
A shepherd once	*The Cherokee*	Longman & Broderip	A shepherd wandered ̃
		Birchall	A shepherd wandered
		Preston	A shepherd wandered
		Goulding	A shepherd wandered

Few contemporary pirated editions are extant. Most unauthorized London editions date from the nineteenth century, when, even though the pieces may not have been strictly out of copyright, Storace was dead and Dale was probably not interested in prosecuting or otherwise discouraging the activities of other publishers. Most of the surviving eighteenth-century pirated editions were in fact altered, as Dale described in his condemnation of such habits, by having new or modified words. Table 4.1 gives a list of the few extant pirated editions of Storace's music that date from the 1790s. All nine have new texts, some barely disguised versions of the original, such as 'Adieu my Lorenzo' and 'Adieu my Fernando', where the point was obviously to make the public realize what they were buying while allowing the publisher to evade copyright law. Occasionally the new words were sufficiently different from the original to require alterations to the word-setting, as in 'Attune the pipe', taken from 'Tho' pity I cannot deny' (*The Haunted Tower*, no. 3). Example 4.1 gives the openings of the two versions, showing the differing text underlay.

The music of 'Would you taste joys pure and ample' is an exact copy of 'Peaceful slumbr'ing on the ocean'. Published by Laurence Ding of Edinburgh, the purpose of this version was probably not to avoid copyright difficulties but rather to provide a vehicle for the verse of a certain Lady Willoughby, who bashfully hid behind the omitted vowels in her name. The title stands merely as 'The Advice. By Lady W—ll—ghby', and the words, which run to four verses and are followed by a flute arrangement, give advice on how to model oneself on the family of George III, each verse ending with the line 'Be advis'd by W—ll—ghby'.

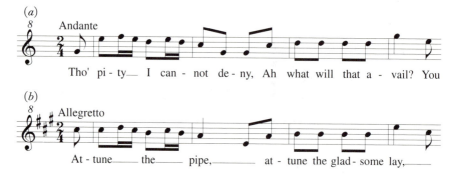

Ex. 4.1(*a*) 'Tho' pity I cannot deny' (*The Haunted Tower*, no. 3); (*b*) 'Attune the pipe'

The alteration of texts by pirating publishers was not confined to songs. The overture to *Lodoiska*, which Storace had himself borrowed from Kreutzer, was renamed *Dodolska* by the same London publisher—Preston—who had changed the texts of two of Storace's songs listed in Table 4.1. The overture was immensely popular and clearly tempting to pirates. In Parke's words: 'The overture, by Kreutzer . . . became so popular, that several of our minor composers published most barefaced copies of it; while others, more wary in making it their model, disguised their plagiarisms, "as gipsies do stolen children, to make them pass for their own!" '[53]

Dublin publishers printed extracts from all Storace's published operas except *The Glorious First of June* and *The Three and the Deuce*, his least popular operas in print and which were probably never performed in Ireland. Some of the others, at least *The Doctor and the Apothecary*, *The Haunted Tower*, *No Song, No Supper*, and *The Siege of Belgrade*, were performed in Dublin.[54] Naturally the most popular songs were those actually performed in Dublin, and the sphere of some had already spread beyond the theatre, as is indicated by the subtitle of Hime's version of 'From hope's fond dream' (*The Haunted Tower*, no. 2). It reads in part: 'Sung with universal applause by Mr. Small at Docr. Doyle's Concerts.' Hime's address indicates that he published this edition in about 1790, only a year after the London première and less than a year since its first Dublin performance.

Irish editions vary greatly in quality of presentation and accuracy. Two versions of 'My native land' (*The Haunted Tower*, no. 8) by Henry Mountain show both extremes. Figure 4.3 gives the earlier edition, dating from about 1790, which is a good and accurate copy in which Mountain even made

[53] *Musical Memoirs*, i. 190.   [54] Walsh, *Opera in Dublin 1705–1797*, app. C.

Fig. 4.3. 'My native land' (Dublin: Mountain, *c.*1790), from *The Haunted Tower*

minor corrections to the score of the complete opera. The later edition, Figure 4.4, printed on paper watermarked 1795, is of an entirely different quality: it is hard to read, the notes are clumsily squashed together between crooked barlines, and small notes are often indistinguishable from large. Both the song and its arrangement for flute or guitar are squeezed on to one page, a spacing common in Irish editions.

One Dublin edition differs radically in notation from the complete score because it appears to have been transcribed by ear. Elizabeth Rhames of Dublin (actually her son Francis carrying on in her name between 1778 and 1806)[55] published 'Sweet little Barbara' from the 'new Opera' *The Iron Chest*. As there is no evidence that *The Iron Chest* was performed in Ireland, 'new' must refer to the London première in March 1796 (presuming, of course, that the expression was not just publisher's licence). Dale did not publish the complete opera until a year later, so the Rhames edition probably dates from before then. With no print or manuscript to copy, someone must have transcribed the song by ear. Example 4.2 illustrates many of the differences between Dale's version and Rhames's, including the different keys, time signatures, and tempos. Rhames also enlarged the introduction and modified the word-setting, the structure, and the melodic shape of some of the vocal parts.

While Rhames's edition was obviously transcribed by someone musically literate, editing was not always performed so accurately. In an anonymous American edition of 'From aloft the sailor looks around' (*No Song, No Supper*, no. 9), which is transposed from B flat to C, many erroneous accidentals suggest that someone performed the transposition purely by rote.

Transposition is fairly common in American editions, as is simplification (omission of inner parts, slurs, dynamics, and extra orchestral notes). There also exist some one-line editions. The quality of printing is, as in Dublin editions, inconsistent. Incidentally, the New York publisher Hewitt, who printed a number of pieces by Storace, was the same James Hewitt who had been a string-player in the Drury Lane orchestra in the early 1790s, and who, like Storace, composed an Indian opera in 1794, his being entitled *Tammanny, or the Indian Chief*.

Music publishers covered the market by printing many arrangements of popular tunes, most often as glees and sets of variations for harp- and keyboard-players. They used any melody in vogue, including several by Storace. His two most popular songs, 'Peaceful slumb'ring' from *The Pirates* and 'A shepherd once had lost his love' from *The Cherokee*, often entitled

---

[55] Humphries and Smith, *Music Publishing*, 272.

Fig. 4.4. 'My native land' (Dublin: Mountain, WM 1795), from *The Haunted Tower*

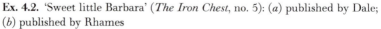

Ex. 4.2. 'Sweet little Barbara' (*The Iron Chest*, no. 5): (*a*) published by Dale;
(*b*) published by Rhames

116

'Fal Lal La' and sung by a Welsh maid in the opera, were both published in several versions in the eighteenth and nineteenth centuries. Dale published arrangements of both as glees whose subtitles indicate that they were not purely for private enjoyment. 'A shepherd once' reads: 'Harmoniz'd for three Voices, And Sung at the Ladies Private Concerts.'

Dale's arrangement of 'Peaceful slumb'ring' is entitled 'Lullaby: A Favorite Glee for Four Voices as sung with the greatest Applause at Harrison & Knyvetts Concerts, Willis's Rooms. Harmonized by Mr. Harrison.'[56] The instrumental sections are omitted; otherwise Harrison remained true to the original except for different dynamics and alterations necessary in an *a cappella* arrangement. The song continued to be popular into the nineteenth century, appearing both as a solo and in glee arrangements, sometimes with its familiar title 'Lullaby' and even with such fanciful ones as 'Reverie Maritime, Nocturne, Pour le Piano, Melodie composée Par Storace'. This version, freely treated but quite recognizable, was published in London by Addison & Hollier around 1860.

'A shepherd once', on the other hand, lost its popularity rapidly in the nineteenth century, even though its fame in the late eighteenth century was sufficient to provoke two 'replies'. The first, entered at Stationers' Hall on 22 February 1796 by the publishers Culliford, Rolfe & Barron, is entitled 'Leap Year or an Answer to the Favorite Welch Air of Fal, lal, la, Sung with the greatest applause by Mrs Bland in the Cherokee. Composed by J. T.' The air bears certain family resemblances to 'A shepherd once' in key and text, though it is in a faster tempo. The other reply, entered at Stationers' Hall on 27 August 1796, is not so clearly linked to the original. It is entitled 'The Ladies Answer to the new Fal, lal, la! the words of this Glee by J. C. Pratt, Esqr. Author of the Gleanings &c, in answer to those written by the late Duke of Dorset, and set to music by Mr. Calcott, composed for and most respectfully inscribed to the Revd. J. Baker by his most obliged Humble Servant T. Essex'.[57] There is no musical relationship between this and 'A shepherd once' and the similarities of the titles may be accidental.

By the early nineteenth century the tune of 'A shepherd once' had passed into the realm of popular song. The Scottish music publisher George Thomson commissioned Beethoven to arrange the melody as one of 'a Select Collection of Original Welsh Airs' (WoO 155 No. 3). Oddly, Beethoven's set of variations on the same tune for flute (or violin) and piano (Op. 105

---

[56] Samuel Harrison (1760–1812) was a tenor, who in 1791 founded the Vocal Concerts at Willis's Rooms with Charles Knyvett (Mollie Sands, 'Harrison, Samuel', *New Grove*, viii. 256).

[57] Neither is listed in *RISM*, but the British Library holds copies of both.

No. 1) is labelled 'Air Ecossais'. The more common idea that the melody was Welsh in origin, recently dismissed by Fiske as inaccurate, was none the less entrenched by the end of the eighteenth century.[58] On the Drury Lane playbill for 12 June 1798, for instance, Mrs Bland was announced as singing 'the Favourite Welch Air of "Fal lal," From the Cherokee'.

A number of composers used these same two melodies as themes for sets of variations. Daniel Steibelt, 'a Lady', Thomas Valentine, and Joseph Dale himself published variations on 'Peaceful slumb'ring' for piano. Joseph Elouis and Madame de Ronssecy wrote sets for harp. The melody was also used in unpublished concertos by the violinist Giovanni Mane Giornovichi in 1794 and the flautist Andrew Ashe in 1795.[59] Giornovichi performed his composition as a prelude to *The Glorious First of June*; it was described in the *Oracle* on 3 July 1794 as follows: 'Giornovichi then played a concerto, the grounds of which were *Hearts of Oak! Lullaby!* and *Rule Britannia!* varied with much taste and brilliancy of execution.' 'A shepherd once' was used as the theme for sets of variations by Jan Ladislav Dussek, John Field, and John Hammond in the 1790s, as well as by Beethoven.

Finally, two puzzling publications exist, both apparently by Storace but neither derived from any of his surviving operas or chamber works. The earlier is a piece arranged by Dale himself, entered at Stationers' Hall on 28 February 1798, entitled 'O Strike the Harp, for One, Two, or Three Voices, with an Accompaniment for the Harp or Piano Forte (The Poetry from Ossian) The Music from the Compositions of Stephen Storace'. It was performed at least once, on 5 June 1800 at Drury Lane. The other oddity appeared in *Choral Harmony* in about 1857 and is headed 'Harvest Time. Adapted from Storace'.

Some of Storace's operas continued to be performed at Drury Lane until the 1830s, and a few extracts were published even later in the century. A mixed selection also appeared in a London publication in 1820 by Goulding, D'Almaine, Potter & Co. whose title reads: 'Ivanhoe or The Knight Templar, A Musical Drama . . . Written by S. Beazley Esqr. The Music Composed & Selected chiefly from Storace's Works, by Dr. Kitchiner.' The work was first performed at Covent Garden on 2 March 1820.[60] It includes numbers from at least five operas by Storace.

[58] Roger Fiske, *Scotland in Music: A European Enthusiasm* (Cambridge, 1983), 75.

[59] Thomas B. Milligan, *The Concerto and London's Musical Culture in the Late Eighteenth Century* (Ann Arbor, Mich., 1983), 201.

[60] Eric Walter White (comp.), *A Register of First Performances of English Operas and Semi-Operas from the 16th Century to 1980* (London, 1983), 67, lists the composer of *Ivanhoe* as John Parry.

By the mid- to late nineteenth century, cheap editions of song books had become increasingly common in England, both unison songs with piano accompaniment and *a cappella* arrangements for more skilled vocal groups. A few of Storace's songs survived long enough to be included in these, thus lasting beyond the memories of his contemporaries. 'Peaceful slumb'ring' and the overture to *Lodoiska*, the two most popular pieces in the 1790s, continued to be published fairly regularly. The only complete opera score to date from the second half of the nineteenth century is a vocal score of *No Song, No Supper*, published by Boosey in 1874. A few other songs were published several times after 1840: 'The sapling oak' (*The Siege of Belgrade*, no. 8) appeared in three editions, and 'Five times by the taper light' (*The Iron Chest*, no. 1) in at least seven. This last was mentioned by Spencer Braham, Nancy Storace's son, in a letter from Winchester College dated 7 December 1817. He wrote that 'the Boys here, among one another sing "5 times by the Taper light" & take Parts, I generally take the second.'[61]

Songs did not have to be published in many editions to become absorbed into the popular repertoire. 'Should e'er the fortune be my lot' (*The Three and the Deuce*, no. 13) was published in only three English editions, where it became known by the title 'Little Taffline' after the character who originally sang it. It had lost its operatic context by 1802 when, on 18 June, the Drury Lane playbill listed 'the favourite Ballad of "Little Taffline" ' to be sung between acts in the mainpiece. *The Three and the Deuce* continued to be performed occasionally at Drury Lane until the mid-1820s, but Storace's music may not have featured large in the nineteenth-century productions. The song, however, continued to be popular. In the middle of the century, Charles Dickens wrote in *David Copperfield*:

Mrs Micawber was good enough to sing us ... the favourite ballads of 'The Dashing White Sergeant', and 'Little Tafflin'. For both of these songs Mrs Micawber had been famous when she lived at home with her papa and mama. ... When it came to Little Tafflin; [Mr Micawber] had resolved to win that woman or perish in the attempt.[62]

A study of editions of Storace's works emphasizes the immense popularity of theatrical music in the English-speaking world, and the healthy state of

---

[61] Spencer Braham to Hannah [Burchell], 7 Dec. 1817 (London, Sir John Soane's Museum, Correspondence Cupboard (1), Division IV (6), no. 68).
[62] *David Copperfield* (London, 1966), 483–4. Another reference to *Little Tafflin* is made on p. 879 as the Micawbers are about to sail for Australia.

amateur music-making that supported the publishing industry. Storace's music was some of the most popular of the operatic music of the time, and his publications are representative of publishing procedures in late eighteenth-century London.

PART II

THE MUSIC

5

QUESTIONS OF GENRE

In the eleven years of his career, Storace composed twenty stage works, most of them English operas with spoken dialogue. Unfortunately there has never been a consensus about what constitutes an English opera, nor any consistent terminology with which to discuss the genre. We therefore need to understand the flexibility of eighteenth-century attitudes, so that we can specify criteria by which to distinguish and name the various types of theatrical music of the period.

In eighteenth-century London there was no compelling need to distinguish an English-language opera from a play with music, because both were performed in the same theatres with cast members in common, and usually on the same programmes. Critics used a variety of descriptive terms, each appropriate to individual works but not necessarily applicable to a broader group. A few recent writers, viewing the same works from a historical perspective, have tried to create suitable categorizing terminology.

A slight sense of shame often clouds discussion of works that offer a national variant to the 'pure' genre of all-sung Italian opera. Thomas Baumann provides a counterbalance to this attitude with his concept of a 'special idiom which blended musical and literary values under the compelling imperatives of the region's distinctive theatrical institutions', which he applies to north German opera of the late eighteenth century.[1] Applied to English opera, this emphasizes its national individuality while not demeaning it by comparison with the all-sung Italian opera which now dominates our thinking.

Eighteenth-century critics had no such problem: they accepted as normal the fact that Italian opera used recitative for dialogue while English opera used the spoken word. There was no question of English opera being

---

[1] *North German Opera in the Age of Goethe* (Cambridge, 1985), 1.

inferior on that count (though it certainly was in terms of its social status); in fact strong factions of intellectuals ever since the early years of the century had preferred English over Italian. English playhouse audiences considered recitative an unacceptable (unnatural and unintelligible) substitute for speech. Kemble gave a strong practical reason when, in relation to Storace's all-sung *Dido, Queen of Carthage*, he wrote in his diary, 'N.B. It was wrong not to print the Words; for the audience cannot understand recitative Dialogue.'[2]

Eighteenth-century Views

Eighteenth-century English critics were pragmatic about distinguishing the various combinations of music and drama staged at the Theatres Royal, which ranged from operas with spoken dialogue to plays with songs. A work could be given several different labels, each appropriate to some of its attributes. One distinction, however, was always clear. To audience, critics, and readers alike, the difference between a mainpiece and an afterpiece was common knowledge and never ambiguous. The mainpiece was always the first and longer of the two shows on an evening's bill; the afterpiece was the second, shorter piece, which typically lacked a serious plot. Indeed Kemble, when he was manager at Drury Lane, consistently called the afterpiece 'the farce' and the mainpiece 'the play' in his diaries, even when one was an opera.

Storace's works were given various designations on playbills, musical scores, and other contemporary publications. Most labels combine indications of genre with the type of plot and imply the distinction between mainpiece and afterpiece. His mainpieces are almost all called 'opera', 'comic opera', and, in the case of *Dido, Queen of Carthage*, 'grand opera' and 'serious opera'. The unfinished opera *Mahmoud* was also called a 'musical romance', a term used for more serious and melodramatic subjects at the end of the century. Only one of Storace's mainpieces is not an opera, though this label is implicit in the score. *The Iron Chest* was normally called a 'play' or 'play with music'. It contains only twelve vocal numbers (as opposed to twenty-two or more in his other mainpieces), all of them in the subplot.

Storace's afterpieces were usually called 'musical entertainment', 'musical farce', or sometimes 'comic opera'. The words 'farce' and 'entertainment'

---

[2] Memoranda A, 23 May 1792 (continued on 27 May).

were always reserved for afterpieces and indicated their more frivolous nature. Less specific (and musical) terms such as plain 'farce' and 'comic drama' were also used, suggesting to some critics that the music was fairly unimportant. Again, one of Storace's afterpieces is exceptional. *Lodoiska* resembles a mainpiece in its serious and spectacular plot and use of chorus. It is an early example of an escape opera with no comic plot, and the eighteenth-century designations 'musical romance' and 'musical spectacle' reflect its contents.

Few eighteenth-century critics attempted to define English opera, though some had strong feelings about its quality. John Adolphus, Jack Bannister's biographer, made a particularly sweeping generalization when he stated that 'an English opera is, properly, a comedy enlivened by music'.[3] This definition fails to distinguish an opera from a play with music, although it is certainly appropriate to the vast majority of English operas of the late eighteenth century. It is also less suited to some of Storace's more Italianate operas and melodramatic pieces than to his lighter, shorter works.

Although newspaper reviewers were not prone to confront the definition of opera directly, a few general statements appeared in eighteenth-century publications. In 1795 one reviewer made the following simplistic distinction between play and opera when discussing Storace's *The Three and the Deuce* (called variously a 'musical entertainment' and 'comic drama'): 'Mr. Hoare's Play was exhibited last night for the first time; but whether to call it a *Comedy with Songs*, or *Opera*, it is impossible to determine, for it was preceded by both *Prologue* and *Overture*.'[4] This writer thought a spoken prologue indicated a play while an overture signified an opera. He also opposed 'comedy with songs' to 'opera', unlike Adolphus, who considered them synonymous. The presence or absence of a prologue or overture can generally be used as an indicator of genre, but a substantial number of exceptions should make one wary of being definitive. For instance, *The Mountaineers* (1793) by Colman and Arnold was normally called a play, but it included an overture with its other music; other works, like Storace's musical afterpiece *The Glorious First of June* (1794) and Kelly's *Of Age Tomorrow* (1800), included both overture and prologue.

Eighteenth-century critics sometimes made parenthetical remarks that help us understand their attitude to operatic works. A favourite topic was the relationship between words and music. Critics liked to point out that they judged the plots and texts of operas by more relaxed standards than

---

[3] *Memoirs of John Bannister, Comedian*, 2 vols. (London, 1839), i. 233.
[4] *Times*, 3 Sept. 1795.

plays. Storace's first piece in English, the afterpiece *The Doctor and the Apothecary*, was seen as having a 'loose and operatical plan':[5]

The plot of the Doctor and the Apothecary, which we shall not attempt to unravel —lays in Spain—and making that kind of allowance, which an author, either of Opera or Farce, is entitled to—not either improbably or unskilfully conducted— whim and laugh are in general all that can be expected—to be merry and *not* wise.[6]

A view prevailed that the plots of operas were weaker than those of spoken dramas because of the emphasis on (and distraction provided by) music:

Since the writing of an Opera became the mere vehicle of music, much intricacy of plot has neither been studied by the author nor expected by the audience.[7]

The Fable [of *The Cherokee*], like most of the Dramas of this species, was a tissue of episodes; not always connected with probability, and very opposite to that delightful species of composition which has a distinct beginning, middle, and end, and the progressive incidents of which contribute to form a whole.[8]

These two quotations indicate that critics did not regard operas (at least Storace's) as mere plays with music, but as works in which music was an essential, if distracting, ingredient. Even so, drama critics used spoken drama as their reference point, by comparison with which librettos naturally suffered. Of course many deserved censure. It is all too easy to criticize the librettos of Storace's operas, for instance, for the confusions of their plots, not to mention the weaknesses of their dialogue; however, it is also misleading to imply that only operas of the period suffered from such weaknesses. Many plays failed for the same reasons after one or two nights on stage; unluckily for them perhaps, they had no music to counterbalance their worst aspects. Indeed, if we are to believe reviewers, the music of Storace's operas often compensated for their literary poverty.

A rare commentator in the daily press of 1790 (when Storace's *The Haunted Tower* was still his only mainpiece) praised English opera at the expense of Italian:

English Operas, and Theatrical Entertainments, thanks to the good sense of this country, which will bear down at length the impositions of folly and fashion! have had the greatest success;—witness the Beggar's Opera, Love in a Village, and the Haunted Tower—whether it be owing to the abolition of the Recitative,

[5] *Morning Chronicle*, 22 Dec. 1794.   [6] *Times*, 27 Oct. 1788.
[7] *Morning Chronicle*, 3 Jan. 1791: review of *The Siege of Belgrade*.
[8] *Morning Chronicle*, 22 Dec. 1794.

so tiresome and so irksome to the ear; or to their uniting sound with sense in the national language.[9]

The notion that English operas were becoming increasingly like their Italian counterparts may surprise some readers, but a few eighteenth-century commentators were perceptive enough to observe just such a trend in Storace's works, for better or worse. The oboist William T. Parke saw the development of the genre as positive: '[*The Siege of Belgrade*] presented a marked instance of the rapid transition which the English opera had made, from the simplicity of the ballad farce to the captivating splendours of the Italian drama.'[10] A critic from *The Oracle* had more difficulty accepting the concept: '[*Mahmoud*] is one of those strange and fantastic medleys called modern Opera, partaking of all the five species of dramatic exhibitions, and classing with no one. It is after the Italian mode, which it only forsakes by giving dialogue for recitative.'[11] A far harsher criticism of the same trend appeared in the *Oracle* in relation to *The Cherokee*:

Modern Opera is really, by the madness of the people after *gew-gaw*, forced into something which the finest talents can accomplish no better than the meanest—there is no lesson of conduct; there is no preservation of manners—there is no connexion.

. . . Pieces now are written upon system—Certain Singers must always be hero and heroine—Certain Performers always lovers—then they must in this place *always* have a *bravura* song, and in that a *duett*—Such a man drops finely from B, who could think therefore of forcing him to take a *new drop*?

Until these shackles are burst, Opera must be an incoherent farago of perhaps *beautiful* parts, but wanting the connexion exquisite, which reflects upon atoms the perfection resulting from Unity.[12]

If we are left with the impression that critics disliked English (and Italian) operas, we must remember that many were drama critics who saw music as corrupting the purity of spoken drama and who had little interest either in the finer distinctions between operas and other musical stage works or in any other musical matters.

All of these views, in which English operas are compared with either spoken drama or foreign opera, are based on implicit ideas as to what an opera should be, ideas moulded to some extent by those very operas upon which judgement was being passed. For instance, when a critic wrote that 'this [second] Act concludes lamely with the single song of Kelly. An Opera of Spectacle should always have grand finales',[13] he was comparing Storace's

[9] *Diary*, 15 Apr. 1790.   [10] *Musical Memoirs*, i. 135.   [11] *Oracle*, 2 May 1796.
[12] *Oracle*, 22 Dec. 1794.   [13] *Morning Chronicle*, 11 June 1794.

Lodoiska to an ideal of the 'opera of spectacle' which was undoubtedly influenced by his earlier works, particularly the elaborate finales and battle scenes of *The Siege of Belgrade* and *The Pirates*.

Critics devoted far more space to discussions of the plot and performers than to the music, which was usually mentioned only in general terms by reporting the audience's response. Instead they sometimes reproduced the words of the most popular songs. As a result, many song texts appeared in print which, when dissociated from their musical settings and dramatic contexts, are trite at best. John Ambrose Williams, who published satirical writings under the pseudonymn Anthony Pasquin, drew attention to the disparity in quality between words and music, though he probably exaggerated the vanity of the librettists (two of them Storace's):

The songs written by Hoare, O'Keefe, and Cobb, are passing despicable. Yet we have no doubt that when either of those gentlemen hears them sung, and applauded, he attributes it all to his verses, if they may be so called, and never to the voice of the singer, or the taste of the composer.[14]

Surprisingly, Pasquin made no comments about their prose dialogue, which today seems as weak as the verse. At least one modern critic agrees with Pasquin, writing: 'Music was the inspiration, and the danger, for a good tune may carry off poor verse.'[15]

Modern Approaches

Modern approaches to the designation and definition of eighteenth-century English operas have differed little from earlier ones. Literary historians have not paid much attention to operas or their librettos, though some include them in surveys of drama of the period.[16] Some recent music scholars have provided more or less appropriate designations but, though they simplify the terminological confusion of the eighteenth century, they too usually fail to provide a clear demarcation between operas and plays with some music.

---

[14] *The Pin Basket to the Children of Thespis*, 48 n.

[15] William L. Renwick, *English Literature 1789–1815* (Oxford, 1963), 10.

[16] e.g. Allardyce Nicoll, *A History of Late Eighteenth Century Drama 1750–1800* (Cambridge, 1937), 195–208. As the title of the section 'Opera, Comic Opera and Kindred Forms' implies, Nicoll makes little attempt to explain or categorize the wide variety of terms he uses and quotes. For criticism of Nicoll's approach, see Robert D. Hume, *The Rakish Stage: Studies in English Drama, 1660–1800* (Carbondale, Ill., 1983), 224–5; Stephen Hannaford, 'The Shape of Eighteenth-Century English Drama', *Theatre Survey*, 21 (1980), 94.

At the beginning of the twentieth century the term 'ballad opera' was current among historians of music for all eighteenth-century operas in English. Now long dismissed as inaccurate except when applied to the particular genre related to *The Beggar's Opera*, it is still used occasionally.[17] The term 'comic opera', in vogue in mid-century, is less than appropriate to some operas from the end of the eighteenth century for the same reason as Adolphus' definition: while individual operas may indeed be comic, a trend towards melodramatic, romantic, even tragic mainpiece operas had begun. More recently Roger Fiske coined the term 'dialogue opera'.[18] If one assumes, as Fiske did, that spoken dialogue is indicated, then 'dialogue operas' are usefully distinguished from burlettas and other all-sung works. However, the point is moot with regard to the patent theatres, where spoken dialogue was used almost exclusively. As general terms, then, both 'comic opera' and 'dialogue opera' are broadly valid.

Some modern commentators have deliberately avoided the terms 'mainpiece' and 'afterpiece', with resulting confusion. Eric Walter White, for instance, in his *Register of First Performances of English Operas and Semi-Operas* instead gives the number of acts. The reader should beware of using his numbers as an indicator because, although mainpiece operas were invariably in three acts, afterpieces were much more flexible and can be found in one, two, and three acts.[19] Fiske uses mixed terminology in his list of Storace's works in *New Grove*, where he distinguishes between a 'full-length opera' and an 'afterpiece'. Perhaps as a result, he lists *Lodoiska* as full-length (and it was indeed long) instead of as an afterpiece (which is how it was always performed).

In his *History of English Opera*, White adopts 'pasticcio' as a general term, making statements such as 'After *The Iron Chest* there was still one more pasticcio of Storace's to come', and 'The majority of Storace's operas were written to the pasticcio formula.'[20] His approach is problematic for two reasons. First we should consider whether the term 'pasticcio' is

---

[17] W. J. Lawrence, 'Early Irish Ballad Opera and Comic Opera', *MQ* 8 (1922), 397, drew attention to the difference between ballad opera and what he termed 'comic opera'. As an example of later use of the term, H. C. Robbins Landon in his edition of *The Collected Correspondence and London Notebooks of Joseph Haydn*, 254, writes that 'Stephen Storace was a well-known composer of English ballad operas'.

[18] *English Theatre Music* (1st edn., London, 1973), ch. 5: 'The One-Composer Dialogue Opera, 1764–1776'. Fiske's terminology was adopted by Sharyn Lea Hall, 'English Dialogue Opera: 1762–1796', Ph.D. diss. (University of Toronto, 1980).

[19] Most afterpieces are in two acts, but Storace's *Lodoiska* and *The Three and the Deuce* are in three acts, while *The Glorious First of June* is in one.

[20] *A History of English Opera*, 224, 225. *The Gazeteer*, 5 Feb. 1791, called *The Siege of Belgrade* a pasticcio.

appropriate at all (which it certainly is not for *The Iron Chest*), then ask whether a work's construction by the 'pasticcio formula' (whatever that means) matters more than its role as mainpiece or afterpiece, opera or play with music.

Writing about Italian operas in London, Curtis Price describes the eighteenth-century 'pasticcio' as 'literally made up of bits and pieces of other works' and 'often written by committee'.[21] One of the important factors in the creation of these composite works is that they were easily adapted by the substitution of different arias for each production, and rarely lasted more than a season in one form. The operas of Storace and other English composers differ completely in approach, except in so far as they regularly included some borrowed music in their operas. English operas were, as far as we can tell, presented intact every season, and over half the music in Storace's operas was original.

The English word 'pastiche' has been used appropriately for works such as Arne's *Love in a Village* (1762) and Arnold's *The Maid of the Mill* (1765), in which most of the material is borrowed and merely rescored.[22] However, a simple count of how many individual numbers include borrowed music in later operas is too rough an estimate of the amount of borrowed music and ignores the composer's role as adapter. For instance, a composer who borrows half his numbers with minimal alteration produces a different kind of opera from one who borrows less and (like Storace) reworks the borrowed material, often adding large amounts of original material within 'borrowed' numbers. The whole question of Storace's borrowings is the subject of Chapter 8.

The mode of gathering musical material for an opera, whether composing afresh or borrowing something old, usually matters less than the work's role in the theatre as opera or play, mainpiece or afterpiece. There is generally no need to call a work with a substantial percentage of music anything other than 'opera', or, to distinguish it from Continental genres, 'English opera', with the modifier of 'mainpiece' or 'afterpiece' when useful. The following guidelines represent an attempt to provide a working definition of English opera that includes both mainpieces and afterpieces, that avoids the inconsistencies of eighteenth-century terminology, and that delimits the genre by excluding at least some of the stage works in which music played a subsidiary role.

The first criterion for whether a work is an opera is its use of music at structurally significant moments. An opera always opens with an overture,

---

[21] 'Unity, Originality', 17.   [22] Fiske, *English Theatre Music*, 327–42, 605–8.

a fact recognized by the eighteenth-century critic quoted above. It also ends with a vocal ensemble, and a variety of vocal numbers are performed in the course of the drama. In other words, music provides a structural framework and is dispersed throughout the spoken dialogue.

The second criterion needs specifying to distinguish opera from the profusion of English plays with music, and from genres in which music plays a different function such as the masque. The majority of the main dramatic roles should be played by the principal singers. This criterion provides an important limiting factor, and excludes Storace's *The Iron Chest* because, although music plays a reasonably significant role in the work's overall plan and it therefore fits the first criterion above, it is confined to specific groups of subsidiary characters, while the main plot is entirely spoken.

These criteria—structurally significant music performed by the main characters—are met by all of Storace's stage works in English except *The Iron Chest*.

Storace in Context

To most composers of Storace's generation, an English opera was a work in which spoken dialogue dominated and was ornamented by music that elaborated upon but did not further the plot. Storace, however, was educated in Naples and his early career in Vienna involved operas in which music was an integral part of the drama, dominating the dramatic structure. His two youthful Italian operas for Vienna, *Gli sposi malcontenti* (1785) and *Gli equivoci* (1786), conform to the contemporary conventions of Classical *opera buffa*, as does what survives of his first London opera, *La cameriera astuta* (1787).

At the other extreme, the English tradition to which Storace conformed on his return from Vienna in 1787 was essentially insular, although not devoid of influences from other European operatic forms. The most successful composers of the time—William Shield at Covent Garden, Samuel Arnold at the Little Theatre in the Haymarket, and Storace's predecessor at Drury Lane, Thomas Linley—had all been educated in Britain; their knowledge of foreign opera came mainly from the Italian operas staged at the King's Theatre (where Shield played the viola for a number of years). Their own operas, which became Storace's models, used spoken dialogue to carry the plot, interspersed with self-contained solos and ensembles. Their music varied in style from a few elaborate numbers for professional singers to a larger number of simpler pieces suitable for professional actors who were also amateur singers.

When Storace started work at Drury Lane, he decided to follow English operatic traditions, at least until he became established as a composer. His works therefore fall into clear divisions: Italian operas, English mainpiece operas (which increasingly approached the Italian in terms of their musico-dramatic involvement), and English afterpieces (which remained firmly in the English tradition throughout his career). His modifications are most evident in his alteration of the balance between drama and music in main-pieces, where he emphasizes music by integrating music and drama more closely. As the authors of *Biographia Dramatica* recognized in 1812: 'Hitherto little had been done beyond the introduction of single airs, or duets, to relieve the dialogue; but [James Cobb], aided by the ever-to-be-lamented Stephen Storace, formed the bold idea of telling the story of the scene in music.'[23] The changes were, of course, Storace's idea, though Cobb carried out his wishes. The greater importance of the role of music is indeed the funda-mental difference between Storace's operas and those of his contemporaries. *The Thespian Dictionary* (1805) claims to quote Storace's view that music should dominate the words:

Mr. Storace openly declared in a music-seller's shop in Cheapside (then Longman and Broderip's) 'that it was impossible for any author to produce a good opera without previously consulting his intended composer; for, added he, the songs must be introduced as *he* pleases, and the words (which are a secondary consideration) be written agreeable to *his* directions'. This is the modern mode of writing operas, which are therefore deservedly called *vehicles for music*; but formerly the music was provided for the words, and not the words for the music.[24]

Storace certainly put into practice what he stated in principle, by giving a much greater emphasis to large-scale finales and especially by incorporat-ing action into ensembles. He made more consistent use of complex forms for airs and of sonata form in overtures; he relied more on music at struc-turally significant points in the opera. His works therefore bear compari-son both with works in the English tradition in which they were performed and with operas in the Italian tradition in which he had been educated.

In order to achieve these modifications, Storace guided James Cobb

---

[23] *Biographia Dramatica*, comp. Baker *et al.*, ii. 285. The authors were referring, with hindsight, to *The Haunted Tower*, the first and least Italianate of Storace's mainpieces. However, their point should be taken in principle.

[24] *The Thespian Dictionary* (2nd edn., London, 1805), s.v. 'Storace, (Stephen)'.

towards writing musical sections that involved action, more like those of *opera buffa* in structure, though smaller in scale. Cobb had never written such numbers in the past; he obviously complied willingly with Storace's requests, as they collaborated on four mainpieces. Storace's afterpieces on the other hand (most with librettos by Prince Hoare) are in the mainstream of English domestic comedies with dramatically inessential music and only small-scale ensembles.

Storace's relationships with his English librettists must have been pleasantly different from his Viennese experiences. We know nothing directly about his relationship with his first librettist Brunati, but as a novice Storace would have had little influence on him. Lorenzo Da Ponte, his second librettist, had by his own account minimal consultation with Storace about *Gli equivoci*. Although Storace suggested *The Comedy of Errors* as a subject, the highly experienced Da Ponte then tossed off a completed libretto in standard *buffa* form.[25] By contrast, Storace's English librettists were active collaborators. We have anecdotal evidence of collaboration between Storace and Cobb, as well as clear indications of Storace's influence on the librettos themselves. Storace's working relationships with Hoare and Kemble were probably similar, as they were both his friends, and their librettos, like Cobb's, disclose Storace's influence. We know less about his relationship with Colman, but there is musical evidence that the two men collaborated on song texts for *The Iron Chest*.

Storace and Cobb do seem to have shared a common outlook on the use of structurally significant musical ensembles, one not shared by all of their contemporaries. Cobb's librettos for other composers (before and after Storace) differ slightly from Storace's in that music is not quite so consistently used to mark beginnings and ends of acts. In particular all internal acts start with speech. Storace's influence upon Cobb can be seen most clearly in their design of complex action finales, which Cobb wrote exclusively for Storace. Given the mediocre quality of Cobb's librettos in other respects, we can also deduce that their common interest in and convictions about structurally significant music helped sustain their partnership. Cobb's efficiency in providing what Storace needed in the placement of music, its involvement with the action, and its potential for musical characterization is good; the quality of the plots and dialogue, however, is sometimes regrettably bad.

We can form a useful picture of Storace's operas by comparing the number of musical items, their positioning, and the proportions of solos to

---

[25] Kelly, *Reminiscences*, i. 233–4; Da Ponte, *Memoirs*, 144.

ensembles to those in operas by his contemporaries. During the years 1788 to 1796, when Storace was at Drury Lane, thirty-three musical stage works in English, in addition to Storace's, were first performed at the London theatres. They range widely in their musical contents. For instance, Arnold's mainpiece play with music *The Mountaineers* (1793) contains only ten vocal numbers, whereas at the other extreme, Shield's opera *The Woodman* (1791) has thirty-five. A mainpiece typically averages more than twenty numbers, with Storace's at the high end. A similarly wide range can be found in afterpieces: from Storace's *The Prize* (1793) with only six pieces to Shield's *Sprigs of Laurel* (1793) with a massive twenty-two.

We can make some generalizations about the proportion of solo vocal numbers to ensembles (including duets and solos with chorus). The particular importance of ensembles derives from their ability to advance the story through interaction between protagonists, and therefore to become an essential part of the drama rather than just an ornament to it. Musical characterization is also important, though it need not further the plot. In operas with more than twenty numbers, Arnold's and Shield's ensembles average less than a quarter of the total; Linley's (from the 1780s) have a slightly higher proportion. In Storace's mainpieces, on the other hand, ensembles typically account for half of the total, a proportion reached by only a few individual works by other composers.[26] If we then take into account the size and complexity of several of Storace's finales, which are without parallel in English works, it becomes immediately apparent that Storace offered the London public something unique in English opera, by elevating music into a primary role.

Storace was more rigorous than his contemporaries in beginning and ending each act with music, especially in his mainpieces. Convention dictated that all operas begin with an overture and end with an ensemble or chorus. Beyond that there were many possibilities. In Storace's case, all his mainpieces begin with an ensemble after the overture and their acts all end with an ensemble. He applied the principle a little less strictly in his afterpieces: five out of eight open with speech (including *Lodoiska* after cuts); all end in an ensemble. Other composers felt free to end acts with solos, and occasionally with speech. Storace's least musically structured afterpiece is *Lodoiska* in its 'final' form, because major cuts were made after the première to shorten it to an acceptable length.

London playhouse audiences accepted both long stretches of spoken

---

[26] Roughly equal numbers of solos and ensembles can be found in Arnold's *New Spain* (1790), Shield's *The Woodman* (1791), and Mazzinghi and Reeve's *Ramah Droog* (1798).

dialogue and several pieces of music in close proximity. Storace's placement of musical numbers is dictated by the course of the drama, with the sole exception of *Dido, Queen of Carthage* which observes the rigid conventions of *opera seria* whereby exit arias alternate meticulously between soloists, carefully spaced, and linked by recitative rather than speech. In works with spoken dialogue, speech and music generally alternate, though occasionally dramatic interests dictate that one musical number should follow another immediately. For instance, in the opening scene of *The Doctor and the Apothecary*, Carlos's air 'When wilt thou cease' (no. 4) is directly followed by Juan's 'Sighing never gains a maid'. Most of Storace's operas also contain at least one scene without music. Sometimes its absence was a dramatic ploy to heighten the effect of the next musical number, as in the lengthy opening scene in *My Grandmother* which precedes the heroine's first entrance, singing.[27]

The importance of Storace's operas in the context of late eighteenth-century London is their musical enhancement of an admittedly short operatic tradition in which music plays an inessential role, one apart from the drama. Storace successfully brought Italian influences to bear on his English operas in integrating drama and music. His works are therefore at the same time the most musical of English operas and the least close to the norms of English opera. None the less, although his achievements were recognized by contemporary critics, he had disappointingly little influence on his colleagues and successors.

---

[27] Scene divisions in English works of the period occur at real changes of scene, not, as in most Continental operas, with spoken dialogue, after each main character's exit.

6

MAINPIECES

Storace moved to Drury Lane in 1788, after returning from Vienna a year earlier then working at the King's Theatre for a year or so. He composed a total of six mainpiece operas in English, at first deliberately conforming to English operatic conventions, later approaching the dramatically integrated form of *opera buffa* that had been his first love.

Storace wrote most of his mainpieces to librettos by James Cobb, along with afterpieces and a few other mainpieces with other librettists. His first mainpiece with Cobb, *The Haunted Tower* (1789), and to a lesser extent the second, *The Siege of Belgrade* (1791), follow the English traditions of spoken dialogue interspersed with dramatically inessential music. They were both immensely successful and were staged well into the 1820s. Next came *Dido, Queen of Carthage* (1792), an all-sung work in the *opera seria* tradition with a libretto by Prince Hoare. This experiment was a failure, closing after only five performances; no music survives. Storace then returned to working with Cobb for his next two full-length works: *The Pirates* (1792) and *The Cherokee* (1794). Both were moderately successful, though neither survived for long after its first season. Even so, these are Storace's two most important operas in terms of their introduction of musical innovations to the London stage. With Cobb's help, Storace increased the integration of drama and music, and the complexity of the ensembles, well beyond the inclination or capacity of any other English composer. Storace did not live to complete his next mainpiece opera, *Mahmoud*, with a libretto by Hoare. His sister Nancy (possibly with other help) fashioned a performance version of the unfinished opera by incorporating large sections of music from his first opera, *Gli sposi malcontenti*. *Mahmoud* was performed fifteen times towards the end of the 1795/6 season.

This chapter will focus on two mainpieces, *The Haunted Tower* and *The Pirates*, which represent the two extremes of Storace's English operatic style.

136

The first was Storace's attempt to work within the English tradition; the second shows his move towards the more complex genre of *opera buffa* while remaining within the boundaries of what the London audience would accept.

The Haunted Tower

Storace's first English mainpiece, *The Haunted Tower* (1789), was his second collaboration with James Cobb. Their working relationship had begun a year earlier with the afterpiece *The Doctor and the Apothecary*, in which we know Cobb collaborated actively with Storace. Michael Kelly reports:

Storace introduced me to Mr. Cobb, the late secretary to the East India Company, who had written two successful farces for Drury Lane. . . . Cobb was adapting, with Storace, Baron Dittersdorf's 'Doctor and Apothecary', for Drury Lane; they wished to consult me upon the kinds of songs I should wish to be written for me.[1]

Although we have no further anecdotal evidence of their continuing consultation, all the later operas show Storace's direct influence on Cobb's writing. Their close working relationship provoked Anthony Pasquin to remark, soon after Storace's death: 'We flatter ourselves with the idea that Mr. Cobb has concluded his career with the death of Storace, and that we shall have no more patchwork from this gentleman.'[2] In fact, Cobb wrote only one further mainpiece libretto, *Ramah Droog*, in 1798. Writing had always been his secondary occupation and he continued working for the East India Company throughout his career as a dramatist.

Many adverse comments were made by newspaper reviewers about the quality of Cobb's librettos, and indeed they abound in confused plots and clumsy prose. However, critics often missed Cobb's great virtue, which Storace appreciated: Cobb was prepared to follow Storace's lead in structuring librettos with dramatically essential music and multisection ensembles along the lines of *opera buffa*.

The première of *The Haunted Tower* on 24 November 1789 represented an important moment for Storace. He hoped to prove himself to the London audience (and the theatre management) with a full-scale work in the mainstream tradition of English opera. It was also his sister Nancy's début on the English stage. She had never before performed in an English opera,

---

[1] *Reminiscences*, i. 309–10.   [2] *The Pin Basket to the Children of Thespis*, 44 n.

and still (as throughout her life) was billed as Signora Storace. Her name headed the playbill (a most unusual circumstance, as men were almost invariably listed first). *The Haunted Tower* was also the work that first brought together the group of four singers who became Storace's regular principals: Nancy Storace partnered by Jack Bannister, and Michael Kelly partnered by Anna Crouch. Kemble commented in his diary that *The Haunted Tower* 'was received with prodigious Applause, and, with Signora Storace's Help, will, I think, be very successful'.[3] He was right. It stayed in the theatre's repertoire for over thirty years, and was often chosen by Nancy Storace, Michael Kelly, and (later) John Braham for special performances such as benefit nights. Its success was undoubtedly instrumental in encouraging Storace and Cobb to become more adventurous in their later collaborations.

The Haunted Tower is set in the time of William the Conqueror. The medieval set, designed by Thomas Greenwood, was indicative of a growing interest in Gothic drama on the London stage, which had developed from the popularity of the Gothic novel in the last quarter of the century. Although the term 'Gothic' was only applied to plays with hindsight, certain settings such as 'mountains, precipices and torrents, lakes, forests and caverns' had begun to appear so regularly towards the end of the century that they were becoming quite conventional.[4] Man-made elements, such as 'the spiral staircase, the grated windows, the secret panel, the trapdoor, the antique tapestries, the haunted chamber', and many more added to the Gothic atmosphere.[5]

The Haunted Tower opens with the perfect natural Gothic phenomenon, a storm at sea. It is portrayed in the overture during which the curtain rises on a seashore scene. The engraving on all but the earliest editions of the score shows an abandoned tower on the right, a castle on the left,[6] and the sea with two lighthouses in the distance. This set comes either from the opening scene or from Act 2, scene 3. The tower of the opera's title is not directly involved in the plot until Act 3, scene 4, when it is described as having a 'Gothic Chamber'.[7] In fact the 'haunted tower' is quite inessential to the plot (though it does give rise to one of the finest airs), and conceals nothing more than inebriated men scared by a 'ghost'.

The Cornish setting is less exotic than Storace's later mainpieces. *The*

[3] Memoranda A, fo. 60[v].

[4] Paul Ranger, *'Terror and Pity Reign in Every Breast': Gothic Drama in the London Patent Theatres, 1750–1820* (London, 1991), 40.

[5] Bertrand Evans, *Gothic Drama From Walpole to Shelley* (Berkeley and Los Angeles, Ca., 1947), 1.

[6] Dover Castle, according to *The Times*, 25 Nov. 1789.

[7] James Cobb, *The Haunted Tower* (London, n.d.), 43.

Haunted Tower is set in the definite past (the time of William the Conqueror) like his next mainpiece, *The Siege of Belgrade* (set at the time of Mehmet II's siege of Belgrade in 1456). The scenery and some of the events on stage were planned to appeal to the audience's more sensational tastes. The description 'Opera of Spectacle', applied by one eighteenth-century critic to *Lodoiska*,[8] is appropriate to all Storace's mainpiece operas, although *The Haunted Tower* has the most modest ending, with an offstage battle conveyed to the audience by suitable military music. Later works such as *The Siege of Belgrade* and *Lodoiska* end with battles presented in full view. *Lodoiska* is particularly spectacular when Princess Lodoiska is rescued from a flaming tower by her lover amid the battle.

The libretto exists in several versions, including the manuscript sent to Larpent before the première and John Cumberland's early nineteenth-century edition. Some reorganization and rewriting of scenes took place in between these two, though none is critical to an understanding of the plot. The earliest edition of the music was published by Storace himself, shortly after the première. The report that 'the music of this opera is now published, and may be had at the theatre', which appears in the book of songs, published by J. Jarvis in 1789, and most likely available on the first night, may have been a trifle optimistic, because although Storace's score is dated 1789 it was not entered as copyright until January 1790.

The Haunted Tower opens with the landing of Lady Elinor de Courcy, who has been sent by her father to meet her prospective husband Edward, the son of a newly titled Baron of Oakland. Her suspicions of Edward's character persuade her to arrive at the baron's castle disguised as her own maid. She is accompanied by her lover Sir Palamede (who has stowed away on the boat) in the guise of a jester. What Lady Elinor does not know is that he is really Lord William, rightful Baron of Oakland. Edward meanwhile introduces his own lover, Adela, to his father, but disguised as Lady Elinor, in the hope that they can be married before his ploy is discovered. After Lord William obtains proof that he is the real Baron, he takes the castle by force and regains his title. Both pairs of lovers are allowed to marry.

Disguise is obviously the most important device of the plot, one with an honourable history both in English theatre and Continental opera. Disguises contribute to the progress of almost all of Storace's plots, but nowhere more elaborately so than here, where double disguises allow the protagonists to show off a wide range of acting and singing skills. Lady Elinor pretends to be her maid; Lord William disguises himself first as Sir Palamede, then—

---

[8] *Morning Chronicle*, 11 June 1794.

as Sir Palamede—dresses as a jester, and finally—as Lord William—disguises himself in his father's armour and is taken for a ghost. Edward's lover Adela reluctantly disguises herself as Lady Elinor (whom she does not know). The present Baron was originally a ploughman, and in the opera tries to hide his crude manners through exaggerated pomposity. Only Edward, the Baron's son, is himself throughout.

The plot unfolds in predictable fashion. In Act 1 all the protagonists are presented, the scene is set, and we are left on the very brink of action. The entire act takes place outside the castle, the interior of which will become the setting for most of what follows. In Act 2 the play of disguises begins. The Baron is confused when he and Adela (as Lady Elinor) both try to act like aristocrats, each thinking the other is high-born, and both appearing absurd to the audience. He then converses with a maid (really Lady Elinor) who insists her mistress follows, although he is sure she has already arrived. The Baron never really recovers from his confusion; Lady Elinor on the other hand (who is equally puzzled by 'Lady Elinor') takes the situation calmly, instructing her servants to treat Adela as their mistress. Finally, tension is heightened when Lady Elinor's brother, who is not in his sister's confidence, arrives at the castle. Act 3 focuses on Lord William's preparations for taking the castle. Once his right to the title of baron is established and the women reveal their true identities, the end falls into place.

The music of *The Haunted Tower* comprises a total of twenty-six vocal numbers, fifteen solos and eleven ensembles, which is a slightly lower proportion of ensembles than Storace used in most of his later operas. Storace acceded to the English operatic tradition of mixing original and borrowed music. Exactly half the vocal numbers are entirely or partly borrowed.[9] The playbill for the première spelled out his sources in some detail: 'The New Musick, composed By Mr Storace, the rest compiled from Linley, Purcell, Sarti, Paesiello [*sic*], Martini, Pleyel, &c. &c.'

The music opens with a descriptive one-movement overture which leads without break into the opera. A long introduction in G major ('allegro maestoso', 2/2) cadences into an allegro assai in G minor, 3/4. The form of the allegro assai is highly individual, characterized by abrupt tonal jumps between G minor, B flat major, and G major, and several reprises of the first theme in different keys, which alternates with and is eventually combined with a second melody.[10] Storace adapted the main movement from

---

[9] See Appendix 5 for details of Storace's borrowings.

[10] Fiske, *English Theatre Music* (2nd edn., Oxford, 1986), 503, implies the presence of sonata elements by calling the second theme in the overture to *Gli equivoci* a 'second-subject group'. However, that theme does not function as part of a sonata movement in either version.

Ex. 6.1. Overture to *The Haunted Tower* (opening)

his overture to *Gli equivoci*, which had also included a storm; he probably suggested the opening scene to Cobb precisely in order to use his old overture. The entire overture portrays rough water, with sweeping arpeggios and rushing scale passages, abrupt dynamic contrasts and sudden swells. Example 6.1 includes some of these features in the opening phrase of the overture. Example 6.2 is taken from the second part of the overture, and includes one of several jumps between keys a third apart plus the rising of the curtain, which is marked by an ascending chromatic scale some eighty bars before the end of the overture. The thunderstorm erupts thirteen bars after the curtain rises, with the marking 'thunder' given in the score and probably played on an unspecified percussion instrument.[11]

Only the two-stave keyboard score of *The Haunted Tower* survives, so our information about Storace's scoring is limited to his labelling of some motifs for specific instruments or families. He used oboes, either flutes or clarinets or both, plus bassoons, horns, trumpets, and drums, and the usual string and continuo section. Oboes are cued in the score, as are high four-note chords for 'wind instruments' in both the overture and opening chorus. He could have been writing for oboes and clarinets (as in *No Song, No Supper*) or oboes and flutes (the scoring of *Gli equivoci*). Wind instruments

---

[11] The score of the overture to *Gli equivoci*, from which the storm section of this overture is adapted, has a separate stave for 'tuono' (thunder), 'lampi' (lightning), and 'grandine' (hail). The section involving hail is omitted in *The Haunted Tower*.

141

Ex. 6.2. Overture to *The Haunted Tower* (part 2)

feature prominently, both as a group to contrast with the strings and as soloists accompanied by the strings.

The overture leads straight into 'To Albion's genius raise the strain', a chorus of peasants and fishermen giving thanks for the end of the storm. Their comparatively simple, through-composed ensemble describes the aftermath of the storm just portrayed in the overture. Indeed, the orchestral introduction to the chorus is directly related to the opening of the overture. The last line of the chorus, 'in hollow murmurs dies away' is particularly effective.

The role taken by the chorus here, setting the scene rather than its members acting as participants in the drama, is typical of *The Haunted Tower*. Act 1 contains one other chorus, 'Hark! the sweet horn proclaims afar' (no. 5), which is also scenic and both visually and musically spectacular. Offstage horns call, the huntsman answers; his followers reply in three parts and are echoed by a three-part offstage chorus before the entire chorus joins together. The scene is attractive, though dramatically inessential.

Like the choruses, the ensembles do not further the plot. Rather each enhances the mood of a scene or a group of characters, whereas the action is advanced by the spoken dialogue. Act 1 ends with a simple trio, 'Against the shaft of cruel fate' (no. 9). Lord William, Lady Elinor, and her maid Cicely have just set the plot in motion, Lord William by sending a letter to prove his title to the baronetcy, and Lady Elinor by agreeing to her maid's suggestion of disguising herself as her own maid. Their contemplative trio is a complaint that they have to go to such lengths to subvert 'capricious destiny'; to the audience it promises action to follow.

In Act 1 all the main characters are introduced in music, apart from the present Baron and De Courcy, both of which are non-singing roles. *The Haunted Tower* shows its English heritage because solos predominate, and because they interrupt rather than further the action. Lord William (sung at the premiere by Michael Kelly) starts in a romantic vein with 'From hope's fond dream' (no. 2), which establishes 'Sir Palamede' (Lord William) as an essentially serious character—an important consideration for some- one who is about to be disguised as a jester but will be the rightful baron in the end. It is a formal number, lyrical and melismatic, with a long intro- duction and an oboe obbligato part to enhance its serious nature.

Lady Elinor (sung by Anna Crouch) follows with a lively but trivial strophic song, 'Tho' pity I cannot deny' (no. 3), in which she declares she will obey her father despite her love for Sir Palamede. Storace borrowed the tune from Pleyel, and neither music nor text convince us that Lady Elinor has any depth of character. In later operas Storace tended to make Anna Crouch's roles pathetic rather than superficial. As a strophic song, 'Tho' pity I cannot deny' again belongs firmly to the English opera tradition. Two attributes made strophic songs particularly suitable for English (or, indeed, French or German) operatic works. First, their repetitive form and simple style made them comparatively easy to learn for actors who were indif- ferent musicians. Secondly, they were easily remembered by the audience, who were not necessarily musically cultivated. It is no coincidence that Storace's most popular published songs were strophic, because the publishing business directed sales of operatic songs to amateur performers.[12]

Storace always included at least two strophic songs in his English works. Because of his Italian training (and the lack of strophic songs in *opere buffe* generally), it is not surprising that he used fewer than most of his English contemporaries, particularly William Shield. In the fifty strophic songs in

---

[12] 'Peaceful slumb'ring on the ocean' (*The Pirates*, no. 9) and 'A shepherd once had lost his love' (*The Cherokee*, no. 15) are the most striking examples of Storace's popular strophic songs.

his operas, Storace consistently chose texts that either had refrains or were narrative ballads, with only three exceptions. All types of character, and all the Drury Lane singers, were regularly given strophic songs, except for the serious hero (sung by Michael Kelly). Storace only once gave Kelly a strophic song, for a special situation in *The Haunted Tower*.

After the hero and heroine have been introduced in Act 1, the other main characters take their turns. Lady Elinor's maid Cicely (sung by Ida Romanzini) sings 'Nature to woman still so kind' (no. 4), which is labelled 'Welch tune' in the score.[13] This lilting folk air establishes Cicely as a servant, while its text shows her to be a thoughtful character. Indeed, she later invents the plan for her mistress to disguise herself. The next two solos belong to Edward's lover Adela (sung by Nancy Storace) and Charles (sung by Sedgwick), servant to De Courcy. They soon became the two most popular songs from the opera, published many times in the eighteenth and nineteenth centuries. Adela's 'Whither my love!' (no. 6) originated as Paisiello's 'La rachelina molinara' from *La molinara*, and 'My native land I bade adieu' was an original number by Storace. Neither is specific to a character or situation, a fact that, combined with their attractive melodies, would only enhance their popularity later.

Most of the airs in Act 1 offer little beyond catchy tunes, superficial characterization, and the setting of each character's mood. The 'dialogue' sung by Adela and Edward, 'Will great lords and ladies' (no. 7), fulfils the same function. There is no differentiation between the singers (who are in complete accord), and their duet simply establishes them as a pair of down-to-earth comic lovers. In summary, then, Act 1 displays the singers in attractive songs in a wide variety of musical styles, interspersed with choruses and ensembles that give atmosphere and provide some visual and aural excitement. There is little integration between the drama and music, nor much sense of stylistic relationship between the separate pieces of music.

In Act 2 the characters develop musically as the plot begins to unfold. Adela's first air establishes Nancy Storace's pre-eminence among the singers. In 'Be mine tender passion' (no. 10), she summons her courage to meet the

---

[13] Storace used the borrowed melody as the main theme of a short 'da capo' song. The melody is similar to one labelled 'Lacrum cush' in the 'Overture and Irish Medley' from Giordani's *The Isle of Saints* (1785). However, there are many differences in detail. Fiske, *English Theatre Music*, 603, thinks that Giordani's overture may have been the source. However, without more substantial evidence to the contrary, I think it more likely that the two composers independently selected the same tune from a popular source, especially since Storace thought the melody Welsh, and Giordani gave it an Irish title. In addition, Storace borrowed only the melody, not the harmonies, which supports the idea that he was using a popular tune. Another similar tune was used by Kane O'Hara in his burlesque *Midas* (1760) to the text 'As soon as her doating piece'.

Baron disguised as Lady Elinor. Her appropriately serious and virtuosic two-tempo air outshines Kelly's 'From hope's fond dream' from Act 1. On the other hand, Lady Elinor's air 'Hush, hush, such counsel do not give' (no. 11) is a light, lyrical number, attractive but adding little depth to her character, and borrowed from an unidentified piece by Sarti.

As the characters go about establishing their disguised personas, Lord William reveals his individuality further. Dressed as a jester, he takes the opportunity to mock the Baron's social position in a strophic song, 'Tho' time has from your Lordship's face' (no. 12). The satirical edge, which the Baron at least partly recognizes, is also ironic in light of William's own aristocratic lineage. Some of the dialogue surrounding his song was censored from the manuscript libretto (and is quoted above in Chapter 2) to remove the more direct criticisms of the aristocracy; the less explicit ones remain. The song (which was borrowed from Champein's *Les dettes*) is also remarkable for being the only strophic song Storace ever gave to Kelly. Kelly, who was usually typecast in Storace's English works as a serious hero, was able to step out of his normal role briefly, and therefore sing the kind of song that was normally beneath his dignity.

The most complex musical number in Act 2 is undoubtedly the sextet 'By mutual love delighted' (no. 15), an original piece by Storace and one of the few occasions in *The Haunted Tower* when characterization takes on any depth. Lady Elinor and her entourage are celebrating the nuptials of Edward and 'Lady Elinor' (Adela). Adela is thus required to keep up her pretence of being a lady with only Edward for support. Asides like 'Whom can they mean? not me' alternate with their dignified public mien. Example 6.3 quotes from the end of the penultimate section. The conspirators offer their own asides, both cynical and sympathetic, while they watch Adela's façade crack. In the final section Adela is pitted alone against the others, thus enhancing her musical status yet again beyond that, in particular, of Lady Elinor. In a later opera this number might have made a successful (if small-scale) finale, with its inclusion of acting and dialogue, and its gradually increasing tempos; instead the real finale is a less dramatic celebratory chorus for the impending nuptials. Its instrumentation includes a carillon, which echoes the following text:

> While the merry bells resounding
> shall in pleasure's chorus chime

Storace's other uses of the carillon are discussed in Chapter 7.

Towards the end of Act 2 Storace made a rare choice to include a popular song as a stage song. Richard Leveridge's 'The Roast Beef of Old

Ex. 6.3. 'By mutual love delighted' (*The Haunted Tower*, no. 15)

Ex. 6.3. *continued*

England' ('Now the mighty roast beef is the Englishman's', no. 16) precedes the finale in the score, although both numbers were cut from later editions of the libretto. The song had proved popular since its first publication in 1735, and would certainly have been recognized by the audience.[14] Storace therefore left it virtually unchanged.

Act 3 contains some of the most interesting music of the opera, most of it in scene 3. This is a domestic interlude, dramatically extraneous but musically powerful. It comprises three musical numbers with very little dialogue in between. First Lady Elinor shows her anxiety for Lord William in 'Dread parent of despair' (no. 21), a highly virtuosic air borrowed from another unidentified piece by Sarti, in which Storace finally allows Anna Crouch to show off her vocal agility. Cicely's simple lyrical song about the privileges of poverty follows almost immediately. Lastly, Lady Elinor and Adela clash head-on when Adela tries to fire Lady Elinor as her maid.

The duet 'Be gone, I discharge you' (no. 23), which ends scene 3, is a heated exchange between the two women. Both are characterized in their disguises and, when they sometimes forget their new roles, as themselves. Adela in particular has previously expressed her doubts about sustaining her disguise for long. Their opening exchange is given in Example 6.4. Storace gives each woman a melody which is stylistically appropriate to her disguised role. As 'Lady Elinor', Adela carries herself with bold, sweeping dignity until her agitation begins to show through (bars 13–16). Lady Elinor replies with a smoother, subdued, syllabic phrase which rises over sustained bassoon lines and the repeated string pedal that started at the end of Adela's phrase.

The duet ends with a typical closing section in which the women sing an almost identical text homophonically, apart from one brief exchange of dialogue, each scorning the pretentions of the other. Whereas in the earlier part their contrasting melodic lines indicated their antagonism, now their conflict is expressed by the visual effect of each turning away from the other and towards the audience. The audience understands that Adela is still pretending to be aristocratic and thus contemptuous of her maid's overfamiliarity, while Lady Elinor is singing in her real character to mock Adela's airs. It is perhaps the most dramatically convincing ensemble of the opera, concluding a scene in which we are treated to virtuosity, simplicity, and real musical characterization.

The remainder of the opera involves the male members of the cast, in particular Lord William reclaiming his castle. His 'Spirit of my sainted sire'

---

[14] Olive Baldwin and Thelma Wilson, '250 Years of Roast Beef', *MT* 126 (1985), 203–7.

Ex. 6.4. 'Be gone, I discharge you' (*The Haunted Tower*, no. 23)

Ex. 6.4. *continued*

(no. 24), a multi-tempo battle song, summons appropriately military imagery as he girds himself in his father's armour to win back the castle by force. As he dresses in the haunted tower where the armour had been stored, he calls on his dead father's memory for inspiration. Example 6.5 illustrates his resolution with the sweeping vocal range and trumpet fanfares of the opening section.

Another diversion delays the final resolution of the plot. We are finally introduced to the workings of the 'haunted' tower, which is actually a drinking club for the baron's servants. While Lord William dons his armour in the next room, a small farce takes place. Drunken servants are first frightened by a ghost (Lord William, who echoes their song from behind the door) then caught in the act of drinking by their employer. They sing the catch 'As now we're met', which Storace adapted from Purcell. He altered

Ex. 6.5. 'Spirit of my sainted sire' (*The Haunted Tower*, no. 24)

Ex. 6.5. *continued*

Purcell's text, making it clearly a drinking song; he simplified his harmonies, and regularized the harmonic rhythm, making it less fussy and more theatrically effective.

Finally the plot is wound up when Lord William takes the castle (off-stage) and is betrothed to Lady Elinor, with her brother's approval. The finale, 'The banished ills of heretofore', is a typical closing chorus, in which all the characters celebrate their new-found happiness and look to the future. The main characters, some alone, others in groups, summarize their own situations. The ensemble, headed 'Storace From Vive les fillettes', alternates a rondo theme borrowed from Krumpholtz with newly composed episodes.[15]

The Haunted Tower is as typical an English mainpiece as Storace ever composed. The action takes place in spoken dialogue, and the plot takes many by-ways; the setting is fashionably Gothic. The music follows the English tradition, with ensembles and choruses that are short and scenic rather than complex and dramatic. Most of numbers are solo songs, and include at least one virtuosic number for each of the three professional singers in the cast. Thus two-tempo airs take their place beside strophic songs. Two English stage songs (actually a chorus and a catch) are introduced, at least one of them already well known to the audience.

Occasional gleams of originality can be found. The overture follows the Continental norm rather than the three-movement form typical of English mainpieces; musical characterization takes place in two ensembles (both involving Nancy Storace as Adela). The overall effect, musically and dramatically, is of diversity of style rather than unity of purpose, of a series

---

[15] Storace probably derived this tune from Krumpholtz's arrangement in his Harp Concerto, Op. 9 No. 6, which he had published in *Storace's Collection*. In *The Haunted Tower* he used Krumpholtz's spelling of the song's title, 'Vive les fillettes' unlike the only other recorded but undated version, by P. J. Meyer entitled 'Vivent les fillettes. Ariette françoise' (London [*c.*1785]), *RISM* 2533. Fiske, *English Theatre Music*, 603, gives the probable source as P. J. Meyer, perhaps because it is the only song with similar title that he could find. Storace several times borrowed a rondo tune on which to build his own rondo, as for instance in 'My rising spirits' (*The Pirates*, no. 21), and the overtures to *My Grandmother* and *The Three and the Deuce*.

of enjoyable moments rather than a directed drama. No doubt because of its spectacular scenes, and despite a certain lack of dramatic and musical coherence, *The Haunted Tower* caught the imagination of the Drury Lane audience. Their enthusiasm must have encouraged Storace and Cobb to begin to integrate music and drama more closely, first in *The Siege of Belgrade* then further still in *The Pirates*.

The Pirates

Many of the conventional aspects of *The Haunted Tower* are modified in *The Pirates*. In the three years between their composition, Storace made significant progress towards the integration of drama and music, something revealed particularly in *The Pirates'* complex and highly dramatic internal finales. His achievement was recognized by his contemporaries, as a comment in his obituary reveals: 'His chief merit seems to have been in his Quartettos and Finales, in which he introduced the method of the Italian School upon the boards of our Theatre, with more success than perhaps any other Composer.'[16]

Cobb designed texts for *The Pirates* which included large-scale action finales and other complex ensembles, while at the same time indulging his penchant for convoluted plots to an extreme. Kemble, who was no musician, thought merely that 'the dialogue is very dull'.[17] Other critics found excellence in the music, particularly the finales and other ensembles. As one reviewer wrote, 'The author has not much depended on plot or interest. The chief merit is in the Scenery and Music.'[18] The work ran for thirty performances in its first season and enjoyed a few sporadic performances in later years. It was reworked in 1827 with new words but most of the original music as *Isidore de Merida or, The Devils Creek*, first performed on 29 November 1827 and lasting just one season.

The following discussion relies on the manuscript libretto of *The Pirates* sent to the Lord Chamberlain for censorship.[19] The dialogue was probably tightened up before the première, and we know cuts were made between the first and second performances, so the Larpent version does not always represent what was actually spoken on stage. The published score includes

---

[16] *Oracle*, 18 Mar. 1796.   [17] Memoranda A, fo. 206ᵛ.   [18] *Times*, 22 Nov. 1792.
[19] 'The Pirate' [*sic*] (Larpent MS 961). Another MS (BL Add. MS 25,913) survives that may have been used by the prompter (Fiske, *English Theatre Music*, 516).

almost all the numbers planned in the manuscript libretto and, like most of Storace's operas, it was published in two-stave format a month after the première. The music includes an overture, sixteen solo songs (which include the first section of the finale to Act 1, printed separately from the rest), twelve ensembles, and a group of four instrumental dances.

The Pirates had been preceded by two failures by Storace with Hoare, the afterpiece *The Cave of Trophonius* and the serious all-sung opera *Dido, Queen of Carthage*. *The Pirates* marked a return to the type of mainpiece opera with spoken dialogue that he and Cobb had made successful in both *The Haunted Tower* and *The Siege of Belgrade*. It was first performed on 21 November 1792 by the Drury Lane company at the King's Theatre, with the same principal singers who had by now become well established at Drury Lane: Nancy Storace, Michael Kelly, Anna Crouch, and Jack Bannister.

Cobb wrote an entirely original plot, as he had for *The Haunted Tower* and did later for *The Cherokee*. The story is based on the traditional premiss that a pair of lovers is thwarted in love by someone in authority. Disguises are less important here than in *The Haunted Tower*, but they are still used in the series of failed attempts at escape and rescue. The following outline vastly simplifies the complex plot. Don Altador (with his servant Blazio) sets out to rescue his love Donna Aurora (who has a maid, Fabulina) from her guardian Don Gaspero de Merida (a wicked pirate) who wants her to marry his nephew Guillermo (also a pirate). Several failed attempts lead to Gaspero hiding Aurora in his castle. Altador and his supporters (who by then include his servants, Aurora's servants, her long-lost maid Fabulina, and the coastguard) infiltrate the castle and rescue Aurora.

The action takes place around Naples, which was probably Storace's idea. Kelly says that the backdrop, a view of Naples with Mount Vesuvius in the background (which appears on the title-page of the score), was based on one of Storace's youthful sketches,[20] though Thomas Greenwood executed the designs. The principal characters, however, are Spanish. The scenes take place in everyday places such as gardens and houses, with a fairground scene and a vineyard to add visual interest. A Gothic touch is added by setting Act 2, scene 6 on 'the Road to Pausilippo near Virgils Tomb', another detail that suggests Storace's local knowledge.

The Pirates opens conventionally with an overture in three movements. Two of Storace's other mainpiece overtures, to *The Siege of Belgrade* (1791) and *Mahmoud* (1796), also use the three-movement overture form that remained the norm in England into the nineteenth century. Thus they

---

[20] *Reminiscences*, ii. 32.

follow Thomas Busby's dictum that 'if the piece be intended for an overture to a three-act opera, an orchestral concerto, a full symphony, or a grand sonata, it ought not to consist of fewer than three movements'.[21]

The overture to *The Pirates* starts with a movement in unexceptional sonata form; its slow movement is short and through-composed, borrowed from his Piano Quintet in D (1784); the rondo finale is also adapted from Storace's quintet. Its use of three movements for the overture is perhaps the only respect in which *The Pirates* is more typically English than *The Haunted Tower*. Even so, sonata form (Storace's favoured first-movement form) was a less common first-movement form in England than on the Continent. The only other opera composer to use it consistently and fairly conventionally was Thomas Linley, Storace's predecessor at Drury Lane.

The curtain rises on a chorus which begins the action, thus contrasting with the purely scenic chorus of *The Haunted Tower*. The opening chorus also draws our attention to the major weakness of *The Pirates*: the dichotomy between the quality of text and music. Cobb's dialogue is trite and at times farcical. After Don Altador and his companions give thanks for their safe arrival in port, the number continues with the innkeeper Genariello greeting them as follows:

> Come my Lads get on—be steady,
> Is the Macaroni ready?
> Where's the Omelet—don't stand staring,
> Zounds, these Rogues are past all bearing.

The chorus then ends as a drinking song. The quality of this opening speech is representative of that of the entire libretto, which includes many conversations whose humour or wit were presumably thought to outweigh their dramatic insignificance. A typical example is Genariello's play on words in 'You know, my Lord, every Man has a Character to support—Gaspero happens to have a bad Character, but he has uniformly maintain'd it—Now there is some merit in that'.[22] Verbosity and lack of direction are also common, as when Fidelia babbles: 'Well and Genariello says he heard Guns fire at Sea an Hour ago, & he thinks—I don't understand Exactly what he thinks, but I am certain we may Expect great News, tho' I dont know what it is—so I just came to tell you all about it—and now I must run back to Genariello.'[23] Some quite lengthy dialogues suffer from similar problems. No doubt sections were removed or abbreviated during rehearsals and after the première, but the Larpent libretto is both verbose and confusing.

---

[21] *A Grammar of Music* (London, 1818), 476. [22] 'The Pirate', p. 8. [23] Ibid., p. 81.

Another reason for the plot's lack of direction and urgency is the sheer number of ineffectual rescue plans that Cobb included. Some plots are turned against the instigators, while others introduce new characters very late in the opera. Fabulina's first plan for Altador and Aurora to meet (in which Altador is to disguise himself as Gaspero) is foiled by Gaspero before it starts; the second (in which they intend to escape by sneaking out past the drunken watchman) almost succeeds. This plan, which takes place as the finale to Act 1, becomes a dramatic highpoint of the opera. Gaspero turns the third plan, in which Altador and Aurora are to meet at the fair, into a trap for Altador. It is concluded in the finale to Act 2 when Altador and Blazio are imprisoned on a pirate ship and Aurora is removed to her guardian's castle in the country. The final rescue is initiated in Act 2 when Gaspero dismisses Fabulina; then Fidelia, a former servant of Aurora, arrives. In Act 3 they are joined by a third servant, Marietta, who provides access to Gaspero's castle. The final rescue goes no more smoothly than the earlier ones because Altador—who enters the castle with Fabulina and Fidelia disguised as an entertainer with a magic lantern—is quickly recognized and imprisoned. He is therefore unable to fire the signal shot to summon the coastguard. In the end, sheer goodness is made to win the day, because trickery is certainly the prerogative of Gaspero and his pirates.

The music of *The Pirates* stands in direct contrast with that of *The Haunted Tower*. By 1792 Storace was a more mature composer and more experienced in the London theatre. In almost every way, the music of *The Pirates* is intrinsically more dramatic, better integrated with the action, and stylistically more unified. This is partly because Storace borrowed far less material for *The Pirates*, a mere seven (or possibly eight) pieces out of twenty-seven. Many of those were either adaptations of his own earlier music or small sections of music by other composers which he reworked significantly.

In Act 1, Storace introduces the main characters more effectively, giving us some real understanding of their characters, their standing, and their dilemmas. For instance, Don Altador, sung by Kelly, opens with 'Some device my aim to cover' (no. 3), borrowed from *Gli sposi malcontenti*. The music portrays him as the confident hero, with sustained arpeggio lines, but also reveals the unsure lover, with faster, more hesitant music (Ex. 6.6). In other words, the hero is no longer a type, as in *The Haunted Tower*, but becomes a real personality. Donna Aurora, sung by Anna Crouch, is introduced with a very elaborate romantic air, 'Love like the op'ning flow'r' (no. 6), quite unlike her weak first number in *The Haunted Tower*. Fabulina, played by

Ex. 6.6. 'Some device my aim to cover' (*The Pirates*, no. 3)

Nancy Storace, is first presented as a character actor in the duet 'What sounds are these' (no. 4). Storace makes no attempt to match her musical style to the serious, virtuosic vocal styles of the hero and heroine. Instead she has a more active presence on stage and a larger share of the dramatic music in most of the ensembles.

Storace's ability to cast character in music is most often shown in ensembles, but one song for Fabulina deserves detailed study. Her song 'A saucy knave' (no. 13) shows her quick-wittedness and the underlying panic when she interleaves a ballad tale with two kinds of personal asides. She has just been leaning over the balcony making plans with the hero's servant Blazio for Donna Aurora to escape. Blazio enters the house to collect a letter from Aurora to Altador when Aurora's guardian Gaspero appears unexpectedly, demanding to know who Fabulina was talking to. She invents the tale of the 'saucy knave', whom she claims never to have seen before, occasionally making desperate asides to Aurora for help as her invention fails (lines indented), and stumbling over her story (lines indented and italicized):

> A saucy knave who pass'd the door,
> would needs, forsooth make Love to me,
> but, as I've often said before,
> you know, Sir, that must never never be.
>
> Of flames & darts, despair and death,
> in vain declaim'd the silly youth;
> I laugh'd and sneer'd, till almost out of breath,
> believe me, Sir, I tell you truth.
>
> I frowning vow'd, without your leave,
> his face again I ne'er would see,
>> Dear Aurora help me out,
>> I shall betray myself I doubt,
> So kind a Master to deceive!
> Oh! fie! Oh fie! no that could never be,
>
>> *I said to him, no, no, 'twas he,*
>> *'twas he spoke next, Ay he said, says he to me,*
>> my dearest Fabulina hear me,
>> Indeed, indeed you need not fear me,
>>> Dear Aurora help me out,
>>> I shall betray myself I doubt,
>> *Says I to him no no 'twas he,*
>> *'twas he spoke next, Ay ay says he to me,*
>> *says I, says he, says I, says he, says I, says he,*

at length enrag'd my maiden pride
my heart I cried is not for you,
in vain your betters oft have tried,
you know, dear sir, that's very very true.[24]

The first two stanzas of text seem to be a typical ballad. Stanza 3 opens like a continuation of the story, then Fabulina begins her asides, which are directly connected with the awkward situation in which she finds herself. Storace reflects her three different levels of speech with distinct melodic styles. They can be represented as follows:

Stanza	Text	Musical section
1	Ballad	A
2	Ballad	B
3	Ballad, asides	A, interrupted by C, A
4	Asides, attempts to continue	D, interrupted by C, D
5	Ballad completed	A

Although this outline suggests the song is a rondo, the ballad itself (that is, stanzas 1, 2, part of 3, and 5) suggest a modified strophic song (in the shape ABAA), while the interruptions provide the material C and D. Example 6.7 gives the settings of stanzas 1, 3, and 4. The ballad itself (A and B) is a regularly phrased melody based on simple harmonic progressions. Fabulina's calls to Aurora (C) are faster and more declamatory. Her stumbles (D) are short, hesitant figures, rhythmically similar to the ballad (which she is trying to continue) but distinguished from it by the broken chord accompaniment figures. It is no coincidence that Storace wrote the song for his sister Nancy, who was well known for her lively stage presence and ability to act while singing.

Storace composed one ensemble in *The Pirates* that resembles the twofold characterization in the duet 'Be gone, I discharge you' in *The Haunted Tower*. The trio 'Past toils thus recompensing' (no. 7) takes place when Altador's first plan for meeting Aurora has just been foiled because her guardian and his nephew (her suitor) have arrived home unexpectedly. Altador comes within hearing distance (but out of sight), not knowing that his plan has been discovered. Gaspero forces Aurora to pretend to be in love with his nephew Guillermo, who plays his role with fervour. Aurora does as she is told by her guardian but also makes asides that echo the style of Altador's horrified gasps. Example 6.8 illustrates her dual role.

---

[24] Stephen Storace, *The Pirates* (London [1792]), 50–1.

(*a*) Stanza 1

Ex. 6.7. 'A saucy knave who pass'd the door' (*The Pirates*, no. 13)

Out of all the ensembles and choruses in *The Pirates*, Storace wrote only one simple chorus, which he linked to the drama in an unusual way. The libretto directs that Act 3 open with the chorus 'To the vineyard's praise the chorus raise' (no. 20), then that the chorus be repeated at the end of the scene in the innkeeper's vineyard. Storace instead wrote two slightly different numbers, which together make one unit, giving the impression of music continuing (though receding into the background) during the scene and re-emerging at the end. One introduction and one postlude serve for the two numbers, as follows:

Introduction A B   INTERRUPTED BY   A1 Postlude
  (no. 20)   DIALOGUE AND AIR (no. 21)   (no. 22)

Thus the two numbers form a balanced unit with an instrumental surround, and again integrate music and drama more closely.

Even though there are many individual musical numbers of interest in

(*b*) Stanza 3

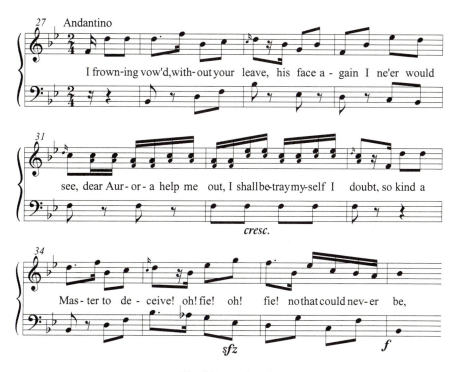

Ex. 6.7. *continued*

The Pirates, the single most important and effective aspect of its music comes in its internal finales. These exemplify better than any other opera by Storace (with *The Cherokee* a close second) his success in integrating drama and music. Previously Storace and Cobb had avoided Italianate finales, probably because neither librettist nor audience was familiar with operatic music that gave more than expressive or entertaining breaks from the drama. Instead, in *The Haunted Tower* and *The Siege of Belgrade*, Storace and Cobb had introduced a moderate amount of action into other ensembles. By 1792, audiences' and reviewers' reactions must have convinced them that the time was ripe for more complex finales. They wrote finales in *The Pirates* and *The Cherokee* that resemble those of *opera buffa* in structure, though they are closer in size to those of *opéra comique*.[25]

Storace's approach to composing finales was undoubtedly influenced by

[25] Charles E. Koch Jr., 'The Dramatic Ensemble Finale in the Opéra Comique of the Eighteenth Century', *Acta Musicologica*, 39 (1967), 79–80.

(*c*) Stanza 4

Ex. 6.7. *continued*

Ex. 6.8. 'Past toils thus recompensing' (*The Pirates*, no. 7)

Mozart and other Viennese composers, as well as Lorenzo Da Ponte, who wrote the libretto for his second opera. Da Ponte gave a now famous decription, partly tongue-in-cheek, of the formula for an *opera buffa* finale:

The finale, besides having to be closely bound up with the rest of the opera, is a kind of little comedy or play by itself, demanding a fresh plot and some special interest. It is here chiefly that the genius of the Kapellmeister, the worth of the singers and the greatest dramatic effect must show themselves. There is no recitative, everything is sung, and every kind of singing has to be introduced: *adagio*, *allegro*, *andante*, *amabile*, *armonioso*, *strepitoso*, *arcistrepitoso*, *strepitosissimo*, with which nearly always the finale closes. This in technical language is called the *chiusa*, or *stretta*, I know not whether because in it the play draws to a close, or because it generally puts the brain of the poor poet who has to write the words into such straits not once but a hundred times. According to theatrical dogma, in the finale all the singers must appear on the stage, even if there were three hundred of them, one at a time, or two, or three, or six, or ten, or sixty at a time, to sing solos or duets or trios or sestets or sessantets. And if the plot of the play does not allow of it, then the poet must find a way to make it do so, in despite of good sense and reason and all the Aristotles on earth. And if then it proves to go badly, so much the worse for him.[26]

The two internal finales of *The Pirates* follow Da Ponte's precepts fairly closely by comprising several distinctive musical sections that incorporate

[26] *Memoirs*, 114.

action (and in the case of Act 1 a whole escape plot), and form the climax of each act. They differ greatly from the typical English finale, which is in one section, visually spectacular rather than dramatic, and performed after the action has been completed in spoken dialogue.

Contemporary critics recognized Storace's achievement, usually with brief comments along the lines that he 'formed the bold idea of telling the story of the scene in music'.[27] Occasionally they acknowledged the influence of *opera buffa*: 'The Composer [of *The Cherokee*], in this and former instances, has laudably, in our opinion, endeavoured to introduce the Italian style of mingling the persons of the Drama in musical conversation; and in this instance has performed his task with great effect.'[28] There can be no doubt that Storace derived his finale structures from *opera buffa*.

Viennese *opera buffa* finales between 1781 and 1790 (including Storace's first two operas) have been analysed by John Platoff with reference to what he calls 'action-expression' cycles of text and music.[29] These linked pairs parallel the relationship between recitative (or spoken dialogue) and aria in the rest of an opera. The action-expression cycle is a useful point of departure for discussing Storace's English finales because, while they fit the conventions of Viennese operas less closely than those of his Italian operas, there is nevertheless a fundamental similarity. Besides, action-expression cycles involve the relationship between words and music intimately while not presupposing a particular size of finale, which is the area in which Storace's finales differ most from *opere buffe*.

In a typical cycle, action (that is, sung dialogue) is followed by an expressive section in which the characters comment together (not necessarily in agreement). Librettos do not always distinguish between active and expressive sections of text; the composer draws the distinction in his setting. In music, active passages are characterized by rapid delivery of text, little word repetition, musical continuity, short, declamatory vocal lines, and prominent orchestral support. In expressive passages the vocal parts are dominant, stability is important, and text repetition is common. They can therefore be distinguished from the preceding active passages by the change in vocal texture from dialogue to tutti and by their tonal stability and harmonic closure. An action-expression cycle is, however, normally one continuous section.

In his individual approach to setting finales, Storace makes more use than normal of separated action and expression sections. In most *opere buffe*, such

---

[27] *Biographia Dramatica*, ii. 285.   [28] *Morning Chronicle*, 22 Dec. 1794.
[29] 'Music and Drama in the *Opera buffa* Finale: Mozart and his Contemporaries in Vienna, 1781–1790', Ph.D. diss. (University of Pennsylvania, 1984), chs. 2–4 *passim*.

sections are exceptional, and take place for specific reasons. Most occur at dramatically important points, such as an interruption by a new and unexpected action before the characters can comment on the first. Distant tonal shifts sometimes emphasize such passages; they can also signify a strong emotion or a surprising event, a change of location, the introduction of a new group of characters, or the return to normal after a shock passage. A shock passage is conventionally a slow, soft, and static section; a *stretta*, the last and often longest section, is usually fast and loud, the boiling-point of agitation. Self-contained expressive passages can also be general in sentiment, providing a break in the forward drive of the finale. Storace was partial both to self-contained expressive passages and to the juxtaposition of keys a third apart. A few come about because of Cobb's text, but most are purely musical choices. The finale to Act 1 of *The Pirates* shows Storace's preference for these features, as well as his dislike of lengthy expressive passages.

The finale to Act 1 of *The Pirates* was published as two separate numbers. The first part, 'Peaceful slumb'ring on the ocean' (no. 9, in C major), is a stage song, introduced by the drunken watchman's invitation to Fabulina, 'Sing away! Sing away! Sing away!', and is also the beginning of the finale, so labelled in the libretto and elsewhere.[30] It became Storace's most popular song, and was often called 'Lullaby'. No doubt Nancy Storace's performance was applauded; there would then have been a natural break between the air and the continuation of the finale, which may have been Dale's reason for publishing it as a separate number.[31] Figure 4.2 reproduces Dale's edition of 'Peaceful slumb'ring'. 'Hist, hist, Fabulina' (no. 10, starting in G major and ending in C major) is the continuation of the finale.[32]

Table 6.1 gives an outline of the finale to Act 1. The sections are marked by double barlines in the score. With only six sections, it is shorter than the typical Viennese finale (including Storace's own), and follows the action-expression pattern rather loosely. None the less, it bears comparison with the plan of a typical *opera buffa* finale in its alternation of action and reaction.

Section 1 (published as no. 9) is a stage song sung by Fabulina to lull the drunken watchman, Sotillo. It is perceived to be the beginning of the finale only when the following section starts. It is an independent

---

[30] e.g. *Diary*, 22 Nov. 1792.

[31] In *The Cherokee* a similar printing convenience probably dictated that the finale to Act 2 should be printed as four separate numbers, 19 to 22. Here the score is clearly labelled.

[32] See John Platoff, 'Tonal Organization in "Buffo" Finales and the Act II Finale of "Le Nozze di Figaro"', *ML* 72 (1991), 387–403, for an overall view of tonal plans.

Table 6.1. Outline of *The Pirates*, finale to Act 1

First line	Key	Metre	Tempo	Characters	Text type
1. Peaceful slumb'ring on the ocean	C	6/8	'soave'	Fabulina	Expression
2. Fabulina, hear me	G	3/4	—	Fabulina, Aurora, Altador	Action— expression— action
3. Stir not resistance is in vain	E♭ to B♭	4/4	'allegro maestoso'	As for sect. 2	Action— expression— action
4. We're lost beyond the help of art	G to D	3/4	'allegretto'	As for sect. 2 + Gaspero, Guillermo, Genariello	Expression— action
5. What means this brawl? Peace I command	G	3/4	'largo'	As for sect. 4 + officer	Action
6. Hear oh hear the simple story	C	2/2	'allegro'	As for sect. 5 [+ chorus?]	Expression

expressive section but an essential part of the overall tonal plan, establishing C major firmly. The action begins in section 2 with the separate entrances of heroine and hero. Action is combined with momentary expressiveness in the form of a love duet, followed by Fabulina's interruption to encourage haste.

The beginning of section 3 is marked by an abrupt move from G to E flat which signifies the first thwarting of the trio's plans to escape when Sotillo wakes from his drunken stupor. As in section 2, an expressive passage in which the two women pacify Sotillo is followed by a return to action as Don Altador hurries them along. Example 6.9 gives the last (active) part of section 3, the shift of a third to G major, and the first half of the brief expressive passage in section 4.

The key shift that begins section 4 matches the second frustration of the trio's plans. At first the only indication of a new obstacle is this key change, because Gaspero and his nephew, accompanied by the innkeeper, are still offstage. The section therefore opens with an expressive section as the women, who have seen them drawing near, exclaim in horror. As they continue and Altador joins them, the reason for their fright is explained. When their opponents arrive on stage a fight ensues (the active part of

Ex. 6.9. 'Hist, hist, Fabulina' (*The Pirates*, no. 10)

section 4), and the innkeeper calls the guard in Altador's defence. Again the women express their despair as the men confront each other.

Section 5 is brief, consisting entirely of the officer's entrance and exhortation for peace. This incites the closing section, in which everyone tells their 'simple story' in fugal texture, interrupted by the audible arrival of official support for the officer (drums) and everyone's comments.[33]

---

[33] See Fiske, *English Theatre Music*, 516–17 for the opening bars.

Ex. 6.9. *continued*

The opening and closing sections are both independent expressive passages, the first because it is a stage song, the last because it is an independent *stretta* with section 5 as its preceding (short) active section. The middle sections, 2 to 4, take unusual forms. Sections 2 and 3 both add a final section to the usual action-expression cycle, while section 4 reverses the normal order. All the sections are through-composed except for the opening strophic song.

Tonally the finale stays in closely related keys with an interruption for section 3. The more distant tonal juxtapositions at the beginnings of sections 3 and 4 match the two real surprises in the action—Sotillo's awakening and Gaspero's appearance:

Section: 1 2 3   4   5 6
Key: C G E♭ to B♭   G to D   G C

Table 6.2. Outline of *The Pirates*, finale to Act 2

First line	Key	Metre	Tempo	Characters	Text type
1. Unhand me cowards/ Bear him away	E♭ to c	4/4	'allegro'	Altador, Guillermo, Gaspero, Aurora	Action
2. Ah! if compassion marks	C	3/4	'andante'	Altador, sailors	Expression
3. Be gone, and to the castle bear	G to g	3/8	'allegretto'	Gaspero, Aurora, Guillermo	Action
4. Whatever path pursuing	E♭	4/4	'allegro'	Fabulina, Fidelia, Genariello, Guillermo, Gaspero, chorus	Expression

Storace's finale also differs from its Italian models because most of the expressive passages are just momentary pauses in the action. Cobb provided fairly conventional expressive texts, which Storace chose to set concisely, without text repetition, thus achieving dramatic drive at the expense of lyrical contemplation. As a result the finale is fast-paced, not too long for an audience to whom it was novel, and culminates in an exciting choral conclusion.

The finale to Act 2 is shorter, with only four sections. Originally it was shorter still, because the manuscript text approximately matches only the first two sections in the score. Sections 3 and 4 were expanded from one much shorter section in the libretto, which indicates that Storace wanted a longer, differently balanced finale than Cobb at first provided. The finale is no less sensational than the first, though it includes less action. It takes place when the lovers' second plot to escape has just been foiled, Altador is captured by the pirates, and Aurora is being taken to her guardian's castle. It ends when a storm springs up.

Table 6.2 summarizes the four sections, which make up two action-expression cycles. In the first cycle, Don Altador is captured by the pirates who are encouraged by Aurora's guardian in the face of Aurora's despair; they reject Altador's pleas. In the second, Aurora is borne off while her captors worry about their merchandise (rather than their human burden, Altador) because a storm is approaching. Finally the characters all describe the storm's progress according to how it will affect their various fates. This finale, like the previous one, differs from the conventional *opera buffa* action-expression pairs, this time because all the passages, both active and expressive, are musically differentiated. The separations give the number an extra weight and musical variety that two undifferentiated cycles would not provide. The pairs of sections match; each uses both triple and quadruple metre and moves between keys a third apart; each active section moves from a major to a minor key. The two cycles have a more conventional relationship between them, with a close key relationship and no change of metre, though the tempo speeds up. The result is less active but more pictorial than the finale to Act 1.

Storace wrote some of his most exciting music in *The Pirates*, both in the finales and elsewhere. In the end the disparity between the quality of words and music is too wide to justify calling *The Pirates* an overall success: the excitement of the music sits oddly with the poor dialogue. Even so, *The Pirates* is extremely important in the history of English opera because here Storace came nearest of any composer of his generation or the next to achieving the integrity of music and drama for which he so clearly strove.

7

AFTERPIECES AND OTHER STAGE WORKS

During his London career Storace composed eight afterpieces plus music for a number of other staged pieces. The scores of all but one of his afterpieces survive, along with some of the other larger works. His only ballet, *Venus and Adonis* (1793), was published in reduced score, and the play with music, *The Iron Chest*, was published posthumously in a volume with *Mahmoud*. Several individual arias, along with his music for *Poor Old Drury* and the numbers he contributed to a revival of *Comus* are lost. Only three individual arias and airs date from after 1786: 'Care donne' (1787) and two songs about Marie Antoinette (1793). This chapter gives a brief overview of Storace's afterpieces followed by a detailed discussion of two pieces, the afterpiece *No Song, No Supper* (whose musical emphasis is solo songs) and the mainpiece play with music *The Iron Chest* (in which the emphasis is on ensembles).

The Afterpieces

Storace's afterpieces are his most typically English group of stage works. They take the conventional form of spoken dialogue alternating with dramatically inessential music. Shorter and simpler than mainpieces, they are typically domestic comedies, so are relatively unaffected by literary fashion or other external influences. Storace embraced the English genre wholeheartedly, particularly in collaborations with his old friend Prince Hoare. It suited their view of the afterpiece as a lighter, shorter work suitable for focusing on one singer and less appropriate for serious or dramatic music. Over half of Storace's afterpieces were originally performed at singers' benefit performances, and most of them stayed in the Drury Lane repertoire for decades, thus giving the lie to one critic's remark that 'pieces brought forth at Benefits are rarely permanent in the Theatre'.[1]

Storace composed afterpieces throughout his London career, starting with his first English work, *The Doctor and the Apothecary* (1788), to a text by James Cobb. Cobb then found his niche in mainpieces, and Storace formed a comfortable working relationship with Hoare for writing afterpieces. *No Song, No Supper*, their first collaboration, was performed at Michael Kelly's benefit performance on 16 April 1790. It was followed by a series of works written specifically for singers' benefits. *The Cave of Trophonius* was written for Anna Crouch's benefit on 3 May 1791, *The Prize* for Nancy Storace (11 March 1793, Drury Lane company at the King's Theatre), and *My Grandmother* was also for his sister, this time at the Little Theatre on 16 December 1793. Storace interrupted the sequence in the summer of 1794 with two afterpieces with other librettists, first *Lodoiska* to a libretto by Kemble (9 June 1794), then less than a month later *The Glorious First of June* to a libretto by Cobb. He then returned to benefit pieces, setting as his last afterpiece Hoare's libretto *The Three and the Deuce* for Jack Bannister (2 September 1795 at the Little Theatre).

The Doctor and the Apothecary was Storace's first piece for Drury Lane, and it must have been in the nature of a test piece. After all, turning from *opera buffa* to English opera was an unusual step to take (as was being an English composer of Italian operas). It seems that Storace deliberately tried to conform to English traditions to prove himself to the Drury Lane management and audience. Cobb translated and adapted Gottlieb Stephanie's libretto for Dittersdorf's *Doctor und Apotheker*; Storace adapted some of Dittersdorf's music (mostly in Act 1), added some of his own (almost the whole of Act 2), and made a few other borrowings. Among the deliberate concessions to his native genre, Storace borrowed other composers' music for the first time. He also wrote strophic songs (virtually unused in *opera buffa*) and kept his ensembles simple. Cobb even broke up Stephanie's complex finale to Act 1 into several separate musical sections and spoken dialogue to keep the English finale small-scale.

However, Storace did not adopt the English style completely. He used a one-movement overture (as opposed to the English norm of three movements) and used fewer strophic songs than are typically found in English works. The result was a fairly successful opera: it was performed twenty-five times in its first season and stayed in the repertoire for several years;

[1] *Morning Chronicle*, 18 Dec. 1793.

there were sporadic revivals until 1816/17. It was certainly successful enough for Storace and Cobb to continue their working relationship. They then wrote *The Haunted Tower*, an immensely popular mainpiece that became the first of several mainpiece collaborations. Cobb only returned to writing shorter works for special occasions, notably the prelude *Poor Old Drury* (1791) and *The Glorious First of June* (1794). He seems to have been the librettist on call when the theatre wanted texts for such occasional pieces.

Once Storace and Cobb had started writing mainpieces together, Storace turned to his old friend Prince Hoare for afterpiece librettos. Their success was nicely summed up by a reviewer of *The Three and The Deuce* (1795): 'The knowledge of farce-writing is one possessed by very few.—Mr. Hoare's productions in this way have usually some very striking incident—some oddity of *equivoque*, and much whimsicality of *character*.'[2] Each afterpiece does indeed focus on a particular trick or device that makes it memorable among the many afterpieces on the London stage. *No Song, No Supper* was named for the song that provides the denouement. It was perhaps his most popular afterpiece and is discussed in detail later in this chapter.

Hoare employed a different device for his next work. *The Cave of Trophonius* (1791), which takes place in the land of faerie, involves two sisters of opposite personalities who reverse their characters by magic. The sisters were played by Nancy Storace and Anna Crouch, and, as befits a piece written for her benefit, Anna Crouch had a role of equal importance to Nancy Storace. The piece was not a success and was performed only a few times. Kemble succinctly wrote: 'Dull—dull.—'[3] *The Times* reported, only a little prematurely, 'The Cave of Trophonius seems to have been consigned to the Cave of Oblivion!'[4] Neither libretto nor score was published; only the manuscript libretto sent to Larpent and the published song words survive.[5]

Some writers have stated that Storace borrowed music from Salieri's opera *La grotta di Trofonio* (1785) for *The Cave of Trophonius*.[6] This notion can easily be disproved by the song text which states unequivocally: 'N.B. The few Pieces not composed by Mr. Storace are marked with the Names of the respective Composers.' Of the twenty numbers, one is by Attwood and one by Paisiello, with a melody each by the singers Nancy Storace and Richard Suett (presumably harmonized by Storace). Salieri is not mentioned.

---

[2] *Oracle*, 3 Sept. 1795. [3] Kemble, Memoranda A, fo. 130ᵛ. [4] *Times*, 9 May 1791.

[5] Larpent MS 899; *Song, Duets, Trio, and Finales, in The Cave of Trophonius* (London, 1791).

[6] e.g. Adolphus, *Memoirs of John Bannister*, i. 252; 'Memoir of Stephen Storace', *The Harmonicon*, 6 (1828), 2; Richard Graves, 'The Comic Operas of Stephen Storace', *MT* 95 (1954), 531; Alfred Loewenberg (comp.), *Annals of Opera 1597–1940* (Totowa, NJ, 1978), 417–18; Brace, *Anna . . . Susanna*, 84.

In between *The Cave of Trophonius* and his next afterpiece, Storace composed music for the occasional prelude *Poor Old Drury*, written by Cobb for the Drury Lane company's opening night at the King's Theatre on 22 September 1791. By this time Storace was house composer in practice if not in name, so the task of providing songs fell to him. The main characters were actors played by themselves in a farcical version of the disruptions caused by moving to a new theatre. The prelude was never published in any form, and no music survives. The manuscript text, which includes neither song texts nor spaces for them, suggests that the only music in the play proper was a stage song or two for the Italian singer (played by Ida Bland).[7] However, the piece did close with a masque, described in the *Diary* as presenting a view of Parnassus, with the Gods in the surrounding clouds, Apollo standing in front, to whom Mercury introduced Melpomene, Thalia, Euterpe, and Terpsichore in recitative with most charming symphonies by Mr Storace.[8]

As a strictly occasional piece, *Poor Old Drury* was performed only sixteen times, all early in the 1791/2 season. Nevertheless, it set a fashion for similar pieces at the other theatres. The following year, *Poor Covent Garden* was intended for the opening of the new theatre but never performed; *Poor Old Haymarket* was then written by George Colman junior at the Little Theatre in the Haymarket to mock the fashion for new larger theatres at Drury Lane and Covent Garden.[9]

After the failure of *The Cave of Trophonius*, Hoare and Storace returned to domestic farce. They wrote *The Prize* for Nancy Storace's benefit on 11 March 1793 at the King's Theatre (while Drury Lane was being rebuilt). The plot hinges on the song 'Beaux yeux', which Nancy Storace had originally sung in Storace's *La cameriera astuta* at the King's Theatre in 1788. A song in spoof French (with Nancy's character disguised as a foreigner), it was the perfect match for Nancy: a piece that required acting ability as well as a dramatic (even exaggerated) delivery. In *The Prize* the point of the song was to prove that her poor suitor (her true love) preferred the impoverished Englishwoman, whereas her supposedly rich suitor was a fortune-hunter who would desert the heroine for a rich 'Frenchwoman'. Despite the focus on Nancy, Kemble reported only that 'Bannister makes this nonsense diverting'.[10] Even so, it was staged every season for an impressive nineteen years, then sporadically for another fifteen.

Nancy's next benefit work, *My Grandmother*, is based on a portrait

---

[7] Larpent MS 918.   [8] *Diary*, 23 Sept. 1791.
[9] *Biographia Dramatica*, iii. 172, 174.   [10] Memoranda A, fo. 223ᵛ.

'coming to life'. The hero falls in love with the portrait of the heroine's grandmother, thinking it is the girl he met at a masquerade. First performed on 16 December 1793 at the Little Theatre, it transferred to Drury Lane when it reopened the following year, and survived for over twenty years.

The opening of the new Drury Lane theatre towards the end of the 1793/4 season brought about many changes. The new theatre was vastly larger and therefore less intimate than the old; sets from the old theatre were too small so no longer fitted; Kemble had a strong interest in producing Gothic shows with historically accurate sets.[11] Storace's first work for the new theatre was *Lodoiska*, an afterpiece with a libretto by Kemble. We know Kemble and Storace were on friendly terms from occasional remarks in Kemble's diaries, including his heartfelt comments on Storace's death and burial.[12] The project was undoubtedly Storace's idea in part, as *Lodoiska* was Kemble's only attempt at a libretto. Storace's hand can be seen in its plan, particularly in a scene designed to introduce a virtuoso air by Master Thomas Welsh (Act 3, scene 1). Kemble adapted Dejaure's libretto for Kreutzer's *Lodoiska* (Paris, 1791), and Storace borrowed music from both Kreutzer and Cherubini, who had also set the story to a libretto by Fillette-Loraux in Paris in 1791.

Lodoiska was in many ways far better suited to being a mainpiece than an afterpiece: its plot was serious, and its spectacular final scene outclassed even *The Siege of Belgrade*. It was highly topical: an escape opera laden with Gothic overtones. Because of its enormous length, many cuts had to be made early in the production, which altered its shape significantly. Despite the practical difficulties it was a great success. Several major revivals took place in the nineteenth century, and it was still in the Drury Lane repertoire in the 1830s.

On 1 June 1794, while *Lodoiska* was still in rehearsal, Earl Howe won a naval victory against the French. He instantly became a national hero and the subject of many tributes, including music, poetry, panoramas, and exhibits of documents relating to the battle. *The Glorious First of June* was designed both to celebrate Howe's victory and to raise money for the families of men lost in battle. It succeeded beyond all expectations: on its opening night of 2 July (when it was performed after *The Country Girl*), it raised the immense sum of £1,526. 11s. 0d. It was the only benefit night allowed during that very short season at the new Drury Lane.

---

[11] Sybil Rosenfeld, *Georgian Scene Painters and Scene Painting* (Cambridge, 1981), 20–1, 37.
[12] Memoranda B, fos. 12ᵛ, 13ᵛ.

The rushed production must have been truly chaotic. The entire piece was written, composed, and rehearsed in only a few days. Many people helped out, including a long list of aristocratic and influential people who, according to the playbill, had 'obligingly undertaken to attend to the arrangements of the Evening'. Some even contributed to the writing, including the duke of Leeds, Lord Mulgrave, and the playwright Mary Robinson, all of whom wrote song texts, and Joseph Richardson, who wrote the prologue. Cobb and Sheridan worked on the dialogue, which takes the form of a loose sequel to Hoare's *No Song, No Supper*. According to Kemble, 'Mr Cobb wrote the greatest part of the Dialogue—Mr Sheridan contributed a Scene or two.'[13] The plot was suitably patriotic, and ended with a final gala scene which took the form of a fireworks display and the House singing 'Rule Britannia'.[14] Storace was responsible for the music, for which he composed some numbers and sensibly borrowed others with minimal alteration. The piece was in fact a huge and impressive spectacle, with many sea songs and naval effects, including a sea fight (illustrated on the title-page of the score). It ran for five nights at the end of the 1793/4 season and two the next, while patriotic fervour ran high. It was then retired until 6 March 1797 when, shortly after another British naval victory, this time over the Spanish on 14 February, it was adapted to the new occasion as *Cape Saint Vincent*. After ten performances that season, its useful life was finally over.

Hoare's last afterpiece, *The Three and the Deuce* (2 September 1795, Little Theatre in the Haymarket), was designed entirely for Jack Bannister. It was first performed at his benefit at the Little Theatre (the only piece Storace wrote specifically for the summer company there), then after eleven nights transferred to Drury Lane for one performance. In keeping with the more casual state of affairs in the summer theatre, it opened with both Storace's overture and a prologue by George Colman junior, the proprietor. Bannister, who was an excellent character actor, performed all three of the triplet heros, Pertinax Single and his brothers Peregrine and Percival. None of Storace's other singers took part, because they were resting or performing elsewhere during the summer. It was less successful than some of Storace's other afterpieces (and of course required a strong actor in the lead), but it was revived in 1806 at Drury Lane, then stayed in the repertoire sporadically until 1823/4. It might not have lasted so long if the actor Robert William Elliston (who was also manager between 1819 and 1826) had not claimed the triple role for himself.

---

[13] Memoranda B, fo. 265. [14] *Thespian Magazine*, 3 (1794), 313.

No Song, No Supper

No Song, No Supper is one of the few afterpieces Storace wrote without a specific agenda such as a performer's benefit or another special event. Although it was first performed at Michael Kelly's benefit, it was not written specifically for that occasion. Storace had originally hoped that Kemble would approve it for the regular season; Kelly chose it as the afterpiece for his benefit night on 16 April 1790 because it was the only way Kemble would agree to stage it.[15] Kemble admitted drily in his diary that 'the Farce was very well rec[eive]d'.[16] It was an immediate success and was adopted into the regular repertoire, with performances every season until 1814/15.[17] One of the reasons for its survival may be that, unlike some of Storace's benefit afterpieces, it is easy to stage with an ordinary cast. There are many small singing roles and most of the songs are simple; only one main character has more than two solos. *No Song, No Supper* is also Storace's only English opera to survive in full score. A scholarly edition is available, which makes it by far his most accessible work today.[18] As in Storace's other early works, borrowings are specified in the score, with the original composer's name printed at the beginning of each number. Fiske describes and reproduces the borrowed music in its original form in his edition.

No Song, No Supper was Prince Hoare's first libretto. According to Benjamin Haydon, a well-known painter in the early nineteenth century, Hoare was 'one of Steven Storace's intimate Friends', so they were natural partners.[19] Apparently they had originally met in Florence in 1779,[20] but Richard Ryan's claim that Hoare had written the words then is very unlikely.[21] Indeed, at that time Hoare had ambitions to be a painter (he stopped exhibiting in 1785), and Storace was thoroughly involved in Italian music. Neither had any reason then to work on an afterpiece for the English stage. Hoare's career as a playwright began with *Such Things Were*, a tragedy performed in Bath in 1788, and his most successful works were unquestionably his librettos for Storace's afterpieces.

---

[15] Kelly, *Reminiscences*, i. 329–30.   [16] Memoranda A, fo. 83ᵛ.

[17] It continued to be in the Drury Lane repertoire at least until 1832/3. According to Kurt Gänzl in *The British Musical Theatre*, 2 vols. (New York, 1986), vol. i., p. vi, it was one of three 18th-cent. operas that were still being performed a century after their premières.

[18] *No Song, No Supper*, copyist's score (Royal College of Music, RCM 597); modern edition by Roger Fiske in *Musica Britannica*, 16 (London, 1959; 2nd edn., 1975).

[19] Haydon, *Diary*, iii. 61. See also Kelly, *Reminiscences*, ii. 79, which states that Hoare 'from his earliest days, was the bosom friend of the gifted composer, both in Italy and in England'.

[20] Gwynn, *Memorials of an Eighteenth Century Painter*, 158, 166–7.

[21] Richard Ryan, *Dramatic Table Talk*, 3 vols. (London, 1825), ii. 12.

Hoare experimented only twice with mainpieces. The first was *Dido, Queen of Carthage*, an *opera seria* in English and a total disaster. The second, *Mahmoud*, was left unfinished at Storace's death and the music 'completed' for one season of performances by Nancy Storace. She reordered some of the libretto to suit the hastily borrowed music. As a result, Anthony Pasquin's acid comments are unfair, despite containing a grain or two of truth: 'Mahmoud, an opera recently produced by Mr. Hoare, shews the vanity of authors. Because Mr. H. had been successful in two or three trifling farces, he aspired to the invention of an opera, in which he has plenarily exposed the weakness of his mind. Stick to your last!'[22] After Storace's death, Hoare never found another regular collaborator and, like Cobb, he eventually gave up working in the theatre altogether. In the early nineteenth century he returned to art and became a respected critic. He wrote a memorial prologue for Storace, delivered at the première of *Mahmoud* in April 1796, as well as the inscription for Storace's monument.[23] He remained a lifelong friend of the Storace family. Nancy Storace left him a legacy of £50 in her will dated 1797, with a request to assist in administering a legacy to her mother. After Nancy's death twenty years later Hoare wrote the inscription for her memorial at her mother's request.[24]

The plot of *No Song, No Supper* revolves around the miseries caused by greed and lack of money. Two sailors, Frederick and Robin, who are shipwrecked on their own coast, hope to reclaim their lovers Louisa Crop and Margaretta. They arrive at the house of Louisa's father, who is also Robin's brother-in-law. An avaricious lawyer is trying to seduce Louisa's stepmother Dorothy into parting with her money; he has already been the cause of both pairs of lovers being separated. Margaretta arrives in search of Robin, only to witness the stepmother first entertaining the lawyer, then hiding him when the men return. The sailors—who are now rich because they have rescued a barrel of gold from their shipwreck—are reunited with their lovers. Margaretta sings a ballad in which she reveals that a leg of lamb, a cake, and the lawyer are all hidden from sight in the house. Peace is made between husband and wife, and the lawyer is sent packing.

Hoare's texts for musical setting are all straightforward. They include many strophic songs, two simple finales, and just a few opportunities for musical characterization in ensembles. Storace and Hoare must have

---

[22] *The Pin Basket to the Children of Thespis*, 46 n.

[23] See Appendix 1 for Hoare's full text for Storace's monument.

[24] Copies of Hoare's inscription for Nancy Storace's memorial, along with correspondence between Hoare and her mother about the inscription, can be seen in Sir John Soane's Museum, Correspondence Cupboard (1), Division IV (6), nos. 65, 66, 77, 78.

discussed the libretto in relation to the kinds of musical texts Storace want-ed, and their positioning. Storace probably asked for musical numbers to open both acts, plus texts that were not obviously strophic for Frederick's (Michael Kelly's) two airs. In fact he probably had Kelly and Nancy Storace in mind for their roles before he wrote the music, as both their musical numbers suit their styles so well. They were the only singers given more than one solo apiece; both texts and musical settings indicate a clear under-standing of their particular skills: Kelly's dignified tenor voice with the high range in true voice, and Nancy Storace's rare ability to act and sing together convincingly. If they were cast early on, the work was either writ-ten after the King's Theatre burned down in June 1789, leaving Nancy free to appear at Drury Lane, or she was already thinking of moving theatre before the King's Theatre burned down.[25]

The opera includes an overture, ten solo songs, and five ensembles. Eight of the songs are strophic; Frederick's two (sung by Kelly) are reca-pitulatory.[26] This is an unusually high proportion of strophic songs for Storace, though not abnormal for his contemporaries. Large ensembles end the two acts; Act 1 also includes a trio and duet, and Act 2 a duet.

The overture in E flat opens with a pompous eight-bar introduction, full of dotted rhythms ('largo maestoso', common time). The main movement ('non troppo allegro', 3/4) is oddly marked 'Chacone' though it is in sonata form.[27] Storace lessens the forward drive of this gentle, lyrical piece by sidestepping heavy downbeats in both primary and secondary themes. Three of Storace's afterpieces have overtures in sonata form, which was the norm in continental Europe though not in England. His others employ a variety of simple structures ranging from a twenty-three-bar 'symphony played while the curtain rises' in *The Prize* to rondos for *My Grandmother* and *The Three and the Deuce*. The latter, composed for the Little Theatre where Samuel Arnold worked, emulates Arnold's practice of repeating the overture's theme in the opera's finale.[28]

Act 1 of *No Song, No Supper* begins like a conventional English after-piece. The first five numbers are solo songs which introduce most of the main characters. Frederick (sung by Kelly) opens the work with a roman-tic air, 'The ling'ring pangs of hopeless love'. Its weighty introduction

---

[25] Price, Milhous, and Hume, *Italian Opera* i. 410.

[26] The term 'recapitulatory' embraces all song forms, both ternary and rounded binary, in which the recurrence of the opening music (and usually text) coincides with a return to the tonic key.

[27] Fiske, in his critical commentary to *No Song, No Supper*, 111, suggests the title Chacone comes from a musical association with a work by Jommelli.

[28] The ternary overture of *The Glorious First of June* was probably not by Storace.

Ex. 7.1. 'With lowly suit' (*No Song, No Supper*, no. 5)

establishes Frederick's seriousness (just like the parallel situation in *The Haunted Tower*), and violin runs in the middle section depict the 'angry strife' and 'whelming billows' of the text. The rest of the cast are given squarely phrased strophic songs, lively but otherwise unexceptional. Only Margaretta's 'With lowly suit and plaintive ditty' (sung by Nancy Storace) has a more individual line, with a catchy rhythm, illustrated in Example 7.1. It became the number most often published, sometimes under the title 'The Ballad-Singer's Petition'. In between the songs, the dramatic situation becomes clear to the audience and the drama begins.

The leisurely alternation of dialogue and music becomes increasingly tense in the last three numbers of Act 1, which are all ensembles, two of

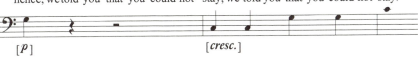

Ex. 7.2. 'Knocking at this time of day' (*No Song, No Supper*, no. 6)

them adapted by Storace from his earlier Italian works. First Margaretta calls at the cottage, only to be sent away by Dorothy and her maid, in the trio 'Knocking at this time of day'. Margaretta's opening phrases are characterized by sighing appoggiaturas which contrast sharply with Dorothy's and Nelly's indignant staccato scales. Example 7.2 is an extract from the final tutti, where the characters sing simultaneously but remain musically and textually distinct. Margaretta, in steady crotchets, despairs at having no roof to sleep under, while Dorothy and her maid, in bustling quavers, berate her.

A comic duet follows in which Dorothy and her husband compete to see who can keep silent longest. This is farce either at its best or silliest, depending on your point of view. The finale 'How often thus I'm forced to trudge' is a sextet that takes place on a darkened stage, with groups of characters going about their business independently. As they arrive on stage, each expounds briefly on his or her unfortunate situation before they finally join in an expressive tutti (borrowed from *Gli equivoci* via *La cameriera astuta*).

In Act 2 the two love affairs are soon resolved; then, after Dorothy's deception with the lawyer is exposed, Crop and his wife make peace. The originality of the plot comes from focusing not on the three couples, who resolve their differences before the final scene, but on the exposure (kindly enough) of Dorothy's plot with the lawyer. Margaretta reveals Dorothy's tricks in the three verses of 'Across the downs this morning' which alternate with dialogue to reveal the hidden lamb, cake, and lawyer. The finale has a simple refrain structure and a lilting and well-articulated melody suitable for everyone to sing.

The overall effect of *No Song, No Supper* is of a well-balanced work with a full singing cast in which no one role or strand of plot dominates, nobody is hurt (except the lawyer Endless, who gets covered with flour and a few bruises), and where musical interest is sustained by a variety of styles and tunes. *No Song, No Supper* is an example of the English afterpiece at its most attractive.

ORCHESTRATION

No Song, No Supper is particularly important today because it is the only English opera by Storace (or indeed by any composer between 1786 and 1799) to survive in full score.[29] Although some two-stave scores give a few orchestral indications and occasional extra staves which hint at his style of orchestration, such labelling varies immensely: some scores, like *The Siege of Belgrade*, include many instrumental indications and extra staves; others, such as *The Prize*, have neither. Many of Storace's borrowed pieces do exist in their original orchestral versions, and we can perhaps assume that he retained their orchestration when preparing such scores for modern performances. However, they tell us nothing about Storace's individual style.

Unfortunately, *No Song, No Supper* dates from fairly early in Storace's career and survives in what may be a modified version. The instrumentation requires a wind section comprising pairs of oboes (doubling flutes),

[29] Fiske, *English Theatre Music*, app. A, lists all the 18th-cent. English operas that survive orchestrally. Apart from *No Song, No Supper*, only Storace's two Viennese operas and the aria 'Care donne' exist in manuscript full scores, and a few extracts from *La cameriera astuta* were published in score. Of his later works only the 'Lamentation of Marie Antoinette' (1793), for voice and chamber group, was published in score.

clarinets, bassoons, and horns, with carillon, strings, and continuo. As appropriate to a short light-hearted piece, it includes no loud brass or timpani. Fiske argues that the surviving score is an adaptation made for performances at the Little Theatre three or four years after its première.[30] He bases his argument on the premiss that the six surviving wind parts were reduced from the original eight at Drury Lane. If so, then this score too can serve only as an approximate indication of Storace's style of orchestration. However, Fiske's evidence that the Drury Lane orchestra included separate pairs of oboes and flutes is weak, and in the context of the discussion in Chapter 3 about reduced bands for afterpieces, such a large wind section seems unlikely even if the players were theoretically available. I prefer to think that the full score of *No Song, No Supper* represents Storace's original intentions.

The score of *No Song, No Supper* clearly indicates Storace's interest in wind instruments, which in turn suggests he had good players available, including William T. Parke on the oboe, plus reliable players on clarinet and bassoon. Twice he calls for the clarinets to open numbers. 'With lowly suit' (no. 5) begins with a clarinet solo over simple accompanying strings, and the duet 'Thus ev'ry hope obtaining' (no. 12) starts with the two clarinets in thirds, entirely unaccompanied. Perhaps the most striking wind introduction of all comes in the first song, 'The ling'ring pangs', where oboes and horns engage briefly in dialogue, followed by bassoon doubling the viola melody an octave lower. The opening is quoted in Example 7.3. Storace particularly liked to double viola lines with bassoons at the octave below. The first half of the Andantino section of 'How often thus I'm forced to trudge' (no. 8, finale to Act 1, borrowed from *La cameriera astuta*) is entirely accompanied by wind instruments. Storace's viola parts also contain a degree of musical interest that suggests he had good players. He uses divided violas in almost every number of *No Song, No Supper*, far more often than other strings. In the opening bars of the finale 'Let shepherd lads and maids advance', two flutes with viola below provide a gentle pastoral introduction.

The two-stave vocal score of *No Song, No Supper* retains some of the most interesting accompaniment figures, such as the billowing string runs in 'The ling'ring pangs', and some of the wind solos are labelled. Many other vocal scores are far less well supplied with such additional details. Even with labels, reduced scores can never give us more than a rough idea of textural detail and motivic intricacies. To illustrate the point, we can compare the reduced

---

[30] Fiske (ed.), *No Song, No Supper*, p. xvii.

Ex. 7.3. 'The ling'ring pangs' (*No Song, No Supper*, no. 1)

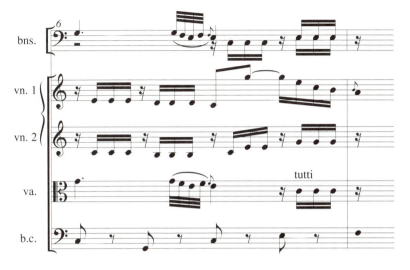

Ex. 7.3. *continued*

score of the overture to *The Cherokee* with the full score of *Gli sposi mal-contenti* from which it was adapted. In *The Cherokee*, even the compara-tively simple texture of the exposition is misleading. The opening eight-bar theme of the Allegro is presented twice, the second time an octave lower. Example 7.4 gives the second phrase. The reduction retains only portions of the string parts and omits entirely two elements that we cannot infer. First, there is a gradual increase of instrumentation in the second phrase, with a pair of flutes added at the original pitch (that is, an octave higher than the pitch of the reduction) and the horns making a brief contribution half-way through. Second, pairs of oboes and bassoons enter imitatively one bar after the flutes, creating an effect entirely omitted from the reduced score. Imitative sections are also omitted from the secondary theme in the exposition and from the beginning of the development. Note also in Example 7.4 that the accompaniment figures in the lower strings are changed in the reduced score to patterns more suited to playing at the key-board.[51] Other predictable omissions include sustained chords for wind and brass, which cannot be satisfactorily reproduced on the piano or harpsichord, and rhythmic punctuation which can only be indicated by dynamic mark-ings. The effect of orchestral colour is therefore largely lost.

---

[51] Another piece by Storace available for comparative studies of full and reduced scores is 'Whither my love!' (*The Haunted Tower*, no. 6), which was published in full score as 'La rachelina' (London [1789]), *RISM* P 571, as well as in the complete reduced score of *The Haunted Tower* (London, 1789).

Ex. 7.4(*a*) Overture to *Gli sposi malcontenti*; (*b*) Overture to *The Cherokee*

(a)

(b)

Ex. 7.4. *continued*

We can reasonably assume that all Storace's stage works required an orchestra at least the size of that for *No Song, No Supper* (without the carillon perhaps) and that most of his mainpieces included parts for trumpets and drums, and sometimes—most unusually for the period—trombones. We can tell from other scores and the Drury Lane account books that brass instruments and timpani were often used in mainpiece operas. Trumpets and drums are listed regularly as 'extras': in other words the performers were paid separately from the regular band but appear frequently in the accounts. Trombones also appear in the account books, though less often than trumpets and drums, and in one instance a trombonist was paid specifically for performing in *The Pirates*.[32] The Duke of York's band also played fairly often at Drury Lane, though *Dido, Queen of Carthage* is Storace's only opera that is specifically linked to it.[33]

The most unusual instrument in Storace's orchestra for *No Song, No Supper* is the carillon. He also called for it in *The Haunted Tower* and *The Siege of Belgrade* (the works immediately before and after *No Song, No Supper*). The regular harpsichordist was probably responsible for playing it at an adjacent keyboard. Storace himself performed on the carillon at the oratorio performance that opened the new Drury Lane theatre on 12 March 1794.[34] All the identifiable instances of its use—that is, where it is named in the reduced scores—involve echoes of vocal lines whose texts mention bells (and imply church bells). In *No Song, No Supper* it enters half-way through the finale to Act 2, immediately after Margaretta sings the words 'While merry, merry bells ring round', then continues playing arpeggio figures to the end. In *The Siege of Belgrade* it is only indicated in 'All will hail the joyous day' (no. 6) where, curiously, the carillon plays scales and arpeggio figures while the voice sings figures derived from genuine church bell peals (illustrated in Ex. 7.5).

We know from the few extant scores that Storace's style of orchestration is conventionally Classical but with a lively sense of colour. Strings predominate; first violins often double the vocal melody, and violas usually play accompaniment figures while cellos and double basses together provide the bass line. His balance is always practical: strings alone often accompany vocalists, with the winds joining in between phrases or on sustained vocal notes. Woodwind soloists, especially oboe and bassoon, often play obbligato melodies; winds and brass together provide harmonic colour and rhythmic punctuation. The bassoons have a more complex role. They

[32] Drury Lane Paybook B, fo. 115.   [33] Drury Lane Paybook B, fos. 86, 92ᵛ.
[34] *Thespian Magazine*, 3 (1794), 128.

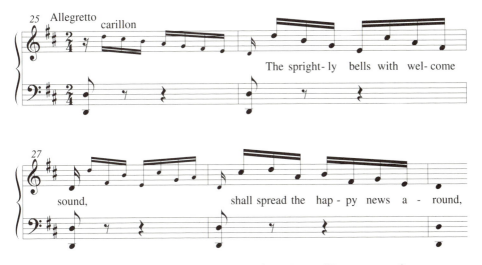

Ex. 7.5. 'All will hail the joyous day' (*The Siege of Belgrade*, no. 6)

act as members of the wind section, as support for the bass line of the strings (especially when the lowest instruments are silent and the violas play the harmonic bass), and occasionally also as melody instruments. Because most of Storace's works do not survive in orchestral versions, we are unable to appreciate the details of his instrumental settings, either in tone colour or motivic subtleties.

The Iron Chest

Storace's most important work outside the operas is *The Iron Chest*, a mainpiece play with music, which contains some of his best mature music. As befits a play with music, Storace made no attempt to integrate drama and music on the scale he had done in his later operas; music is clearly subsidiary to the drama. The surviving text and music indicate that the author, George Colman junior, certainly collaborated with Storace on the words for musical setting.

    The Iron Chest was Storace's last completed work, first performed at Drury Lane on 12 March 1796, just a few days before his death. The text was commissioned by Drury Lane from George Colman junior for an unusually high

189

fee.[35] Colman, who owned and operated the Little Theatre, was an experienced playwright who occasionally wrote for Drury Lane. Indeed, his epilogue to *Macbeth* was delivered at Drury Lane on 21 April 1794, the day the new theatre opened for staged works. Colman based *The Iron Chest* on William Godwin's *Caleb Williams*, a political novel from 1794, to which he added a comic subplot. The subplot was undoubtedly one of the play's major problems. As John Genest and William Hazlitt later described most aptly:

It is one of those jumbles of Tragedy, Comedy, and Opera, of which Colman Jun. was so fond, and which every friend of the legitimate Drama must reprobate.[36]

The two plots (the serious and ludicrous) do not seem to be going on and gaining ground at the same time, but each part is intersected and crossed by the other, and has to set out again in the next scene, after being thwarted in the former one, like a person who has to begin a story over again in which he has been interrupted.[37]

Despite these criticisms, perhaps exaggerated but partly deserved, *The Iron Chest* was in the forefront of fashion, being both a Gothic tragedy and an expression of dissatisfaction with the existing social order.

The Iron Chest was a disaster at its première, however. Colman was so disgusted with the progress of rehearsals and with the opening night that he vented his feelings in a vicious preface to the first edition of the text, in which he described at great length the events leading to the first night.[38] He blamed Kemble the most, and treated Storace the most kindly, no doubt because he died soon after the first performance. Kemble's own assessment, which is confirmed by reviews, was that it was 'very bad indeed. . . . The music is Storace's and was much lik'd.'[39]

The Morning Chronicle blamed its initial failure on the fact that 'the image of the original was fixed too deeply in the heart to admit the faint traces of the copy'.[40] It was much better received at its second performance a week later, when it was cut from four hours to under two and a half, so that it 'now presents, if not a regular plot and connected business, a series

---

[35] [John Genest], *Some Account of the English Stage, from the Restoration in 1660 to 1830*, 10 vols. (Bath, 1832), vii. 234, quotes Colman as saying he was paid 'a larger sum than usual' for *The Iron Chest*. The figure of £1,000 given in the *Oracle*, 14 Mar. 1796, is unsubstantiated. Payments totalling £300 are listed in the Drury Lane account books.

[36] *English Stage*, vii. 233.

[37] William Hazlitt, *A View of the English Stage* (London, 1821), 377–8.

[38] George Colman jun., preface to *The Iron Chest*, quoted in full in Peake, *Memoirs of the Colman Family*, ii. 234–56.

[39] Memoranda B, fo. 11ᵛ.   [40] *Morning Chronicle*, 14 Mar. 1796.

of scenes so powerfully written, recommended by music so various, and some of it so original, that it was received with very general approbation'.[41] Colman modified the work still further and took it to his own theatre in the summer, where it had better success. It continued to be performed occasionally at Drury Lane from 1800/1 into the 1830s, particularly with Edmund Kean in the role of Sir Edward.[42]

The plot revolves around Sir Edward Mortimer's guilty secret that, although he has been cleared of the murder of his lover Helen's brutish uncle, he was actually guilty. His secretary Wilford discovers Sir Edward's secret and decides he cannot live in the house with the burden of his knowledge, but Sir Edward refuses to release him from service. Wilford escapes, only to be found by a band of charitable robbers. One vindictive robber betrays his whereabouts to Sir Edward and he is dragged back to the house and accused by Sir Edward of theft. Because he promised to keep the secret, Wilford cannot defend himself against the charge, but Sir Edward's brother eventually discovers the truth, both of Wilford's innocence and of Sir Edward's guilt. Sir Edward is taken mortally ill; the secretary is reunited with his lover, and the servants rejoice.

The manuscript text sent to the Lord Chamberlain's office is lost, but two short extracts survive that were later submitted to link passages cut by the censor. Their dramatic context suggests that the excised passages involved morally reprehensible speeches by the vindictive robber, Orson. Storace composed music exclusively for the subplot (including the scenes with the robbers, which were adapted from an episode in the novel) and almost entirely for minor characters. The characters in the main plot have speaking roles only, apart from Wilford (played by Jack Bannister) who sings only when he is taking part in the subplot. The Drury Lane singers therefore took minor roles, Kelly playing the robber captain and Nancy Storace playing Barbara, Wilford's peasant lover. Kemble, who has been mentioned most often as manager of Drury Lane but who was primarily an actor who specialized in serious roles, played the speaking role of the anti-hero Sir Edward. The music comprises a series of dramatically inessential numbers, with ensembles predominating over solos; indeed, eight out of twelve vocal numbers are ensembles. The work is a play with music rather than an opera, because the main characters do not sing, and because of the small proportion of music to dialogue overall.

Unlike some plays with music, *The Iron Chest* opens with an overture.

---

[41] *Morning Chronicle*, 21 Mar. 1796.
[42] Fiske, *English Theatre Music*, 534, claims the last performance took place in 1879.

This use of music to frame the play continues in the rest of the work, with the curtain rising on a vocal ensemble, and all three acts ending with ensembles. The overture is closely related to two others Storace had used recently. When he had borrowed Kreutzer's overture for *Lodoiska* (1794) it quickly became popular, and its slow introduction was particularly striking. Storace then copied its style in both *The Cherokee* (1794) and *The Iron Chest*. In *The Cherokee*, he simply added a newly composed introduction in the style of Kreutzer's to an adaptation of his own overture to *Gli equivoci*; for *The Iron Chest* he wrote an entirely new movement. All three open in D minor (Storace transposed *Lodoiska* from Kreutzer's C minor), though only *The Iron Chest* stays in the minor for the main movement. The family resemblances between *Lodoiska* and *The Iron Chest* can be seen by comparing the extracts given in Example 7.6. The overture to *The Iron Chest* is unique in having a second movement but not a third. The Andante (D major, 3/4) therefore ends the overture on a serious note, in keeping with the plot and matching the mood of the closing finale.

In the first two acts, the music centres around specific groups of characters. Act 1 focuses on Barbara's large peasant family, who subsist with help from poaching. Of the five musical numbers in Act 1, the first three are ensembles in which members of the family portray their abject poverty and distressed circumstances. Then follows the only solo of the act, in which Sir Edward's steward remembers his old master. Finally the act closes on a duet for Barbara with her lover Wilford. The music of Act 2 focuses on the robbers who rescue (and in one case betray) Wilford. Armstrong sets the tone with an elaborate air propounding his moral view that thieving from the rich is acceptable, but not killing them. After a song by Barbara's brother, the robbers sing two choruses with Gothic overtones. Act 3 contains only three musical numbers: a duet for Barbara and her brother, Barbara's willow song (a deliberate association of name with *Othello*?), and the finale.[43]

The unusual musical balance of eight ensembles to four solos is in keeping with this work's hybrid nature. All but one of the solos are strophic songs. The exception is the robber captain's 'When the robber his victim has noted', a two-tempo number with a virtuosic ending (sung by Michael Kelly who almost never sang strophic songs). Storace's ensembles are by far the richest musical material in the play: they range from dialogues to glees and choruses. Some include internal action, though none resembles in size or dramatic integration the multisection ensembles of his mainpiece operas.

[43] Ibid. 538, suggests an association with Ophelia.

Ex. 7.6(*a*) Overture to *Lodoiska*; (*b*) Overture to *The Iron Chest*

Among the ensembles are two glees, a genre Storace used only rarely, unlike Shield who was a proponent of the operatic glee. The glee was an indigenous British genre, originally for three or more male voices, designed to be sung (like the catch) by amateurs. Men's clubs were formed for the express purpose of singing glees, catches, and madrigals; they proliferated in the second half of the eighteenth century and some survived into the nineteenth century and beyond.[44] Glees can be loosely grouped by their texts into drinking songs (the majority), pastorals, and serious songs.[45] The glee was readily absorbed into English opera because, like the strophic song, it was usually fairly easy to sing. Some theatrical glees take liberties by putting women's voices on the top parts and adding essential instrumental accompaniment. Others retain the original associations with essentially unaccompanied songs for male voices only.

Storace composed only four glees in his entire career, all of them for comic characters and servants. Three of the four, including 'Five times by the taper light' in *The Iron Chest*, function as opening choruses. This number not only involves female voices but also has an instrumental accompaniment. The finale to Act 2, 'Jolly friars tippled here' (no. 9) is likewise a glee in which abrupt changes of musical style parallel the text, and it approaches many of Henry Bishop's later glees in complexity. In the early nineteenth century Bishop developed the glee into an elaborate form with orchestral accompaniment. He often used these glees as substitutes for the dramatic ensembles that Storace tried so hard to develop.[46] Storace, on the other hand, never considered them more than simple picturesque scenic numbers.

One of the most memorable numbers in *The Iron Chest*, 'Sweet little Barbara' (no. 5), warrants discussion because of its origin. It is a love duet between Wilford and Barbara, and acts as the finale to Act 1. Its position is not dramatically significant—the couple have been in love throughout Act 1—but it provides musical closure to the act. It is the only borrowed number in *The Iron Chest*. Storace took the vocal version from the second movement of the first of his own *Six Easy and Progressive Sonatinas* (1791), which in turn he had borrowed from Mozart's 'Se vuol ballare' from *Le nozze di Figaro* (1786). When he had originally adapted Mozart's aria for piano he added decorative quaver figurations. For the vocal version in *The*

---

[44] J. G. Craufurd, 'The Madrigal Society', *PRMA* 82 (1955–6), 37; David Baptie, *Sketches of the English Glee Composers* (London [1896]); David Johnson, 'The 18th-Century Glee', *MT* 120 (1979), 200–2; Percy M. Young, Introduction to id. (ed.), *The English Glee* (Oxford, 1990), pp. v–ix.

[45] J. Merrill Knapp, 'Samuel Webbe and the Glee', *ML* 33 (1952), 350–1.

[46] Bruce Carr, 'Theatre Music: 1800–1834', in Nicholas Temperley (ed.), *Music in Britain: The Romantic Age 1800–1914* (London, 1981), 295.

Ex. 7.7(*a*) Mozart, 'Se vuol ballare' (*Le nozze di Figaro*); (*b*) Storace, Sonata No. 1, *Six Easy and Progressive Sonatinas*; (*c*) Storace, 'Sweet little Barbara' (*The Iron Chest*, no. 5)

Iron Chest five years later, Colman created a text appropriate to the quaver figures. Example 7.7 gives extracts from all three versions: Mozart's original, Storace's decorated version for piano, and 'Sweet little Barbara', in which the melody seems a perfect match for its new text, though obviously Colman added words to music that already existed. That he captured the style so well is to his credit.

The quintet 'The sun has tipt the hills with red' (no. 3) is a study in realism, but difficult to bring off in performance without being unintentionally farcical. In a household with everyone talking at once, two separate but simultaneous events take place: the lovers sing farewell in concord while the children ignore them, instead nagging their elder brother Samson, who replies with curses. Example 7.8 shows the contrasting musical styles of the lovers' duet against the short outbursts of dialogue between Samson and his siblings.

The finale to Act 3 is strikingly unusual. It takes place when Sir Edward (who has been exposed as a murderer) is taken mortally ill. A joyful celebration is therefore not deemed appropriate, even though his secretary Wilford is exonerated and reunited with his lover. Instead Wilford rejects the normal celebratory (and often self-congratulatory) finale by announcing: 'Clamour not now your congratulations to me, I entreat you: Rather, let the slow, still voice of gratitude be lifted up to Providence, for that care she ever bestows upon those deserving her protection!' The text of the finale reads:

> Where Gratitude shall breathe the note,
> To white-robed Mercy's throne,
> Bid the mild strain on aether float,
> A soft and dulcet tone.
>
> Sweet, sweet and clear the accents raise,
> While mellow flutes shall swell the song of praise.
> Melody! Melody!
> A soft and dulcet melody!
>
> Where fever droops his burning head;
> Where sick men languish on their bed;
> Around let ev'ry accent be,
> Harmony! Harmony!
> A soft and dulcet harmony![47]

Storace's music was described by James Boaden as 'built upon the idea of surrounding seraphs whispering peace to a departing spirit'.[48] The setting is a concise homophonic four-part chorus with some solo (or unison) soprano phrases and little internal text repetition. The work ends in calm, regretful, peace.

The Iron Chest shows Storace's mastery of the small-scale ensemble, as does *The Pirates* of the large. His response to words is immediate, his settings are concise with little musical or word repetition, and he draws characters in small domestic scenes. His sound theatrical sense is shown by

---

[47] George Colman jun., '*The Iron Chest*', in Michael R. Booth (ed.), *Eighteenth Century Tragedy* (London, 1965), 394.

[48] *Memoirs of the Life of John Philip Kemble, Esq.* (Philadelphia, Pa., 1825), 347.

Ex. 7.8. 'The sun has tipt the hills with red' (*The Iron Chest*, no. 3)

the fact that music remains firmly subsidiary to the dialogue, even though it was written for some highly skilled singers. While we cannot judge *The Iron Chest* as a whole on the basis of Storace's music, we can certainly appreciate his musical settings and dramatic understanding.

8

BORROWINGS

An opera without some borrowed material was a rarity in late eighteenth-century England. Composers of English operas regularly borrowed, arranged, and adapted existing material for their own operas. Storace was no exception, taking his cue from William Shield and Samuel Arnold, though they used different types of source material. They most often chose popular melodies to which they added new accompaniments, whereas Storace borrowed most of his material from *opere buffe*. Sometimes he used borrowed music with little alteration, but more often he made significant modifications to the original, fashioning the borrowed material to his own requirements and combining it with new music. Because of his innovative choice of material and its adaptation, Storace's borrowings are more rewarding to study than those of his English contemporaries.

The first part of this chapter surveys some eighteenth-century views on operatic borrowing and investigates Storace's choice of borrowed material; the second part focuses on individual operas in which he took different approaches to adapting his borrowed music. *The Siege of Belgrade* and *Lodoiska* illustrate two ways of borrowing libretto and music together; *The Glorious First of June* and *Mahmoud* are presented as exceptional works in which the borrowed music was only minimally modified, in one case because of time constraints, in the other because someone else 'completed' the opera.

Storace incorporated borrowed material into slightly over half the numbers in his first three operas and into slightly less than half in the fourth. In his later works the proportion of borrowed to new numbers dropped dramatically. Three of his later afterpieces, *The Prize* (1793), *My Grandmother* (1793), and *The Three and the Deuce* (1795), are entirely his own composition, though he did use some old music of his own. A complete list of Storace's borrowings is given in Appendix 5, including those pieces whose sources have not yet been identified.[1] He gave credit to the original composer even when he used only a small portion of borrowed music in an otherwise newly composed piece, or made major structural modifications to the borrowed piece. We must therefore take into account his process of adaptation when evaluating the proportion of borrowed music.

Storace always acknowledged his sources, though he did not identify self-borrowings. Occasionally we find descriptions in the scores such as 'Paesiello Accomp: by Storace' (*The Doctor and the Apothecary*, no. 12), or 'Storace from Vive les fillettes' (*The Haunted Tower*, no. 26), which indicate that Storace had added substantial amounts of new material to the borrowed piece. In the early scores, publishers acknowledged the original composers of individual numbers; however, Dale stopped doing so after *The Siege of Belgrade* (1791). In *The Pirates* he omitted their names entirely, then for later operas he listed them on the title-page only. Fortunately, the playbill for *The Pirates* supplies the missing information. Dale may have been trying to simplify his opera scores, because he simultaneously stopped providing figured basses and most orchestral cues. Coincidentally, William Shield (who was not published by Dale) also stopped labelling individual numbers in the early 1790s.[2]

We cannot be sure which numbers need identification in the later works because composers' names appear only on title-pages and playbills, which are generally accurate as far as they go. Not all opera composers (or publishers) were so specific. For instance, the playbill for 8 December 1785 at Drury Lane describes the music to Linley's *The Strangers at Home* as 'Some of the Airs compiled from the best Master; the Rest of the Music, the Overture, Accompaniments, &c by Mr Linley.' Equally vague was the phrase 'partly new and partly Selected' used for Michael Kelly's music to *A Friend in Need* on 9 February 1797 at Drury Lane.

Eighteenth-century Attitudes

Composers of English operas had no compunction about using borrowed music, a procedure which was common knowledge and quite acceptable.

[1] Roger Fiske, Geoffrey Brace, and I have discovered many of the original sources; some remain unidentified. See Fiske, *English Theatre Music* (2nd edn., Oxford, 1986), app. E and *passim*; Roger Fiske, critical commentary to *No Song, No Supper*, Musica Britannica, xvi (London, 1959), 117–30.

[2] Fiske, *English Theatre Music*, 550, 552, states that Shield stopped identifying borrowed pieces after he returned from Italy in 1792.

Most contemporary writers mention borrowings (or 'selections') in a neutral tone, merely acknowledging their presence. True critical comment was rare, but occasionally brief compliments were given. For instance, *The Times* wrote that 'the new and old music [of *The Haunted Tower*] does great credit to the composition and selection of *Storace*.'[3] Michael Kelly also praised his friend's abilities. Referring to *The Pirates*, he wrote that 'whenever Storace selected, his knowledge of stage-effect was so great, that the selections were always appropriate and never-failing'.[4] A particularly striking comment was made by a critic in the *Gazeteer*, who, in a review of *The Pirates*, expounded on the principle of adaptation:

The music has many skilful and valuable harmonies; if, now and then, some part of a melody reminds us of one that has been heard before, the remembrance, perhaps, rather helps than diminishes the effect of the improvement. It is as if Burke had stolen an image from Brook Watson (had he ever one?) and, having varied it by application, enriched it with new qualities, and displayed it with the arts of eloquent arrangement, had placed it in his octavo *poem* upon the French Revolution! Who, that remembered this image in its first state, would not delight more in the improvement than in the original suggestion of it![5]

On the other hand, Georg Forster, a German traveller in England in the 1790s, clearly did not understand the English tolerance of borrowings. Referring wrongly to Nancy Storace as Stephen's wife, he wrote of *No Song, No Supper* that 'die Musik ist von ihrem Manne componirt, von Pleyel, Grétry, Giordani zusammengestohlen' (the music is composed by her husband, stolen from Pleyel, Grétry, and Giordani),[6] saying that it was stolen. The English attitude seemed to have been that as long as borrowings were not underhand they were acceptable and not worthy of comment. John Trusler, Storace's uncle, had a similarly relaxed view of literary borrowings:

Those who are apt to charge others with Plagiarism are not unlike Mr. Bush, the broken merchant, who according to the fable, being transformed into a bramble, seized every passer by, by the garment, fancying it were made out of his Cloth, & thus when he could do no more, picked a hole in his own coat—In short an author is no more to be censured for embellishing his work with any valuable papers which he has met with in his readings, than a traveller for ornamenting his house with pictures he has picked up on his Tour.[7]

---

[3] *Times*, 25 Nov. 1789. [4] *Reminiscences*, ii. 32–3.

[5] *Gazeteer*, 22 Nov. 1792. Brook Watson was a Member of Parliament at the time of writing, and obviously far less eloquent than Edmund Burke.

[6] *Georg Forsters Werke*, xvi: *Briefe 1790 bis 1791* (Berlin, 1980), 147.

[7] 'Memoirs', vol. ii (Bath library, typescript of MS, late 18th cent.), 5–6.

THE MUSIC

Storace's Sources

We can state with some conviction that most of the music Storace borrowed came from works that either he, his sister, or his friend Kelly knew from performance; only occasionally did he rely on scores alone. However, an incontrovertible connection exists between Storace and only two of his sources: Paisiello's *Gli schiavi per amore*, which he directed at the King's Theatre in both 1787 and 1788, and Sarti's *Le nozze di Dorina*, which he directed in 1793. In the first case he borrowed two substitute arias that had been incorporated in the London production, possibly by Storace himself: Mengozzi's 'Donne, donne' which he used in *The Glorious First of June*, and Bianchi's 'Per pietà padron mio' which he used in *The Cherokee*.[8] Sarti's *Le nozze di Dorina* (also known as *Fra i due litiganti*, *I rivali delusi*, and *Les noces de Dorine*) had long-standing associations with the Storaces. Nancy had performed in it first in Milan in 1782, then in Vienna, and finally in London. The music Storace borrowed for *The Cherokee*, 'Compatite mie o signore', starts with virtually the same words as the substitute aria by Storace himself that Nancy had introduced when she sang in Sarti's opera. It is, however, a different setting.

Storace undoubtedly saw most of the operas then in performance during his European travels in the 1780s. He borrowed music from several operas he probably saw in Vienna, many of which had included his sister Nancy and Michael Kelly in their casts: Mozart's *Le nozze di Figaro* (1786), Martin y Soler's *Una cosa rara* (1786), Dittersdorf's *Doctor und Apotheker* (1786), and Paisiello's *I filosofi imaginari* (1783, 1785, and 1786). Similarly, he used material from several operas performed at the King's Theatre while he was in London: Sacchini's *Armida* (1791) which included Andreozzi's aria 'Ah quell'anima che sdegna', and Martin y Soler's *Il burbero buon core* (1794) which included Haydn's aria 'Quel cor umano'.[9] Guglielmi's *La bella pescatrice* was also performed in London in 1791, by an Italian opera company at the Pantheon.

Storace needed to work from published or manuscript scores of his sources in order to make his adaptations. Most of them were available in print, in some cases as an individual aria, in others as part of a complete opera score. Many of the later works were published in London, where they

---

[8] Both arias were published soon after their appearance in *Gli schiavi*. Bianchi, 'Per pietà padron mio', *RISM* B 2555; Mengozzi, 'Donne donne chi vi crede', *RISM* M 2255. William Shield also used Mengozzi's aria as the basis for 'Lovely ladies sprigs of fashion' in *The Farmer* (1787).

[9] Haydn's aria originally appeared with the text 'Quel tuo visetto' in his opera *Orlando Paladino* (1782).

were readily available. We also know he brought music home from Vienna; other works can be traced to Paris either at the time of the Storaces' journey home in 1787 (when, according to Kelly, they attended the theatre there) or to Kelly's later trips. Kelly described one as follows: 'In the summer of 1792 I went to Paris to see what I could pick up in the way of dramatic novelty for Drury Lane.'[10] On another journey, he describes how his companion John Henry Johnstone (a tenor at Covent Garden) 'got the music copied to bring to Mr. Harris, at Covent Garden'.[11] Obviously Kelly was doing something similar, ordering special manuscript copies when prints were not available. Unfortunately, he rarely names the operas he attended and never mentions bringing specific scores back to London.

Storace probably brought home scores of at least three French works that date from around the time of his journey home in 1787. Grétry's *L'Amitié à l'épreuve* and *L'Épreuve villageoise* were both published in or about 1786. Champein's opera *Les Dettes* was first performed in Paris on 11 January 1787 and published the same year. Later works that Kelly may have brought back to England include Kreutzer's and Cherubini's operas *Lodoïska* (1791), which he saw in Paris,[12] and Devienne's *Les Visitandines*, first performed in Paris in July 1792, about four months before Storace used an extract in *The Pirates*. The borrowed song was in turn derived, perhaps unconsciously, from Mozart's *Die Zauberflöte*.

A few of Storace's borrowings come from works that he must have acquired as manuscripts, possibly from the composers themselves. For instance, Paisiello's *La molinara* (Naples, 1788) and Martín y Soler's *L'arbore di Diana* (Vienna, October 1787) are both sources for numbers in *The Haunted Tower* (1789), yet both date from later than Storace's return to England in March 1787. *La molinara* was not performed in England until 1791, *L'arbore di Diana* in 1797.

Storace borrowed some ten pieces from sources other than stage works. Six of these are English songs and were freely available; two others come from works Storace had already published in his *Collection of Original Harpsichord Music* (Krumpholtz's Harp Concerto, No. 6 and Mozart's Piano Sonata, K. 331). Of the remaining two, Pleyel's String Quartet in C had been widely published in the 1780s, with editions in both London and Vienna.[13]

---

[10] *Reminiscences*, ii. 22. See also ibid. i. 284–7.   [11] Ibid. i. 348.   [12] Ibid. ii. 59.

[13] Fiske, *English Theatre Music*, 603, is wrong in saying that 'My little blithsom sparrow' was Storace's source for 'Tho' pity I cannot deny' (*The Haunted Tower*, no. 3). 'My Little Blithsom Sparrow . . . now introduced by Mrs. Crouch, in the Haunted Tower' (London [*c*.1790]), *RISM* P 2717, was obviously a later edition. The melody first appeared in Pleyel's String Quartet in C (Rita Benton, *Ignace Pleyel: A Thematic Catalogue of his Compositions* (New York, 1977), ref. 334).

The last, a number marked 'French tune' in *The Haunted Tower* was identified by John Adolphus, Bannister's biographer, as 'Qui veut ouir, qui veut
savoir', probably a popular song.[14]

Storace sometimes chose borrowed music for a specific singer, but more
often for its related dramatic context, even though the same singer might
coincidentally be assigned the same music in the adapted version. *The Siege
of Belgrade* illustrates the point clearly because words and music were
partly adapted from Martin y Soler's *Una cosa rara* in which both Nancy
and Kelly had sung in 1786. There, Nancy was cast as Lilla and Kelly played
Corrado, the Prince's confidant; in *The Siege of Belgrade*, Nancy again sang
Lilla, but Kelly became the Seraskier (the equivalent of Martin y Soler's
Prince). Storace borrowed eight vocal numbers, retaining all their dramatic
contexts. As a result, Nancy sang two numbers from her original role, 'Lost
distress'd I'm thus driven from home' (no. 2) and 'Blithe as the hours of
May' (no. 9). Kelly, on the other hand, was given none of his old music but
instead sang music previously performed by Martin y Soler's Prince.

When old and new dramatic contexts of a borrowed piece are unrelated,
there is not always an obvious reason for Storace's choice of music. However,
in a few instances Storace borrowed music specifically for his sister Nancy
to sing. In *The Cherokee* he used Bianchi's 'Per pietà padron mio' (which
Nancy had previously sung in Paisiello's *Gli schiavi per amore*) as 'Dearest
youth'. Nancy, or Stephen as director of the Italian production, had probably made the original borrowing, and Stephen surely transferred it to *The
Cherokee* for her. The clearest example of his deliberately choosing material specifically for his sister occurs in *The Prize*, Nancy's benefit afterpiece
of 1793. The entire plot is built around the aria 'Beaux yeux' which Storace
had originally written for her in *La cameriera astuta* (1788) and which had
been a great success.[15] He adapted the aria to its new plot by adding an
extra section in spoof French and directing it to be 'sung to the height of
burlesque and ridicule'. In *La cameriera* Nancy, as the maid, had been
demonstrating to a nobleman how he should woo a lady; in *The Prize* Nancy
was a lady pretending to be a Frenchwoman in order to distinguish her
genuine suitor from a fortune-hunter. Example 8.1 gives the end of section 1 and the beginning of the middle section, newly composed for *The
Prize*.[16]

---

[14] Adolphus, *Memoirs of John Bannister*, i. 234.   [15] *Times*, 5 Mar. 1788.
[16] See Price, Milhous, and Hume, *Italian Opera*, i. 399, for an extract from the original version
in *La cameriera astuta*.

Ex. 8.1. 'Beaux yeux' (*The Prize*, no. 5)

Storace's Methods of Adaptation

The simplest way for a composer to borrow material was to transfer the music into the new opera without regard for its old or new dramatic contexts. The librettist would then provide new words, which could be related to the old ones if desired. All English opera-composers used this technique, some most of the time, others—like Storace—rarely. The provision of a related dramatic context, on the other hand, required collaboration between composer and librettist. Storace was lucky in his librettists, who were often happy to accommodate his choice of music. Equally, when a librettist had adapted an old libretto and Storace was using some of its music, he chose borrowed numbers to fit the same context as the original.

Composers' techniques of adaptation were quite diverse. Often, in contrast to Storace's habitual practice, they barely altered the borrowed music; at other times a composer might use only part of a borrowed number on which to build a new composition, either by adding new music or restructuring the old music into a new form. Storace often took this approach, more frequently than his colleagues.

In three instances, Storace and his librettists took the unusual step of translating and modifying librettos that had already been set to music—one German, one Italian, and one French—then adapting some of the original music to be performed alongside newly composed numbers. These three operas are *The Doctor and the Apothecary* (1788) with a libretto by James Cobb, *The Siege of Belgrade* (1791), also by Cobb, and *Lodoiska* (1794), with a libretto by Kemble. In all three, the librettists carefully retained the dramatic context of borrowed material and provided English words of similar meaning.

As I have noted, Storace always gave credit to the original composers of the music he borrowed. In *The Doctor and the Apothecary* and *The Siege of Belgrade* he named composers at the heads of individual pieces in the scores; his debt to Kreutzer and Cherubini in *Lodoiska* was clearly stated in the announcements of the première. There was no attempt at disguising the titles of the adapted operas. *The Doctor and the Apothecary* came from *Doctor und Apotheker* (also called *Der Apotheker und Doktor*), and *Lodoiska* remained the same, despite temporary pre-production changes to *Czartoriska* and *Lodoviska*.[17] The title of *The Siege of Belgrade*, which is

---

[17] The title *Lodoiska* and the heroine's name were changed to *Czartoriska* in the MS libretto that was submitted to the Lord Chamberlain ten days before the première (Larpent MS 1029). Playbills in late May and early June announced the piece as *Czartoriska*. On 4 June 1794, five days before

partially based on Martin y Soler's *Una cosa rara*, refers to the part of the plot that Cobb wrote himself; in any case, *Una cosa rara* is a vague title, at variance with the more specific ones normal on the English stage.

Cobb's and Storace's adaptation of *The Doctor and the Apothecary* from Stephanie and Dittersdorf's opera was the most straightforward of the three. Cobb divided Stephanie's three multi-section ensembles (two finales and an extended piece in Act 2) into a mixture of spoken dialogue and small musical numbers, so that Storace avoided setting large-scale musical numbers, which were yet not acceptable to the London playhouse audience. His techniques in *The Siege of Belgrade* and *Lodoiska* are more complex.

THE SIEGE OF BELGRADE (1 JANUARY 1791)

The Siege of Belgrade is unique in blending two plots, one old and one new. It was Cobb and Storace's second mainpiece, following *The Haunted Tower* (1789). The idea of borrowing part of the plot from Da Ponte's two-act libretto for Martin y Soler's *Una cosa rara* (Vienna, 1786) was probably Storace's. He must have known it in Vienna, with his sister and Kelly singing. It had also been performed at the King's Theatre in 1789.

Cobb created a three-act mainpiece opera by using the Italian piece as a comic subplot to his own main plot. Main and subplot are fairly equal in importance, though they retain the traditional division between aristocrat and peasant, serious and comic. Cobb changed the location from Spain to Turkey to suit his new plot, which was based on the siege of Belgrade by the Turks under Mehmet II in 1456 and provided an excuse for a spectacular stage battle.[18] Historical accuracy was not a concern. Because he was melding two plots and giving the English work a different focus from the Italian, Cobb made more drastic alterations to the foreign libretto than he had in *The Doctor and the Apothecary*. He also added new twists to some of the characters' personalities. The magistrate (who was Ghita's brother in the Italian version) is now mean, greedy, and deceitful; Lilla's lover has a temper that gets him into tangles. While Da Ponte's Prince showed some conscience, the Seraskier is quite amoral.

The two strands of the plot are easily separable for the first two acts, then become intertwined. In *Una cosa rara* Lilla's brother wants her to marry (against her will) the local magistrate, who is the brother of his own fiancée

the première, the choice of name was still unsettled: the 2-guinea licence was listed to 'Czartoriska or Lodoviska' (Drury Lane Paybook B, fo. 35ᵛ).

[18] *Diary*, 3 Jan. 1791. See also Franz Babinger, *Mehmed the Conqueror and his Time* (Princeton, NJ, 1978), 138–44.

Ghita. In the middle of the opera, Lilla gets her way and marries her real lover. In the second part the Prince and his confidant try various ploys to entice Lilla into the Prince's arms, resulting in misunderstandings between Lilla and her new husband, as well as between her brother and his new wife. Cobb combined this plot with a Turkish political plot; he changed the setting to eastern Europe and transformed the Spanish Prince into a Seraskier. The Seraskier pursues a local girl (who retains the name Lilla), but he has also captured the Austrian colonel's wife Catherine. Colonel Cohenberg, with the help of local peasants and later his army, tries to rescue his wife. He is caught trying to infiltrate the Seraskier's camp and is condemned to death. In a fight between the Austrians and Turks the Colonel is saved but the Seraskier escapes. Catherine flees the seraglio with Lilla, whose husband and brother help the Colonel fight the Turks. After the final battle, the Colonel and his wife are reunited, and the Colonel spares the Seraskier's life in 'Christian revenge'.

Out of a total of twenty-nine pieces in *The Siege of Belgrade*, Storace adapted nine from *Una cosa rara*. One became the second movement of the overture; the eight vocal numbers retain their original dramatic contexts. Martin y Soler's music therefore occurs only in Lilla's plot; the music for the Turkish–Austrian story is either new or derived from other sources.

Storace abbreviated most of the borrowed music, making both large cuts to alter the overall form and small ones to tighten the phrase structure. He retained the melodic and harmonic integrity of Martin y Soler's music throughout. The duet 'Un briccone senza core', which became 'How the deuce I came to like you', serves as an example of both techniques, and is typical of Storace's procedures in other works. The duet introduces Lilla's brother Peter and his fiancée Ghita to the audience by establishing their quarrelsome relationship. Although Storace adapted Martin y Soler's music mainly by cutting sections, he also rewrote Peter's first reply in the interests of simplification, repeating Ghita's opening music exactly instead of using Martin y Soler's slightly different phrase. He made two major omissions: a thirty-three-bar section (bars 39–71 of 'Un briccone') and a thematically related one of seventeen bars (bars 115–31). He therefore made the form more concise without fundamentally altering it. He also made ten small cuts, all of repeated phrases (and most of repeated words), ranging from four bars each to a single bar. Example 8.2 gives the last three cuts from the duet, of two bars, four bars, and one bar respectively.

In three borrowed numbers Storace added newly composed music to old, thereby significantly restructuring the original piece. He borrowed Martin y Soler's 'Più bianca di giglio' for the serene first section of the Seraskier's

Ex. 8.2(*a*) Martin y Soler, 'Un briccone senza core' (*Una cosa rara*); (*b*) Storace, 'How the deuce came I to like you' (*The Siege of Belgrade*, no. 5)

Ex. 8.2 *continued*

Ex. 8.2 *continued*

opening number 'The rose and the lily', keeping Martin y Soler's music intact except for its postlude, then added a second part marked 'allegro furioso', so transforming a simple aria into a much more complex and intensely expressive one. He also transposed it down a tone to B flat. Had he not done so, Michael Kelly would have had to sing several high c''s and b''s in the second (new) part of the air. He took a similar approach, though using less borrowed material and more of his own, in the closing finale, 'Loud let the song of triumph'. Here he composed the opening Maestoso, then borrowed the melody of Martin y Soler's 'Brilli pure in sì bel giorno' for the Allegretto section (which he marked 'Spanish Tune') to which he added material of his own.

Storace borrowed most of the finale of Mozart's Piano Sonata in A, K. 331 (commonly known as the Turkish Rondo), for the third movement of the overture to *The Siege of Belgrade*. He had already published the sonata in his *Collection of Original Harpsichord Music*, giving it the strange tempo marking 'allegrino alla Turca'. In *The Siege of Belgrade* he reverted to the more common 'allegretto alla Turca'. The reason he borrowed this particular movement by Mozart is quite obvious from the title of the opera.[19] However, in a departure from his usual conscientious practice, he did not credit Mozart as the composer of his material. He transposed Mozart's music from

[19] Eve R. Meyer, '*Turquerie* and Eighteenth-Century Music', *Eighteenth-Century Studies*, 7 (1973–4), 474–88. Though she does not mention *The Siege of Belgrade* specifically, she gives an idea of the widespread use of so-called Turkish music in the 18th cent.

Table 8.1. Mozart's 'Turkish Rondo', adapted by Storace

Mozart	Storace's reorganization of Mozart's material
A	B [instrumental]
B	D [new material by Storace, instrumental]
A	B [instrumental]
B	C [Mozart's coda with Storace's extension, as the curtain rises, instrumental]
C[oda]	B [as the chorus enters and begins to sing]
	A ['Dance of Turkish Soldiers']
	B ['Dance of Turkish Women', then chorus]
	C [chorus]

A to D, in keeping with the key of his overture and the vocal ranges of the chorus who enter in the second part of the movement.

Storace treated Mozart's music as three segments of material, which he reordered in alternation with new material of his own. Table 8.1 tabulates the form of Mozart's rondo and its reorganization by Storace. He took one of Mozart's episodes (the major rather than the minor material) for the rondo theme and added a third episode. He used Mozart's coda twice in its original function, first to close the purely instrumental part of the overture, then to close the entire movement (the opening chorus).

These examples of adaptations in *The Siege of Belgrade* demonstrate Storace's skill in abbreviating borrowed music and merging new and old while retaining the dramatic integrity of the music he borrowed. The techniques he used, particularly in adapting 'Un briccone senza core', typify his procedures in other operas.

LODOISKA (9 JUNE 1794)

Unlike the libretto of *The Siege of Belgrade*, that for Storace's *Lodoiska* derives entirely from an earlier opera. Kemble based his work on Dejaure's libretto for Kreutzer's *Lodoiska* (Paris, 1791), making an afterpiece from a full-length *opéra comique*. The result was an extremely long afterpiece. Kreutzer's work was not the only source for the English opera, neither was it the only *Lodoiska* on the Paris stage in the summer of 1791. Cherubini's own version of the same story (an episode from Jean Baptiste Louvet de Couvray's novel *Les Amours du Chevalier de Faublas*) to a libretto by Fillette-Loraux had received its première two weeks earlier. Michael Kelly saw both in Paris and undoubtedly brought the scores (which include the spoken dialogue) back to England.[20] Storace borrowed music from both French versions.

---

[20] *Reminiscences*, ii. 59.

Although Kemble, actor–manager at Drury Lane, was already an effective dramatist, he was an untried librettist, and *Lodoiska* remained his only venture. His biographer James Boaden claimed that his motive was amusement;[21] he may also have wanted to oblige his friend and colleague Storace. However, he was also keen to stage new works at the rebuilt theatre, particularly those with Gothic associations, so the initiative may have been his.[22] He followed Dejaure's libretto scene by scene, though he wrote livelier dialogue. Otherwise the only substantive difference is Kemble's addition of an episode to open Act 3 in which the page sings 'Sweet bird that cheer'st the heavy hours' (no. 12) to amuse his master. The air is the most virtuosic in Storace's opera and clearly the reason for the otherwise extraneous scene. It was composed for Master Thomas Welsh, a treble who featured in various Drury Lane operas of the mid-1790s. Storace must have insisted on its inclusion, and it is a rare instance of his catering to a singer without regard for dramatic integrity.

Some odd, even inexplicable, changes of name occurred between the various French and English versions of the libretto. The temporary—and never published—changes to Czartoriska and Lodoviska of the heroine Princess Lodoiska have already been mentioned. Cherubini's Titzikan first became Titzi Khan, crossed out in Kemble's manuscript and replaced by Kera Khan. The other change is startling, given that Kemble based his libretto on Kreutzer's opera: he used Cherubini's hero's name Floreski for his own, and Kreutzer's hero Lovinski for his villain.

Princess Lodoiska has been sent into hiding at Baron Lovinski's castle by her father who has withdrawn his consent to her marriage to Count Floreski. While searching for her, Floreski and his servant Varbel fall in with Kera Khan, who with his Tartars is preparing to attack the Baron's castle. Floreski and Varbel enter the castle, only to be seized by the Baron, who also captures Lodoiska's father. The Tartars storm and burn the castle, and free the captives. Floreski rescues Lodoiska from the flames and the lovers are united with the Prince's approval.

Lodoiska stands alone among Storace's afterpieces as a serious 'escape' opera, a genre that became increasingly popular after the French Revolution. Apart from complaints about its length, it was a great success.[23] Cuts were made early in the production (after the manuscript had been sent to the Lord Chamberlain's office) to shorten it. These include several significant musical numbers: the opening chorus, the finale to Act 1, and a chorus of

---

[21] *Memoirs of the Life of John Philip Kemble*, 330.

[22] Rosenfeld, *Georgian Scene Painters*, 37.

[23] Roger Fiske, 'Stephen (John Seymour) Storace (ii)', *New Grove*, xviii. 181, lists *Lodoiska* wrongly as a full-length opera (which he opposes to an afterpiece), presumably based on the fact that *Lodoiska* has three acts.

Tartars in Act 3, scene 1. As a result, Act 1—uniquely in Storace's operas—begins and ends without music. The opening chorus may originally have been superimposed over the latter part of the overture, like Kreutzer's original version, but if so, its omission served no useful purpose in shortening the opera. Only two choruses remain: one for the Tartars and the closing finale.

Storace borrowed five pieces from Kreutzer's opera and two from Cherubini, which total slightly under half of the numbers that remained after the cuts. All four instrumental pieces in Storace's opera come from wholly or largely instrumental pieces by Kreutzer; Storace made them all entirely instrumental. In fact *Lodoiska* uses an unusually large amount of instrumental music compared with Storace's other operas, with instrumental preludes for all three acts plus a march. Four out of eleven vocal numbers are borrowed, one from Kreutzer, two from Cherubini, and one from Andreozzi; the other seven are original.

Storace borrowed Kreutzer's overture with little alteration, merely transposing it from E minor to D minor and (in the published version) omitting the chorus parts that Kreutzer had superimposed on the latter part of the instrumental piece. The overture became immensely popular in England. Storace labelled the introductions to Acts 2 and 3 'symphony'. He took the first of these from the opening of Kreutzer's Act 2, which was rather more involved. Entitled 'Récitatif', it contains a substantial orchestral introduction (musically unrelated to the recitative) which Storace borrowed almost note for note. Kreutzer's entr'acte between Acts 2 and 3 became Storace's symphony to Act 3. The directions in Kreutzer's score include soldiers marching across the stage; Storace's version contains none. He made two alterations, cutting twenty-six bars (a modulation to the relative major and back) and altering the dynamics. Kreutzer's 'forte' ending becomes a very gradual diminuendo to 'pianissimo', because Kreutzer starts Act 3 with a rousing chorus of Tartars whereas Storace opens in a more intimate setting—the villain Baron talking to his servants.

The final instrumental piece that Storace borrowed from Kreutzer is a march, purely instrumental in Storace's version but containing vocal parts, 'Qu'entends je', in Kreutzer's. As in the overture, the vocal lines do not contain significant musical material and Storace merely omits them. By adding repeat marks he also converts a two-section but through-composed movement into a regular binary one.

Storace borrowed only one vocal number from Kreutzer, 'Adieu, my Floreski' (no. 9) from 'La douce clarté de l'aurore', which is sung when Lodoiska is told (untruthfully) of Floreski's death. Both Storace's and

Kreutzer's pieces are marked 'Romance', and the texts are similar, with Lodoiska mourning the death of her lover. Storace makes the form strophic by adding a second stanza; otherwise he follows Kreutzer closely. Like the overture, this song became a popular item for unauthorized publication at the end of the century.

Storace made similarly minor adjustments to one of his two selections from Cherubini's rival opera. He barely altered the music of 'Jurons quoi qu'il faille' to become 'We swear and all our hordes' (no. 4), and the texts are related. The Tartars swear friendship, the hero and his companions thank them. Storace made one cut, a trio section in which the hero was joined in his thanks by his two companions before the general chorus.

Storace's final adaptation from Cherubini is far more complex structurally. He refashioned parts of Cherubini's Act 1 finale, 'Floreski / je l'entends', into a trio, 'Floreski! / 'Tis her voice' (no. 5), which takes place within Act 1 when Floreski and his companion discover Lodoiska in a tower. Cherubini's finale contains sections in four main key areas, C major, A major, D major, and C major respectively. Storace borrowed most of his material from the second, A major, section, with small portions from the first and third sections. He therefore transposed all the borrowed music into A major, composed new linking material, and designed a new form by creating a reprise where Cherubini used none. Storace's ensemble is considerably shorter than Cherubini's finale.

Most of Storace's adaptations in *Lodoiska* are straightforward, and, in the case of music by Kreutzer, consist almost entirely of turning partly vocal pieces into wholly instrumental ones. He made unusual selections but straightforward alterations in the music he borrowed from Kreutzer: he omitted two musically insignificant chorus parts, cut some bars from one symphony, and added a second strophe to the air 'Adieu, my Floreski'. Only in using Cherubini's finale did Storace make any major alterations, something which is more in line with his procedures elsewhere.

THE GLORIOUS FIRST OF JUNE (2 JULY 1794)

The genesis of *The Glorious First of June* is a case study in theatrical practicality. It was written hurriedly for one short season, and stands in stark contrast to Storace's usual care in adaptation. Dr William Kitchiner described Storace's normal manner of working in an edition of *Ivanhoe or the Knight Templar* (1820), whose music was mainly based on Storace's:

We have been assured, from excellent authority, that an Opera, generally, occupied [Storace's] attention for many months: moreover, in the department of the

Theatre which he filled, he was the absolute director. When a Piece was given to him, he asked, 'How many minutes do you allow me for the music'. He took care to keep within the time allotted to him; and so, when his work was done, it was finished. Being certain he was not labouring in vain, he was encouraged to take pains with his Compositions, because he was sure they would be performed in such a manner as to produce every effect he intended.[24]

Obviously *The Glorious First of June* was exceptional. It was first performed on 2 July 1794 for the benefit of the surviving families of the men killed while serving under Earl Howe, who had recently fought a sea battle against the French which culminated in an English victory on 1 June 1794. After news of the victory reached England, celebrations began. Music, poetry, panoramas, and exhibits of documents related to the battle were all rushed into the public view. On 23 June the company at the King's Theatre followed their regular performance of *La serva padrona* by an adaptation by Da Ponte of a cantata by Paisiello, now entitled *La vittoria* to celebrate the British triumph. The evening ended with Madame Banti singing 'Rule Britannia'. This last event provoked Parke to comment that 'she was vociferously encored, although her bad English amounted almost to burlesque! This clearly shows that fashion, like love, is blind.'[25]

Of all the celebrations of the British victory, only *The Glorious First of June* was designed as a fund-raiser. According to contemporary reports, the plan to raise money with a benefit performance was not initiated until late June. By 20 June a decision had been made in principle, and was announced on the Drury Lane playbill: 'The Public are respectfully informed that a Play will be speedily performed at this Theatre, with a New and Appropriate Entertainment, commemorating, and founded on, the Glorious Naval Victory of the First of June.' However, serious work may not have started on the piece then, as the *Thespian Magazine* reported that 'the afterpiece [was] written and studied within two days'.[26] This is only partly true. Full rehearsals did indeed take place only on 1 July (for the entire day and evening) then the following day before the première.[27] However, ballet rehearsals had started on 21 June (right after the first announcement) and continued on 26 and 28 June. Even so, the entire creation was so hurried that one reviewer thought it might 'be fairly exempted from passing the ordeal of criticism, as having been written so much on the spur of the occasion, that the copy, we understand, was not delivered to the Prompter till

---

[24] 'Observations on Vocal Music', *Ivanhoe or the Knight Templar* (London [1820]), 1–2.
[25] *London Stage*, 23 June 1794, King's Theatre; Parke, *Musical Memoirs*, i. 190.
[26] *Thespian Magazine*, 3 (1794), 313.
[27] William Powell's playbills, as quoted in *London Stage* for these dates.

Monday morning [30 June]'.[28] The manuscript text was sent to Larpent for licensing the day before the première and he read it the next day.[29] It contains several almost blank pages, including the last, which is merely headed 'Fete'. This title is the only clue to the fact that the work ended with fireworks and the House singing 'Rule Britannia'.[30]

The haste with which the piece was put together explains why Storace made very few adaptations to the music he borrowed. Four borrowed pieces have been identified out of a total of eleven numbers in the score: one Italian aria which was given a new text but was otherwise barely altered, and three English pieces, all of which kept their original texts. With one exception (Richard Leveridge's song 'Now mighty roast beef is the Englishman's food' in *The Haunted Tower*), these three songs are the only instances where Storace took over both text and music into one of his operas.

As we have already seen, Mengozzi's aria 'Donne, donne chi vi crede' had been inserted into Paisiello's *Gli schiavi per amore* for its London season in 1787 (which Storace had directed) and Longman & Broderip had published the score.[31] Storace's version, 'Never, never, when you've won us', comes directly from the printed full score. Storace reproduced the bottom two staves of Mengozzi's score identically in his own two-stave score, even down to the marking 'arco' in bar 31. He made only two alterations, cutting four bars of Mengozzi's internal recitative and repeating one phrase at the end.

Storace took over Linley's 'When 'tis night' complete with text. He merely changed the time signature from alla breve to common time and adjusted the end to omit Linley's short chorus.[32] Joseph Baildon's 'Adieu to the village delights' is similarly presented with little change. Originally for three voices and entitled 'A Pastoral Elegiac Glee', it was popular enough to be published in several editions in the eighteenth century.[33] Storace added a fourth voice, transposed it down a semitone to E flat, and used only the first of Baildon's three stanzas. He added an instrumental bass-line throughout, plus an introduction and postlude.

'When Britain first at Heav'n's command', commonly known as 'Rule Britannia', became the final piece in *The Glorious First of June*. This well-

---

[28] *Times*, 3 July 1794.
[29] Conolly, *The Censorship of English Drama 1737–1824*, 20. 'The Glorious First of June', Larpent MS 1032.
[30] *Thespian Magazine*, 3 (1794), 313.   [31] *RISM* M 2255.
[32] The only version of Linley's score I have been able to find was published by J. Steven of Glasgow, *c*.1795. It is therefore an unreliable source because of its late date and because it was probably pirated. It was not entered at Stationers' Hall.
[33] See *RISM* B 654–60.

known song had long been used to arouse patriotic fervour, so naturally Storace made no attempt to alter it.[34] It originated as the finale of Thomas Arne's masque *Alfred* of 1740, which told the story of King Alfred's victory over the Danes.[35] 'Rule Britannia' was the victory song sung by Alfred, his queen Eltruda, and chorus. It caught the public fancy and was published in over twenty British editions.[36] Storace's publisher Dale advertised his own edition at the catalogue in the front of Storace's *The Pirates* (1792), and it was the obvious choice to end *The Glorious First of June*. Storace's version follows Walsh's early edition remarkably closely, even including a figured bass, which had not appeared in any of Storace's publications since *The Siege of Belgrade* in 1791. He used all six verses of the song and made only minor alterations.[37]

The rarity of unaltered borrowings by Storace cannot be emphasized enough. He rarely neglected to tailor his borrowed music to its new context and to his own liking. The fact that he did so in *The Glorious First of June* is strong testimony that he was a practical man of the theatre, who could sacrifice perfection for speed in a good cause.

MAHMOUD (30 APRIL 1796)

The mainpiece opera *Mahmoud*, with a libretto by Hoare and music by Storace, would have been an unusual work if Storace had lived to complete it. The plot is built on a web of complex interrelationships, involves issues of personal status and Muslim values, and introduces the notion of the 'innocent savage'. The stereotyped casting of earlier operas is more loosely applied here; it includes two tenor roles (Michael Kelly and John Braham in his first role at Drury Lane), no role for Anna Crouch, and Kemble as the non-singing Mahmoud. Nancy Storace and Bannister were cast fairly normally. To judge from the libretto, Storace planned to compose some elaborate ensembles, particularly as finales. However, the manner in which the borrowed music is treated is so unlike Storace's normal practice that it is clear someone else finished the work after Storace's death. The makeshift

---

[34] This is the only occasion in any operatic score by Storace that a vocal piece is headed with a title instead of a singer's name.

[35] Alexander Scott, 'Arne's "Alfred" ', *ML* 55 (1974), 389. See also Thomas Augustine Arne, *Alfred*, ed. Alexander Scott, Musica Britannica, xlvii (London, 1981).

[36] See *RISM* A 1586–1612; *BUCEM* i. 41.

[37] One alteration that persists to the present day is the note e'' for the fifth syllable of the chorus instead of Arne's f'', altering the harmony to match. The alteration may not have been made by Storace, but simply copied by him from a source more recent than Walsh's print. Other modern alterations are not present in Storace's version, such as the beginning of phrase 3 and the end of phrase 6.

completion was a gesture of affection for a dead man and his family, as Bingley described:

Although his death paralysed the work, it did not prevent its being afterwards produced, though in an incomplete state. With the consent of the managers and Mr. Hoare, the author of the opera, the friendly assistance of Mr. Kelly, and some additional music selected by Signora Storace, the composer's sister, it was performed for the benefit of his family.[38]

Although we cannot confirm Nancy Storace's role in the completion of *Mahmoud*, we can tentatively assume that Bingley was correct.

The borrowed music consists of one aria by Haydn in Act 1, and four numbers from *Gli sposi malcontenti*: an aria and part of the finale in Act 2, and a chorus and a trio in Act 3. At least two other borrowings, from Paisiello and Sarti, remain unidentified.[39] As well as borrowing old music, Nancy Storace moved an ensemble from its original position in Act 1 to become the closing finale. Here it is textually and musically inappropriate: only five characters from the cast take part and the text is specific to the early part of the plot. Obviously Nancy needed a finale and chose the most convenient ensemble available.

Most of the music is borrowed from the two finales to *Gli sposi* in several large sections, becoming the last half of the finale to Act 2, part of the chorus which opens Act 3, and the following trio. Table 8.2 lays out the scheme of borrowing. A section-by-section comparison reveals that the borrowings were carried out in an atypical manner, with material simply transferred from one context to the other, one section after another. Some complete sections of the original are omitted, but smaller cuts altering the internal make-up of individual sections are rare.

The borrowing of *a* (the middle column of Table 8.2) is complete and exact, given that *Mahmoud* does not survive in an orchestral version. In *b* the first thirty-eight-bar entry of the ensemble is omitted, so that the opening dialogue is continuous instead of being interrupted after eight bars. Overlapping phrases are occasionally made discrete by the addition of an extra bar; a few individual bars are omitted. Section *c* is borrowed complete; the Più allegro section that follows in the *Gli sposi* finale is omitted and instead new cadential music *d* (in a similar style) ends the *Mahmoud* finale. The finale in *Gli sposi* ends with a separate section, *e*, similar to but by no means the same as section *a*.

Section *f*, the beginning of the opening chorus of Act 3 in *Mahmoud*, is

---

[38] *Musical Biography*, ii. 214.   [39] Playbill, 30 Apr. 1796.

Table 8.2. Sections of *Gli sposi malcontenti* borrowed in *Mahmoud*

Gli sposi malcontenti[a]			*Mahmoud*[b]	
Volume, folio	Section	Text refs.	Section	Pages, no.
2, 61–67ᵛ	Act 1 finale, sect. 5	*a*	Act 2 finale, sect. 6	64–71, no. 16
2, 68–83ᵛ	Sect. 6	*b*	Sect. 7	72–4
2, 84–90	Sect. 7	*c*	Sect. 8	74–6
[2, 90ᵛ–92ᵛ]	[Sect. 8 omitted]	—		
—		*d*	Sect. 8 continued, end Act 2	77–8
[2, 92ᵛ–98]	[Sect. 9 omitted], end Act 1	*e*		
—		*f*	Act 3 opening chorus; sect. 1	79–87, no. 17
3, 73ᵛ–85	Act 2 finale, sect. 6, pt. 2	*g*	Sect. 2	88–91
3, 66–73	Sect. 6, pt. 1	*h*	Trio	92–3, no. 18

[a] 'Gli sposi malcontenti' (Vienna, Österreichische Nationalbibliothek, Musiksammlung KT 425).
[b] *The Iron Chest and Mahmoud* (London [1797]).

new but bears some similarity to *a* and *e*. The second part of the chorus, *g*, comes from the Act 3 finale of *Gli sposi*. Its long orchestral introduction is not used; otherwise the bulk of the section is identical. The orchestral postlude is also omitted; instead *Mahmoud* has a new cadential section which includes a brief return of the opening music. Section *h*, which had originally preceded *g* in *Gli sposi*, now follows *g* in the next, unconnected, trio. The introduction and first singer's section are not used; the piece begins with the second singer (who has the same music as the first); then it continues in an identical fashion. The method of borrowing suggests that Nancy Storace chose suitable ensembles from *Gli sposi*, then filled all the necessary ensembles in *Mahmoud* with that music basically unrevised.

Other music is borrowed similarly. The aria 'Quel ciglio sereno' from Act 1 of *Gli sposi malcontenti* becomes 'From tears unavailing' (no. 12) in Act 2. The two versions are virtually identical except in bar 70, where orchestral and vocal parts are exchanged. Similarly, 'Safe in the word' (no. 6) comes virtually unchanged from Haydn's 'Quel cor umano' with Da Ponte's words. The duet originated in *Orlando Paladino* (1782) with the text 'Quel tuo visetto', and was then interpolated in Martin y Soler's opera *Il burbero di buon core* at the King's Theatre in 1794 with Da Ponte's text. Both Storace and his sister probably heard the duet there; certainly Hoare's English words are more closely related to Da Ponte's than to the original. The London version was published;[40] apart from a few trivial differences the two-stave reduction in Dale's score of *Mahmoud* reproduces Haydn's voice and second violin parts almost note for note. Storace's harmonies sometimes appear to be inversions of the originals because Haydn's bass is omitted; Joseph Mazzinghi (who prepared Storace's score for publication) obviously copied Haydn's score literally.

Because so few modifications were made to any of the identified borrowings in *Mahmoud* and because the adaptations in nos. 16, 17, and 18 are so lacking in detail, it seems certain that these borrowings were not Storace's work, even though he may have planned them before he died. Only in *The Glorious First of June* had he borrowed music with so little alteration, and nowhere else did he borrow such large sections without regard to dramatic context. The refinements of Storace's style of adaptation are missing; the result is an opera that has more historical interest than potential for modern peformance.

Summary

In his use of borrowed material, Storace emerges as a practical composer for the theatre who was at the same time uncompromising as regards his ideals of compositional craft. He was always conscious of the reactions of his audience, who had the ultimate say in the success or failure of his operas. Indeed many of his adaptations rapidly became crowd-pleasers, as we know from both contemporary reports and the number of printings in London.

As a young composer starting his London career, he followed the conventions set by his established older colleagues, incorporating substantial amounts of borrowed material into his operas. Since *Singspiel* and *opéra comique* were the genres most closely related to English opera in their use of spoken dialogue and in the dimensions of their individual numbers, it was natural that Storace should have chosen a *Singspiel* on which to base *The Doctor and the Apothecary*, his first English opera. To his audience, however, the choice must have seemed unusual, since, despite their Hanoverian king, English composers of the period generally had much closer relations with French musical life and culture than with German.

In subsequent works Storace turned back to Italian operas, borrowing music from operas he knew at first hand, though he relied on published

---

[40] *RISM* H 2573.

versions from which to make his adaptations. In the earlier operas he generally used music he had heard and collected on his travels; starting with *The Pirates* (1792), he used music that was available in London or through Kelly's kind offices. He also made increasing use of his own earlier music, especially his three *opere buffe*. Because his background and training differed from those of most other English composers, his choice of music and methods of adaptation were likewise different.

Storace asserted his individuality through his choice of borrowed music and extensive modifications. For both reasons, Storace's approach to musical borrowings was strikingly at variance with that of his contemporaries. His adaptations range from minimal to virtual recomposition. He favoured careful reworking and disliked redundant repetition, both textual and musical. He made the fewest alterations to simple folk-like songs, the most to elaborate Italian numbers. He also took into account his own speed of composition, making few alterations when pressed for time. In general he respected the melodic (and usually harmonic) integrity of the music he borrowed, while feeling able to modify the formal outlines freely.

Finally, it is important to return to the question of identifying operas that borrow existing material—whether they are called 'pastiche', 'pasticcio', or another name—with the knowledge that borrowing music is not simply the removal of a composition from one work directly into another. Storace invested far more compositional skill in his operas than can ever be conveyed by calling them 'pastiches'. Even the earlier ones that contain the highest proportion of borrowed music are far more than collections of unrelated songs from different sources; certainly the later operas display great skill in adaptation, and large amounts of newly composed music incorporated into so-called 'borrowed' numbers. When Storace chose to use old material he took it as his own, with the right to alter and add at will.

9

CONCLUSIONS

It is difficult to evaluate Storace's achievements without first regretting his early death. Thirty years after it, the *Harmonicon* expressed the sentiment plainly:

Had fortune enabled [Storace] to write at leisure, and not on the spur of the occasion, as was too frequently the case,—had he enjoyed better health, and lived but a few years longer, it is reasonable to conclude that he would have proved his claim to a still higher niche in the temple of fame than is now allotted him.[1]

We can only speculate as to how far he would have taken his pursuit of dramatically integrated operas in searching for a comfortable balance between English and Italian characteristics. It is undeniable that Storace's innovations had little impact on English opera, a fact that was recognized in the nineteenth century. The reason that the Victorian critic George Hogarth singled out Storace as outstanding was partly that his lack of successors highlighted his own achievements:

His operas, to this day, are among the most attractive that we possess. He had been educated in the *reformed* Italian school of the close of the last century; and the models on which he formed his style were the works of Piccini, Sacchini, and Paesiello. From the study of these, he not only acquired grace and refinement, but learned to enrich his operas with those concerted scenes and finales, the introduction of which was a new era in dramatic composition. In the beauty and spirit of his concerted pieces, he has not been surpassed by any English composer who has succeded [*sic*] him.[2]

What Hogarth saw as an enriching influence from the Italian to the English school of opera, critics later still have seen in a more negative light. One recent commentator voiced the opinion that Storace's music suffered

[1] *Harmonicon*, 6 (1828), 3.
[2] *Musical History, Biography and Criticism* (1st pub. London, 1835; New York, 1845), 130.

because he was working within a weaker tradition than the Italian, thereby ignoring Storace's attempts to strengthen the English operatic tradition:

A good tradition can sustain the minor craftsman–composer; he will be listened to with pleasure not for his individual voice so much as for the ease and resource with which he exploits the current idiom. Who can doubt that if Arne or Boyce had had the opportunity of writing within the continental tradition his stature would be higher than it is? Likewise the Storace of *The Pirates* or *The Iron Chest* has little more to offer than a handful of pretty tunes; but in *Gli Equivoci*, written for a Viennese public to a libretto by da Ponte, he takes on the strength of the tradition which he serves.[3]

This distinguished writer (like others who believe in the inherent superiority of Italian opera) considers that Storace failed to achieve his potential simply because he was composing in the wrong place and genre, not belonging to an already strong tradition but, rather, trying to reform his own. Equally, if success is measured by historical impact, then he did indeed fail, not for lack of trying but because he had no successors. His innovations passed unnoticed by succeeding generations of English composers, and English opera steadily declined.

Storace's English operas are little known today, in part because only one survives in a performing version. *No Song, No Supper* survives in manuscript full score, along with his two Viennese operas; not surprisingly, *No Song, No Supper* and *Gli equivoci* have been the most often revived in recent years and are the only two in modern edition. *Gli equivoci* has proved most popular, with at least six revivals in recent years. Its latest production at the Wexford Festival in October 1992 confirms its place in the mainstream of Classical *opera buffa*.[4] Because Storace's Italian works belong to an established tradition, producers have no need to justify their performance. The validity of staging his English works, on the other hand, is sometimes questioned.

Revival of an English opera from this period (apart from *No Song, No Supper*) requires complete orchestration, which makes it far more involved to produce and correspondingly less 'authentic'. Most recent performances of Storace's operas have been staged by student groups, whose approaches to making the scores stageworthy range from attempts at historically accurate orchestration to practical arrangements for small ensembles.[5] The issue

---

[3] Julian Budden, *The Operas of Verdi*, ii: *'Il Trovatore' to 'La Forza del Destino'* (New York, 1984), 3.
[4] *Gli equivoci*, ed. Richard Platt (Musica Britannica, forthcoming).
[5] e.g. when Neil McGowan produced *The Siege of Belgrade* with the Royal Holloway College Opera Society in 1981, he reconstructed and orchestrated a score in Storace's style. By contrast, Janet

of editing the spoken dialogue must also be faced, in light of some severe weaknesses.

As an example of a professional musician of the classical period, practising in a city with a flourishing cultural life, Storace fills a fascinating historical position. His role in the theatrical world and his success as a published composer illuminate a way of life that was shared by many musicians of the eighteenth century, and his works allow us entry into theatrical history from an important perspective. As an individual, Storace tried to elevate the state of English opera. That he did not succeed is a fact of history. Nevertheless, in his attempts to achieve new heights of dramatic opera in England, Storace gave us some exciting and attractive music.

Morrow King's production of *The Haunted Tower* at Colorado State University in 1993 used only six players in an instrumental arrangement which, while stylistically appropriate, made no attempt to reconstruct the original score.

APPENDIX 1

Storace's Epitaph by Prince Hoare

Storace's memorial, in which a hand holding a lyre and wreath appears above the text, can be seen in Marylebone parish church, 17 Marylebone Road, London NW1, which was erected in 1817.

IN MEMORY OF
A LIFE DEVOTED TO THE STUDY OF MUSICAL SCIENCE,
AND SHORTEN'D BY UNREMITTED APPLICATION
AND ANXIETY IN THE ATTAINMENT OF ITS OBJECT,
THIS MARBLE IS
INSCRIBED WITH THE NAME OF
STEPHEN STORACE
WHOSE PROFESSIONAL TALENTS COMMANDED
PUBLIC APPLAUSE
WHOSE PRIVATE VIRTUES ENSURED DOMESTIC AFFECTION,
HE DIED MARCH 16TH 1796 AGED 34,
AND IS INTERRED UNDER THE CHURCH,

SILENT HIS LYRE OR WAK'D TO HEAV'NLY STRAINS,
CLOS'D HIS SHORT SCENE OF CHECQUER'D JOYS AND PAINS,
BELOV'D, AND GRATEFUL AS THE NOTES HE SUNG,
HIS NAME STILL TREMBLES ON AFFECTIONS TONGUE,
STILL IN OUR BOSOMS HOLDS ITS WONTED PART,
AND STRIKES THE CHORDS, WHICH VIBRATES TO THE HEART.

P. H.

THIS MARBLE IS PUT UP BY A TENDER MOTHER,
AND AN AFFECTIONATE SISTER.

APPENDIX 2

Contents of Storace's English Operas in Chronological Order

Note: Numbers in the third column are page numbers from the complete scores.

The Doctor and the Apothecary (25 October 1788, Drury Lane)

OVERTURE	1	Instrumental
1. Now the sun so faintly glancing	5	Trio
2. On love's blest altar burns the flame	9	Air
3. SYMPHONY PLAY'D DURING THE SUN SETT	12	Instrumental
4. When wilt thou cease, thou pleasing pain	12	Air
5. Sighing never gains a maid	13	Air
6. Two maidens sat complaining	16	Duet
7. Ye hours that part my love and me	18	Air
8. But see the moon ascending high	19	Quintet
9. Bacchus now his nap is taking	21	Duet (finale 1)
10. Let angry ocean to the sky	22	Air
11. The summer heats bestowing	24	Air
12. This marriage article in every particle	26	Air
13. Am I belov'd? Can you refuse?	28	Air
14. How mistaken is the lover	30	Air
15. This joy inspires the vocal lay	32	Finale 2

The Haunted Tower (24 November 1789, Drury Lane)

OVERTURE	1	Instrumental
1. To Albion's genius raise the strain	8	Chorus
2. From hope's fond dream though reason	10	Air
3. Tho' pity I cannot deny	13	Air
4. Nature to woman still so kind	14	Air
5. Hark! the sweet horn proclaims afar	15	Solo and chorus
6. Whither my love! ah whither art thou gone	22	Air
7. Will great lords and ladies	24	Duet
8. My native land I bade adieu	25	Air
9. Against the shaft of cruel fate	26	Trio (finale 1)
10. Be mine tender passion, soother of care	29	Air
11. Hush, hush, such counsel do not give	32	Air
12. Tho' time has from your Lordship's face	33	Air
13. What blest hours untainted by sorrow	34	Air

14.	Now all in preparation	36	Air
15.	By mutual love delighted	37	Sextet
16.	Now mighty roast beef is the Englishman's food	43	Solo and chorus
17.	Love's sweet voice to Hymen speaking	44	Chorus (finale 2)
18.	Where'er true valour can its pow'r	48	Air
19.	Love from the heart	50	Air
20.	Dangers unknown impending	52	Duet
21.	Dread parent of despair	54	Air
22.	From high birth and all its fetters	58	Air
23.	Be gone, I discharge you	60	Duet
24.	Spirit of my sainted sire	64	Air
25.	As now we're met and a jolly set	66	Trio
26.	The banished ills of heretofore	67	Finale 3

No Song, No Supper (16 April 1790, Drury Lane)

	OVERTURE	1	Instrumental
1.	The ling'ring pangs of hopeless love	4	Air
2.	Go George, I can't endure you	6	Air
3.	How happily my life I led	8	Air
4.	I thought our quarrels ended	10	Air
5.	With lowly suit and plaintive ditty	12	Air
6.	Knocking at this time of day	14	Trio
7.	I think I'll venture to surmise	19	Duet
8.	How often thus I'm forced to trudge	20	Sextet (finale 1)
9.	From aloft the sailor looks around	26	Air
10.	A miser bid to have and hold me	28	Air
11.	Pretty maid your fortune's here	30	Air
12.	Thus ev'ry hope obtaining	31	Duet
13.	Three years a sailor's life I led	34	Air
14.	Across the downs this morning	35	Air
15.	Let shepherd lads and maids advance	36	Finale 2

The Siege of Belgrade (1 January 1791, Drury Lane)

	OVERTURE	2	Instrumental
1.	Wave our prophets fam'd standard	8	Chorus
2.	Lost distress'd I'm thus driven from home	11	Air
3.	Speak I command thee	12	Trio
4.	The rose and the lily	15	Air
5.	How the deuce I came to like you	18	Duet
6.	All will hail the joyous day	22	Air
7.	Seize him, seize him, I say	24	Solos and chorus
8.	The sapling oak lost in the dell	26	Air
9.	Blithe as the hours of May	28	Air
10.	When justice claims the victim due	30	Trio

229

11.	So kindly condescending	36	Chorus (finale 1)
12.	My plaint in no one pity moves	40	Air
13.	Of plighted faith so truly kept	43	Duet
14.	Confusion thus defeated	45	Air
15.	Haste gentle zephyr, o'er the glade	48	Duet
16.	Night that from me concealing	50	Septet
17.	How few know how to value life	55	Air
18.	What can mean that thoughtful frown	56	Air
19.	To mighty love the yielding strings	57	Air
20.	MARCH OF TURKISH SOLDIERS	58	Instrumental
21.	Since victory now like a mistress	59	Finale 2
22.	On the warlike plains descending	64	Chorus
23.	No more I'll heave the tender sigh	65	Air
24.	How provoking your doubts!	67	Air
25.	Domestic peace my souls desire	68	Air
26.	Some time ago I married a wife	72	Air
27.	Tho' you think by this to vex me	73	Duet
28.	Love and honour now conspire	75	Air
29.	Loud let the song of triumph rise	78	Finale 3

The Pirates (21 November 1792, Drury Lane at the King's Theatre)

	OVERTURE	2	Instrumental
1.	Thanks to the brisk and fav'ring gale	10	Chorus
2.	Of a vile lack of honesty	14	Air
3.	Some device my aim to cover	16	Air
4.	Signor! What sounds are these	18	Duet
5.	Oh! the pretty creature	20	Air
6.	Love like the op'ning flow'r	22	Air
7.	Past toils thus recompensing	24	Trio
8.	Lovers, who listen to reason's persuasion	26	Air
9.	Peaceful slumb'ring on the ocean	28	Air (finale 1)
10.	Hist, hist, Fabulina	29	Finale 1 cont.
11.	Hear our suit and don't refuse	44	Trio
12.	There, the silver'd waters roam	48	Air
13.	A saucy knave who pass'd the door	50	Air
14.	What shall I do? What line pursue?	52	Air
15.	FOUR DANCES	54	Instrumental
16.	Let mirth and joy appear	56	Quartet
17.	Mem'ry repeating	58	Air
18.	In childhood's careless happy day	60	Air
19.	Unhand me cowards / Bear him away	61	Finale 2
20.	To the vineyard's praise	70	Chorus
21.	My rising spirits thronging	72	Air
22.	To the vineyard's praise	74	Chorus
23.	As wrapt in sleep I lay	76	Air

24. No more his fears alarming	77	Air
25. Scarcely had the blushing morn	79	Air
26. The jealous don won't you assume	82	Duet
27. When you shall hear the sound of joy	84	Air
28. We the veil of fate undraw	85	Trio
29. Now constancy its need shall gain	88	Finale 3

The Prize (11 March 1793, Drury Lane at the King's Theatre)

SYMPHONY PLAYED WHILE THE CURTAIN RISES	1	Instrumental
1. You care of money, care no more	2	Air
2. Ah tell me softly breathing gale	4	Duet
3. O dear delightful skill	6	Air (finale 1)
4. From my hide and seek chin	8	Duet
5. Beaux yeux qui causer mon trepas	10	Air
6. The changling's fate we've set to view	12	Finale 2
[7. Ah ne'er ungrateful shall he I love	14	Air]

My Grandmother (16 December 1793, Little Theatre)

OVERTURE	2	Instrumental
1. Are ye fair, as op'ning roses	7	Air
2. Cruel fair! who secret anguish	10	Air
3. On the lightly sportive wing	12	Air
4. Ah me! I am lost and forlorn	16	Air
5. Full twenty times you've heard my mind	18	Air
6. Ah! believe these plaintive sighs	20	Trio (finale 1)
7. When I was a younker	23	Air
8. Say, how can words a passion feign	26	Air
9. Tho' now betroth'd in early life	27	Quartet (finale 2)

Lodoiska (9 June 1794, Drury Lane)

OVERTURE	1	Instrumental
1. Ah, Lodoiska, wide o'er the world	6	Air
2. Hark! hark the music	10	Air
3. Yield your arms to noble quarter	12	Quartet
4. We swear and all our hordes	14	Chorus
5. Floreski! / 'Tis her voice	20	Trio
6. MARCH	26	Instrumental
7. SYMPHONY	27	Instrumental
8. Ye streams that round my prison creep	28	Air
9. Adieu, my Floreski, for ever	30	Air
10. Descend some warring angel	32	Air (finale 2)
11. SYMPHONY	36	Instrumental
12. Sweet bird that cheer'st the heavy hours	38	Air

13. When the darken'd midnight sky	42	Trio
14. Oh happy hour! what bliss I feel	44	Finale 3

The Glorious First of June (2 July 1794, Drury Lane)

1. Adieu to the village delights	2	Quartet
2. When 'tis night and the mid-watch	4	Air
3. Oh stay, my love, my William dear	6	Air
4. When in war on the ocean	8	Air
5. Th'eventful hour is near at hand	10	Quintet
6. O'er the vast surface of the deep	14	Air
7. Our hearts with joy expanding	16	Duet
8. Never, never, when you've won us	20	Air
9. Of lovers you'll have plenty	24	Duet
10. The line was form'd, the French lay to	26	Air
11. When Britain first at Heav'n's command	28	Finale

The Cherokee (20 December 1794, Drury Lane)

OVERTURE	2	Instrumental
1. Victory's smiles bid us banish all care	6	Trio
2. Our country is our ship d'ye see	8	Air
3. Oh what a sight it was to see	10	Air
4. Oh! set me free / Those accents dear	12	Quartet
5. Like paint first us'd	16	Duet
6. CHEROKEE MARCH	19	Instrumental
7. BRITISH MARCH	19	Instrumental
8. Sweet sympathy's pleasure	20	Air
9. In praise of peace its martial tone	22	Trio
10. Oh pow'r unknown	23	Chorus (finale 1)
11. Ah! what avails the busy care	30	Air
12. And does a fond emotion	32	Duet
13. A secret pow'r impelling	34	Air
14. Glory firing, fame inspiring	36	Air
15. A shepherd once had lost his love	38	Air
16. Then no more my dearest blessing	40	Duet
17. Fair one those eyes command me	44	Duet
18. A sailor lov'd a lass	46	Air
19. Now cool evening's breeze inviting	48	Quartet (finale 2)
20. From the forest the Indians are coming	50	Duet (finale 2)
21. Fatal news our fears confound us	52	Septet (finale 2)
22. Warriors advance! / The call we obey!	54	Chorus (finale 2)
23. Dearest youth too long dissembling	60	Air
24. In former times the silent bride	62	Air
25. The call of honour I obey	64	Air
26. False hope dissembling	68	Air

232

27. Soon as friendly night beneath	71	Air
28. Storms and various perils braving	74	Septet
29. Let mirth attune th'inspiring strain	78	Finale 3

The Three and the Deuce (2 September 1795, Little Theatre)

OVERTURE	1	Instrumental
1. Around the old oak, right jolly and gay	6	Trio
2. Oh lud! what a dreadful temptation	8	Air
3. To see the fair bride go back	10	Air
4. Go not, my love, ah go not away!	12	Air
5. Behold I'm a simple village lass	14	Air
6. Lead on, I'm resolv'd on a turn	16	Duet (finale 1)
7. Full many a lad in Llewyel's vale	18	Air
8. Right easy of mind	20	Air
9. I'll bid my trembling heart no more	22	Air
10. Musick is the food of love	25	Air
11. Oh wonders that grow in Kilkenny	28	Air (finale 2)
12. This beating heart feels ev'ry fear	30	Duet
13. Should e'er the fortune be my lot	32	Air
14. Oh happy me whose fears now past	34	Finale 3

The Iron Chest (12 March 1796, Drury Lane)

OVERTURE	2	Instrumental
1. Five times by the taper light	9	Quartet
2. Who knocks at this dead hour? / A friend	12	Duet
3. The sun has tipt the hills with red	13	Quintet
4. Sir Marmaduke was a hearty knight	18	Air
5. Sweet little Barbara	19	Duet (finale 1)
6. When the robber his victim has noted	22	Air
7. A traveller stopt at a widow's gate	25	Air
8. Listen! No, it is the owl	26	Chorus
9. Jolly friars tippled here	37	Chorus (finale 2)
10. From break of the morning	44	Duet
11. Down by the river there grows	48	Air
12. When gratitude shall breathe the note	50	Finale 3

Mahmoud (30 April 1796, Drury Lane)

OVERTURE	1	Instrumental
1. Ere we laid our arms by	10	Trio
2. When sleep has clos'd	17	Air
3. Where jealous misers starve in wealth	20	Air
4. Tho' pleasure swell the jovial cry	22	Air
5. Toll, toll the knell	24	Air

APPENDIX 3

Entries in the Stationers' Hall Registers of Storace's Works

Year	Date	First line/title (opera)	Copyright-holder
1787	23 Nov.	*Storace's Collection of Original Harpsichord Music*, vol. i, no. 1	Storace
	21 Dec.	'Care donne che bramate'	Storace
	31 Dec.	'Care donne che bramate'	Longman & Broderip
1788	9 Jan.	*Storace's Collection*, vol. i, no. 2	Storace
	25 Feb.	*Storace's Collection*, vol. i, no. 3	Storace
	31 Mar.	'Beaux yeux' (*Cameriera*)	Storace
	12 Apr.	'Ah perche di quel ingrato' (*Cameriera*)	Storace
	26 Apr.	'E di matti questo mondo' (*Cameriera*)	Storace
		Storace's Collection, vol. i, no. 4	Storace
	7 May	Overture to *La cameriera astuta*	Storace
	3 June	*Storace's Collection*, vol. i, no. 5	Storace
	22 July	*Storace's Collection*, vol. i, no. 6	Storace
	18 Nov.	*The Doctor and the Apothecary*	Storace
	22 Nov.	*Storace's Collection*, vol. ii, no. 1	Storace
1789	19 Jan.	*Storace's Collection*, vol. ii, no. 2	Storace
	24 Feb.	*Storace's Collection*, vol. ii, no. 3	Storace
	30 Apr.	*Storace's Collection*, vol. ii, no. 4	Storace
	23 July	*Storace's Collection*, vol. ii, no. 5	Storace
	2 Dec.	*Storace's Collection*, vol. ii, no. 6	H. Andrews
1790	16 Jan.	*The Haunted Tower*	Storace (sold to Longman & Broderip, 18 Jan. 1790)
	19 May	*No Song, No Supper*	Longman & Broderip
	30 Nov.	'La rachelina' ['Whither my love!'] (*Haunted Tower*)	Longman & Broderip
1791	11 Feb.	*The Siege of Belgrade*	Dale
	27 Oct.	*Six Easy and Progressive Sonatinas*	Storace
1792	24 Dec.	*The Pirates*	Dale

Year	Date	First line/title (opera)	Copyright-holder
1793	7 Feb.	*The Pirates* (flute)	Dale
	19 Feb.	'Captivity'	Dale
	16 Apr.	'Io non era'	Storace
	24 Apr.	'Peaceful slumb'ring' (*Pirates*)	Dale
	4 May	*Venus and Adonis*	Dale
		The Prize	Dale
	17 June	*The Prize* (flute)	Dale
	29 June	*The Pirates* (guitar)	Dale
	13 Aug.	*The Prize* (guitar)	Dale
	4 Nov.	'Will great lords' (*Haunted Tower*) (arranged by Clarke)	J. Clarke
	17 Nov.	'Lamentation of Marie Antoinette'	Storace
1794	20 Feb.	*My Grandmother*	Dale
	20 Mar.	'Peaceful slumb'ring' (*Pirates*) (harmonized by Harrison)	Dale
	15 Apr.	'Peaceful slumb'ring' (*Pirates*) (variations by Elouis)	Dale
	5 May	*My Grandmother* (flute)	Dale
	6 Sept.	'No more his fears' (*Pirates*)	Dale
		'Lovers, who listen' (*Pirates*)	Dale
		'The jealous don' (*Pirates*)	Dale
		'When you shall hear' (*Pirates*)	Dale
	18 Sept.	Overture to *Lodoiska*	Dale
	26 Sept.	*Lodoiska*	Dale
	27 Sept.	*The Glorious First of June*	Dale
	29 Sept.	'When in war' (*Glorious First of June*)	Dale
		'Peaceful slumb'ring' (*Pirates*) (variations by Dale)	Dale
	9 Oct.	'When 'tis night' (*Glorious First of June*)	Dale
	29 Oct.	Overture to *The Glorious First of June*	Dale
	13 Nov.	'There, the silver'd waters' (*Pirates*)	Dale
	24 Nov.	'O'er the vast surface' (*Glorious First of June*)	Dale
	25 Nov.	'The line was formed' (*Glorious First of June*)	Dale
	26 Nov.	'Oh stay, my love' (*Glorious First of June*)	Dale
	4 Dec.	'Ye streams that round' (*Lodoiska*)	Dale
1795	12 Feb.	*The Cherokee*	Dale
	13 Feb.	'A shepherd once' (*Cherokee*) (variations by Dussek)	Dale
	17 Feb.	'A shepherd once' (*Cherokee*) (variations by Dussek)	Corri, Dussek & Co.
	2 Mar.	'Adieu my Floreski' (*Lodoiska*) (arranged by Cramer)	Corri, Dussek & Co.
	6 Mar.	'A shepherd once' (*Cherokee*)	Dale
	10 Mar.	'Adieu my Floreski' (*Lodoiska*)	Dale
	24 Mar.	*Lodoiska* (flute)	Dale

Year	Date	First line/title (opera)	Copyright-holder
	26 Mar.	*The Cherokee* (flute)	Dale
	8 Apr.	Overture to *My Grandmother*	Dale
		'On the lightly sportive' (*Grandmother*)	Dale
		'Are ye fair as' (*Grandmother*)	Dale
		'Cruel fair' (*Grandmother*)	Dale
	17 Apr.	'In childhood's careless' (*Pirates*)	Dale
		'As wrapt in sleep' (*Pirates*)	Dale
		'You care of money' (*Prize*)	Dale
	23 Apr.	'A shepherd once' (*Cherokee*) (harmonized, three voices)	Dale
	27 May	*The Glorious First of June* (flute)	Dale
	7 July	'Sweet sympathy's pleasure' (*Cherokee*)	Dale
	29 July	'Ah me! I am lost' (*Grandmother*)	Dale
		'When I was a younker' (*Grandmother*)	Dale
	7 Nov.	*The Three and the Deuce*	Dale
	17 Nov.	'A sailor lov'd a lass' (*Cherokee*)	Dale
1796	5 Feb.	'Go not my love' (*Three and Deuce*)	Dale
	8 Feb.	'Should e'er the fortune' (*Three and Deuce*)	Dale
	20 May	'Say how can words' (*Grandmother*)	Dale
1797	3 Mar.	*Mahmoud* and *The Iron Chest*	M. Storace
	14 Mar.	*The Three and the Deuce* (flute)	Dale
	10 May	'In former times' (*Cherokee*)	Dale
		'Full twenty times' (*Grandmother*)	Dale
	11 May	'Ah what avails' (*Cherokee*)	Dale
		'And does a fond emotion' (*Cherokee*)	Dale
	12 May	'And does a fond emotion' (*Cherokee*) (variations by Steibelt)	Dale
	10 June	'We the veil of fate' (*Pirates*)	Dale
	20 Nov.	'Though pleasure swell' (*Mahmoud*)	Dale
		'Don't you remember' (*Mahmoud*)	Dale
		'Toll toll the knell' (*Mahmoud*)	Dale
		'From shades of night' (*Mahmoud*)	Dale
		'Where jealous misers' (*Mahmoud*)	Dale
		'Down by the river' (*Iron Chest*)	Dale
		'Oh! hapless youth' (*Mahmoud*)	Dale
		'Sweet little Barbara' (*Iron Chest*)	Dale
		'A traveller stopt' (*Iron Chest*)	Dale
	23 Nov.	'Five times by the taper light' (*Iron Chest*)	Dale
	13 Dec.	Overture to *The Iron Chest*	Dale
	21 Dec.	Overture to *Mahmoud*	Dale
		The Iron Chest (flute)	Dale
	27 Dec.	*Mahmoud* (flute)	Dale

Year	Date	First line/title (opera)	Copyright-holder
1798	7 Feb.	'My plaint in no one' (*Siege*)	Dale
	16 Feb.	'Oh dear delightful skill' (*Prize*)	Dale
	28 Feb.	'O strike the harp'	Dale
	19 Apr.	'A shepherd once' (variations by Hammond)	Hammond
	21 May	'Spirit of my sainted' (*Haunted Tower*)	Dale

APPENDIX 4

Complete List of Works

Stage Works

Gli sposi malcontenti (*opera buffa*)	1 June 1785
Gli equivoci (*opera buffa*)	27 December 1786
La cameriera astuta (*opera buffa*)	4 March 1788
The Doctor and the Apothecary (afterpiece)	25 October 1788
The Haunted Tower (mainpiece)	24 November 1789
No Song, No Supper (afterpiece)	16 April 1790
The Siege of Belgrade (mainpiece)	1 January 1791
The Cave of Trophonius (afterpiece)	3 May 1791
Poor Old Drury (prelude)	22 September 1791
Dido, Queen of Carthage (all-sung mainpiece)	23 May 1792
The Pirates (mainpiece)	21 November 1792
Venus and Adonis (ballet)	26 February 1793
The Prize (afterpiece)	11 March 1793
My Grandmother (afterpiece)	16 December 1793
Lodoiska (afterpiece)	9 June 1794
The Glorious First of June (afterpiece)	2 July 1794
The Cherokee (mainpiece)	20 December 1794
The Three and the Deuce (afterpiece)	2 September 1795
The Iron Chest (mainpiece play with music)	12 March 1796
Mahmoud (mainpiece)	30 April 1796

Other Works

Orfeo negli elisi (cantata for two voices)	1781
A New Recitative and Rondo ('Ah se poro') (solo vocal)	1782?
Eight Canzonetts (solo vocal)	c.1782
'Compatite miei signori' (solo vocal)	c.1783
'Deux quintettes et un Sestette' (for 2 violins, viola, cello, flute, and keyboard)	1784
'Ah! Delia' (solo vocal)	c.1785
'The favorite Overture of Sigr. Haydn from Op. 39' [actually 79; arranged by Storace] (harpsichord, violin, and cello)	1786
'Care donne che bramate' (solo vocal)	1787
Storace's Collection of Original Harpsichord Music [edited by Storace] (various, instrumental)	1787–9
Three sonatas for harpsichord, violin, and cello	1787–9

APPENDIX 4

'The favorite Air in the Heiress . . . with Variations, and an
    Introduction' (harpsichord)   *c.*1790

Six Easy and Progressive Sonatinas (piano/harpsichord)   1791

Music for *Cymon* (various, vocal and instrumental)   1791

'Captivity' (solo vocal)   1793

'Io non era' (solo vocal)   1793

'Lamentation of Marie Antoinette' (solo vocal)   1793

Operas in which Storace used Borrowed Material

THE DOCTOR AND THE APOTHECARY (1788)

Title-page (Birchall & Andrews): 'The Music Adapted from Ditters, and Composed by S. Storace'
Playbill: 'The Music composed by Ditters and Storace.'

No.	Title/first line	Printed score	Source
1.	Now the sun so faintly glancing	'Ditters'	Dittersdorf, *Doctor und Apotheker* (Vienna, 1786), 'O wie herrlich! O wie labend'
4.	When wilt thou cease	'Ditters'	Dittersdorf, *Doctor und Apotheker*, 'Wann hörst du auf'
5.	Sighing never gains a maid	'Ditters'	Dittersdorf, *Doctor und Apotheker*, 'Wenn mann will zu Mädchen gehen'
6.	Two maidens sat complaining	'Ditters'	Dittersdorf, *Doctor und Apotheker*, 'Zwi Mädchen sassen manche Nacht'
8.	But see the moon ascending high	'Ditters & Storace'	Dittersdorf, *Doctor und Apotheker*, 'So ist das Glück uns dan entgegen'
9.	Bacchus now his nap is taking	'Ditters'	Dittersdorf, *Doctor und Apotheker*, 'Wer will lieben'
12.	This marriage article	'Paesiello Accomp: by Storace'	Paisiello, *I filosofi imaginari* (St Petersburg, 1779), 'Salve tu Domine'
14.	How mistaken is the lover	'Storace'	Storace, 'Care donne', in Paisiello's *Il re Teodoro* (King's Theatre, 1787)
15.	This joy inspires the vocal lay	'Ditters'	Dittersdorf, *Doctor und Apotheker*, 'Victoria! Victoria!'

THE HAUNTED TOWER (1789)

Title-page (Longman & Broderip): 'The Music Selected, Adapted & Composed by Stephen Storace'
Playbill: 'The New Musick, composed By Mr Storace, the rest compiled from Linley, Purcell, Sarti, Paesiello, Martini, Pleyel, &c. &c.'

No.	Title/first line	Printed score	Source
	Overture, part 2	—	Storace, *Gli equivoci* (Vienna, 1786), Overture
3.	Tho' pity I cannot deny	'Pleyel'	Pleyel, Quartet in C, 3rd movt. (Benton 334). [The setting 'My little blithsome sparrow' mentioned in Fiske, *English Theatre Music*, 603, is later than *The Haunted Tower*.]
4.	Nature to woman still so kind	'Welch tune'	Possibly Giordani, *The Isle of Saints* (Dublin, 1785), overture; *Midas* (London, 1760), 'As soon as her doating piece'. [Irish tune, 'Lacrum cush', according to Fiske, *English Theatre Music*, 603.]
6.	Whither my love!	'Paesielo'	Paisiello, *La molinara* (Naples, 1788), 'La rachelina molinara'
11.	Hush, hush, such counsel do not give	'Sarti'	Unidentified
12.	Tho' time has from your Lordship's face	'French tune'	Champein, *Les dettes* (Paris, 1787), 'On doit soixante mille francs'
13.	What blest hours untainted	'Linley'	Linley, *The Carnival of Venice* (London, 1781), 'The song of thy love'
14.	Now all in preparation	'French tune'	Unidentified. [Adolphus, *Memoirs of Bannister*, i. 234, says it is 'Qui veut ouir, qui veut savoir'.]
16.	Now mighty roast beef	—	Leveridge, 'The Roast Beef of Old England'
19.	Love from the heart	'Martini'	Martin y Soler, *L'arbore di Diana* (Vienna, 1787), 'Sereno raggio'
20.	Dangers unknown impending	'Sarti'	Unidentified
21.	Dread parent of despair	'Sarti'	Unidentified. [Fiske, *English Theatre Music*, 505 n. 1, thinks it may be from *Giulio Sabino* (Venice, 1781).]
25.	As now we're met	'Purcell'	Purcell, 'I gave her cakes' (catch)
26.	The banish'd ills of heretofore	'Storace from Vive les fillettes'	The melody appears, so labelled, in Krumpholtz, Harp Concerto n. 6.

NO SONG, NO SUPPER (1790)

Title-page: 'The Music Chiefly Composed & Adapted for the Harpsichord or Piano-Forte by Stephen Storace.'

Playbill: 'The Music chiefly composed by Mr. Storace; the Rest selected from Pleyel, Dr. Harrington, Giordani, Gluck, &c.'

No.	Title/first line	Printed score	Source
2.	Go George, I can't endure you	'French air'	Unidentified
4.	I thought our quarrels ended	'Grétry'	Grétry, *L'Amitié à l'épreuve* (1786 revival in Paris), 'Oui, noir, mais pas si diable'
5.	With lowly suit and plaintive ditty	—	[Adolphus, *Memoirs of Bannister*, i. 240: 'Formed, with great alterations, on the daily chaunt of a blind street-beggar.' Parke, *Musical Memoirs*, i. 132: 'The melody taken from an old street ditty.']
6.	Knocking at this time of day	—	[*No Song, No Supper*, ed. Fiske, 118, claims it is similar to the Act 1 finale of *Gli equivoci* (Vienna, 1786). Kelly, *Reminiscences*, i. 234 n., says it is from *Gli equivoci*.]
8.	How often thus I'm forced to trudge	—	Storace, *Gli equivoci* and *La cameriera astuta* (King's Theatre, 1788), 'Ah perche di quel ingrato'
10.	A miser bid to have and hold me	'Grétry'	Grétry, *L'Épreuve villageoise* (Versailles, 1784), 'Bon dieu'
11.	Pretty maid your fortune's here	'Giordani'	Unidentified
12.	Thus ev'ry hope obtaining	'Altered from Pleyel'	Pleyel, String Quartet, Op. 1 No. 2, 3rd movt.
13.	Three years a sailor's life I led	'Dr. Harrington'	Harrington, 'To Beth's fair market'

243

THE SIEGE OF BELGRADE (1791)

Title-page: 'The Music Principally Composed by Stephen Storace.'
Playbill: 'The Musick composed principally by Mr. Storace, With a few Pieces selected from *Martini, Saliezi* [*sic*], *and Paesiello*.'

No.	Title/first line	Printed score	Source
	Overture, 2nd movt.	'Spanish Tune'	Martin y Soler, *Una cosa rara* (Vienna, 1786), 'Non farmi più'
	Overture, 3rd movt., and No. 1, Wave our prophets	—	Mozart, Piano Sonata in A, K. 331, 3rd movt., 'Rondo alla turca'
2.	Lost distress'd	'Martini'	Martin y Soler, *Una cosa rara*, 'Ah pieta de merce'
3.	Speak I command thee	'Martini'	Martin y Soler, *Una cosa rara*, 'Perchè mai nel sen perchè'
4.	The rose and the lily	'Martini and Storace'	Martin y Soler, *Una cosa rara*, 'Più bianca di giglio'
5.	How the deuce I came to like you	'Martini'	Martin y Soler, *Una cosa rara*, 'Un briccone senza core'
9.	Blithe as the hours of May	'Martini'	Martin y Soler, *Una cosa rara*, 'Dolce mi parve un dì'
11.	So kindly condescending	'Martini'	Martin y Soler, *Una cosa rara*, 'Oh quanto un sì bel giubilo'
14.	Confusion thus defeated	'Paisiello'	Unidentified
16.	Night that from me concealing	'Martini'	Martin y Soler, *Una cosa rara*, 'Dammi la cara mano'
18.	What can mean that thoughtful frown	'Saliere'	Salieri, *La grotta di Trofonio* (Vienna, 1784), 'Che filosofo buffon'. See also Fiske, *English Theatre Music*, 510
19.	To mighty love	'Kelly'	[Probably written specifically for *The Siege of Belgrade*]
29.	Loud let the song of triumph rise	'Storace & Martini'	Martin y Soler, *Una cosa rara*, 'Brilli pure in sì bel giorno'

THE CAVE OF TROPHONIUS (1791)

Playbill: 'The Music composed principally by Mr. Storace.'
Songs (London, 1791) labels one piece by Attwood, one by Paisiello, and one melody each by Nancy
Storace and Suett.

DIDO, QUEEN OF CARTHAGE (1792)

Playbill: 'The Musick is chiefly new, and composed by Mr. Storace, The Selections are made from
the most celebrated works of

Salieri,	Sacchini,	Cimerosa,
Pär,	Sarti,	Schuyster,
Rompini,	Giordaniello,	Andreozzi'

THE PIRATES (1792)

Title-page: 'The Music Composed by Stephen Storace.'
Playbill: 'The Music composed principally by Mr. Storace. *With a few Pieces selected from Anfossi, Bianchi and Guglielmi.*'

No.	Title/first line	Source
	Overture, 2nd movt.	Storace, Piano Quintet No. 1 in D, 3rd movt. (London: Author [1784])
	Overture, 3rd movt.	Storace, Piano Quintet No. 1 in D, 4th movt.
3.	Some device my aim to cover	Storace, *Gli sposi malcontenti* (Vienna, 1785), 'Ad un uom versato e cognito'
10.	Hist, hist, Fabulina	'Hear oh' section from Storace, *Gli equivoci* (Vienna, 1786), 'Maldetto sia il momento'
14.	What shall I do?	Opening four bars from Anfossi, *L'Inconnue persécutée* (Rome, 1773), 'Hélas que faire'
17.	Mem'ry repeating	Storace, *Gli sposi malcontenti*, 'Languida voce in seno'
21.	My rising spirits thronging	Mozart, *Die Zauberflöte* (Vienna, 1791), 'Ein Mädchen', via Devienne, *Les Visitandines* (Paris, 1792), 'Enfant cherides'
28.	We the veil of fate undraw	Guglielmi, *La bella pescatrice* (Naples, 1789), 'Al suon soave'

THE PRIZE (1793)

Title-page: 'The Music Composed by Stephen Storace.'
Playbill: 'The Musick by Mr. Storace.'

No.	Title/first line	Source
5.	Beaux yeux	Storace, *La cameriera astuta* (King's Theatre, 1788), 'Beaux yeux'

246

MY GRANDMOTHER (1793)

Title-page: 'The Music Composed by Stephen Storace.'

No.	Title/first line	Source
	Overture	Storace, *Venus and Adonis* (King's Theatre, 1793), polonese

LODOISKA (1794)

Title-page: 'The Music Composed & Selected by S. Storace.'

Playbill: 'The Music composed, and selected from Cherubini, Kreutzer, and Andreozzi, by Mr. Storace.'

No.	Title/first line	Source
	Overture	Kreutzer, *Lodoiska* (Paris, 1791), Overture
4.	We swear and all our hordes	Cherubini, *Lodoiska* (Paris, 1791), 'Jurons quoi qu'il faille'
5.	Floreski! / 'Tis her voice	Cherubini, *Lodoiska*, 'Floreski / je l'entends'
6.	March	Kreutzer, *Lodoiska*, 'Qu'entends je'
7.	Symphony	Kreutzer, *Lodoiska*, 'Comme l'air est tranquille et frais'
9.	Adieu, my Floreski, for ever	Kreutzer, *Lodoiska*, 'La douce clarté de l'aurore'
10.	Descend some warring angel	Andreozzi, 'Ah quell'anima che sdegna', in Sacchini, *Armida* (King's Theatre, 1791)
11.	Symphony	Kreutzer, *Lodoiska*, Entr'acte

THE GLORIOUS FIRST OF JUNE (1794)

Title-page: 'The Music Composed and Selected by S. Storace.'
Playbill: 'The Music composed and selected by Mr. Storace.'

No.	Title/first line	Source
1.	Adieu to the village delights	Joseph Baildon, 'Adieu to the village delights'
2.	When 'tis night	Linley, 'When 'tis night', in revival of *Harlequin Fortunatus* (Drury Lane, 1780)
4.	When in war on the ocean	[*No Song, No Supper*, ed. Fiske, 125, states that the start of the tune is based on an anacreontic song published in 1775.]
8.	Never never when you've won us	Mengozzi, 'Donne, donne' in Paisiello, *Gli schiavi per amore* (King's Theatre, 1787)
11.	When Britain first	Arne, *Alfred* (Cliveden, 1740), 'When Britain first'

THE CHEROKEE (1794)

Title-page: 'The Music Principally Composed By Stephen Storace.'
Playbill: 'The Musick, principally New, composed by Mr. Storace, With a few Pieces selected from Anfossi, Mozart, Bianchi, Ditters and Sarti.'

No.	Title/first line	Source
	Overture	Storace, *Gli sposi malcontenti* (Vienna, 1785), overture
5.	Like paint first us'd	[Graves, 'English Comic Opera', 213, claims a similarity to Mozart, *Le nozze di Figaro*, 'Se a caso madama'.]
19.	Now cool evening's breeze	Sarti, *Le nozze di Dorina* [*I rivali delusi, Fra i due litiganti*] (King's Theatre, 1793), 'Compatite mie o signore' (not Storace's setting)
23.	Dearest youth too long dissembling	Bianchi, 'Per pietà padron mio', inserted in Paisiello, *Gli schiavi per amore* (King's Theatre, 1787)

THE THREE AND THE DEUCE (1795)

Title-page: 'The Music Composed by Stephen Storace.'

No.	Title/first line	Source
	Overture	Storace, *Six Easy and Progressive Sonatinas* (1791), No. 4, 2nd movt.

THE IRON CHEST (1796)

Title-page to Mahmoud and The Iron Chest: 'Composed by Stephen Storace.'
Playbill: 'The Musick composed by Mr. Storace.'

No.	Title/first line	Source
5.	Sweet little Barbara	Mozart, *Le nozze di Figaro*, 'Se vuol ballare', via Storace, *Six Easy and Progressive Sonatinas* (1791), No. 1, 2nd movt.
6.	When the robber his victim	[Kelly, *Reminiscences*, ii. 78, says he (Kelly) finished it.]

MAHMOUD (1796)

Title-page to Mahmoud and The Iron Chest: 'Composed by Stephen Storace.'
Playbill: 'The Musick principally composed by the late Mr. Storace, With a few Selections from Paesiello, Haydn and Sarti.'

No.	Title/first line	Source
6.	Safe in the word	Haydn, *Orlando Paladino* (Esterhazy, 1782), 'Quel tuo visetto', inserted with new text, 'Quel cor umano', in Martin y Soler, *Il burbero di buon core* (Vienna, 1786) at King's Theatre, 1794
9.	Health to your highness	Paisiello, *I zingari in fiera* (Naples, 1789), 'Vi riverisco'
12.	From tears unavailing	Storace, *Gli sposi malcontenti* (Vienna, 1785), 'Quel ciglio sereno'
16.	Follow, follow, boldly enter	Storace, *Gli sposi malcontenti*, 'Che no vita che senta'
17.	To arms	Storace, *Gli sposi malcontenti*, 'L'aurora che colora'
18.	At your feet thus lowly bending	Storace, *Gli sposi malcontenti*, 'Cara sposa perdo nate'

BIBLIOGRAPHY

Archival Sources

Barnard, Lord (Harry Vane), Diaries, 1786–7. Consulted by permission of Lord Barnard, Raby Castle, Staindrop, Co. Durham.

Bath Central Library

John Trusler, 'Memoirs', ii (typescript of late 18th-century MS).

British Library, London

Cobb, James, 'Receipts and Letters of Jas. Cobb, 1787–1809' (BL Add. MS 25,915).
Hoare, Prince, Letter to T. Hill, 18 September [1805/6?] (BL Add. MS 20,081, fo. 187).
Kemble, John P., 'Professional Memoranda of John Philip Kemble, 1788–1795' (BL Add. MS 31,972).
—— 'Professional Memoranda of John Philip Kemble, 1796–1800' (BL Add. MS 31,973).
Storace, Mary, Letter [June 1799?] (BL Add. MS 29,261, fo. 54).
Storace, Stephen, Letter to Sir Robert McKeith, 3 July 1787 (BL Add. MS 35,538, fo. 258).

Folger Shakespeare Library, Washington, DC

'Drury Lane Journal 1788–89' (MS W.b. 291).
'Drury Lane Ledger 1795–99' (MS W.b. 423).
'Drury Lane Paybook 1789–94 [chronological]' (MS W.b. 347).
'Drury Lane Paybook 1790–96 [name-indexed]' (MS W.b. 422).

Harvard Theatre Collection, Cambridge, Mass.

Storace, Stephen, Letter to J. Serres, 21 February 1787 (Autograph V 79).

Huntington Library, San Marino, Ca.

Larpent Collection: MSS of Storace's librettos.

Österreichische Nationalbibliothek, Vienna

Sarti, Fra i due litiganti (Musiksammlung MS 17.888).
Storace, Gli sposi malcontenti (Musiksammlung KT 425).

BIBLIOGRAPHY

Public Record Office, London

Administration Act Books (PROB 6/172).
Affidavits (C31/247/39, C31/247/81).
Recordings of proceedings in Chancery (C33).
Will of Anna Selina Storace, 10 August 1797 (PROB 11/1597).
Will of Elizabeth Storace, 12 September 1817 (PROB 11/1686).

Sir John Soane's Museum, London

Hoare, Prince, inscription for Nancy Storace's memorial.
Storace, Brinsley, indentures.
Various letters by John Braham, Spencer Braham, Prince Hoare, Mary Kennedy, Anna (Nancy) Storace, Elizabeth Storace.

Stationers' Hall, London

Copyright registers of the Worshipful Company of Stationers and Newspaper Makers.

Other Sources

ADOLPHUS, JOHN, *Memoirs of John Bannister, Comedian*, 2 vols. (London, 1839).

ALBRECHT, OTTO, *A Census of Autograph Music Manuscripts of European Composers in American Libraries* (Philadelphia, Pa., 1953).

ARNE, THOMAS AUGUSTINE, *Alfred*, ed. Alexander Scott, Musica Britannica, xlvii (London, 1981).

ARRIGHI, PIER-DOMENICO, *Orfeo Negli Elisi: Cantata a Due Voci, Musica del Signor Stefano Storace Inglese* (Lucca, 1781).

ASPINALL, A., *Politics and the Press c.1780–1850* (Brighton, 1973).

BABINGER, FRANZ, *Mehmed the Conqueror and His Time*, trans. Ralph Manheim, ed. William C. Hickman (Princeton, NJ, 1978).

BAILLIE, LAUREEN (ed.), *The Catalogue of Printed Music in the British Library to 1980*, 62 vols. (London, 1981–7).

BALDWIN, OLIVE, and WILSON, THELMA, '250 Years of Roast Beef', *MT* 126 (1985), 203–7.

BAPTIE, DAVID, *Sketches of the English Glee Composers. Historical, Biographical and Critical, (From About 1735–1866)* (London [1896]).

BAUMANN, THOMAS, *North German Opera in the Age of Goethe* (Cambridge, 1985).

BENTON, RITA, *Ignace Pleyel: A Thematic Catalogue of His Compositions* (New York, 1977).

BINGLEY, WILLIAM, *Musical Biography; or, Memoirs of the Lives and Writings of the Most Eminent Musical Composers and Writers, Who Have Flourished in the Different Countries of Europe During the Last Three Centuries*, 2 vols. (London, 1814; 1834 edn., repr. New York, 1971).

Biographia Dramatica; or, A Companion to the Playhouse, comp. David E. Baker (to 1764), Isaac Reed (to 1782), and Stephen Jones (to 1811), 3 vols. (London, 1812, repr. New York, 1966).

BLACK, JEREMY, *The English Press in the Eighteenth Century* (London, 1987).

BOADEN, JAMES, *Memoirs of the Life of John Philip Kemble, Esq. Including a History of the Stage, From the Time of Garrick to the Present Period* (London, 1825).

BOOTH, MICHAEL (ed.), *Eighteenth Century Tragedy* (London, 1965).

BOULTON, WILLIAM B., *The Amusements of Old London: Being a Survey of the Sports and Pastimes, Tea Gardens and Parks, Playhouses and Other Diversions of the People of London from the 17th to the Beginning of the 19th Century*, 2 vols. (London, 1901).

BOYDELL, BRIAN, *A Dublin Musical Calendar 1700–1760* (Dublin, 1988).

—— *Rotunda Music in Eighteenth-Century Dublin* (Dublin, 1992).

BRACE, GEOFFREY, *Anna...Susanna: Anna Storace, Mozart's First Susanna: Her Life, Times and Family* (London, 1991).

BROOK, BARRY S., 'Piracy and Panacea in the Dissemination of Music in the Late Eighteenth Century', *PRMA* 102 (1975–6), 13–36.

BUDDEN, JULIAN, *The Operas of Verdi*, ii: *'Il Trovatore' to 'La Forza del Destino'* (New York, 1984).

BUSBY, THOMAS, *A Grammar of Music: To Which are Prefixed Observations Explanatory of the Properties and Powers of Music as a Science and of the General Scope and Object of the Work* (London, 1818, repr. New York, 1976).

—— *Concert Room and Orchestra Anecdotes, of Music and Musicians, Ancient and Modern*, 3 vols. (London, 1825).

BYNG, JOHN, *The Torrington Diaries, Containing the Tours Through England and Wales of the Hon. John Byng (Later Fifth Viscount Torrington) Between the Years 1781 and 1794*, ed. C. Bruyn Andrews, 4 vols. (New York, 1938).

CARR, BRUCE, 'Theatre Music: 1800–1834', in Nicholas Temperley (ed.), *Music in Britain: The Romantic Age 1800–1914* (London, 1981).

C. C. T., Letter to the Editor, *Quarterly Musical Magazine and Review*, 4 (1822), 154.

CHARLTON, DAVID, 'Orchestra and Chorus at the Comédie-Italienne (Opéra-Comique), 1755–1799', in Malcolm H. Brown and Roland J. Wiley (eds.) *Slavonic and Western Music: Essays for Gerald Abraham* (Ann Arbor, Mich., 1985), 87–108.

—— *Grétry and the Growth of Opéra Comique* (Cambridge, 1986).

CLARK, T. BLAKE, *Oriental England: A Study of Oriental Influences in Eighteenth Century England as Reflected in the Drama* (Shanghai, 1939).

COBB, JAMES, *The Haunted Tower* (London, n.d.).

COLMAN, GEORGE [jun.], *Random Records*, 2 vols. (London, 1830).

—— *'The Iron Chest'*, in Michael R. Booth (ed.), *Eighteenth Century Tragedy* (London, 1965).

BIBLIOGRAPHY

CONOLLY, LEONARD W., *The Censorship of English Drama 1737–1824* (San Marino, Ca., 1976).

CRAUFURD, J. G., 'The Madrigal Society', *PRMA* 82 (1955–6), 33–46.

DA PONTE, LORENZO, *Memoirs of Lorenzo da Ponte, Mozart's Librettist*, trans. L. A. Sheppard (London, 1929).

DEAN, WINTON, 'Opera Under the French Revolution', *PRMA* 94 (1967–8), 77–96.

DIBDIN, CHARLES, *The Musical Tour of Mr. Dibdin; In which—Previous to his Embarkation for India—He Finished His Career as a Public Character* (Sheffield, 1788).

DOANE, J., *A Musical Directory for the Year 1794* (London [1794]).

DUTTON, THOMAS, *The Dramatic Censor*, 3 vols. (London, 1800–1).

—— *Early English Newspapers*, microfilm series (Woodbridge, Conn., 1983).

EVANS, BERTRAND, *Gothic Drama from Walpole to Shelley* (Berkeley and Los Angeles, Ca., 1947).

FENNER, THEODORE, *Opera in London: Views of the Press, 1785–1830* (Carbondale and Edwardsville, Ill., 1994).

FISKE, ROGER, 'The Operas of Stephen Storace', *PRMA* 86 (1959–60), 29–44.

—— 'The "Macbeth" Music', *ML* 45 (1964), 114–25.

—— *Scotland in Music: A European Enthusiasm* (Cambridge, 1983).

—— *English Theatre Music in the Eighteenth Century* (London, 1973; 2nd edn., Oxford 1986).

—— 'Storace's "Gli Equivoci" ', *Opera*, 25 (1974), 120–4.

FORSTER, GEORG, *Georg Forsters Werke: Sämtliche Schriften, Tagebücher, Briefe*, xvi: *Briefe 1790 bis 1791* (Berlin, 1980).

GÄNZL, KURT, *The British Musical Theatre*, 2 vols. (New York, 1986).

GARLINGTON, AUBREY S., Jr., ' "Gothic" Literature and Dramatic Music in England, 1781–1802', *JAMS* 15 (1962), 48–64.

GASKELL, PHILIP, *A New Introduction to Bibliography* (New York, 1972).

GEIRINGER, KARL, and GEIRINGER, IRENE, 'Stephen and Nancy Storace in Vienna', in Robert L. Weaver (ed.), *Essays on the Music of J. S. Bach and Other Divers Subjects: A Tribute to Gerhard Herz* (Louisville, Ky., 1981).

[GENEST, JOHN], *Some Account of the English Stage, from the Restoration in 1660 to 1830*, 10 vols. (Bath, 1832).

GIRDHAM, JANE, 'The Last of the Storaces', *MT* 129 (1988), 17–18.

—— 'Stephen Storace and the English Opera Tradition of the Late Eighteenth Century', Ph.D. diss. (University of Pennsylvania, 1988).

—— 'A Note on Stephen Storace and Michael Kelly', *ML* 76 (1995), 64–7.

GRAVES, RICHARD, 'The Comic Operas of Stephen Storace', *MT* 95 (1954), 530–2.

—— 'English Comic Opera: 1760–1800', *MMR* 87 (1957), 208–15.

GRAY, CHARLES H., *Theatrical Criticism in London to 1795* (New York, 1931).

GWYNN, STEPHEN, *Memorials of an Eighteenth Century Painter (James Northcote)* (London, 1898).

BIBLIOGRAPHY

HAIG, ROBERT L., *The Gazeteer 1735–1797: A Study in the Eighteenth-Century English Newspaper* (Carbondale, Ill., 1960).

HALL, SHARYN LEA, 'English Dialogue Opera: 1762–1796', Ph.D. diss. (University of Toronto, 1980).

HANNAFORD, STEPHEN, 'The Shape of Eighteenth-Century English Drama', *Theatre Survey*, 21 (1980), 93–103.

[HASLEWOOD, JOSEPH], *The Secret History of the Green Room: Containing Authentic and Entertaining Memoirs of the Actors and Actresses in the Three Theatres Royal*, 2 vols. (3rd edn., London, 1793).

HAYDN, JOSEPH, *The Collected Correspondence and London Notebooks of Joseph Haydn*, ed. H. C. Robbins Landon (London, 1959).

HAYDON, BENJAMIN R., *The Diary of Benjamin Robert Haydon*, ed. Willard B. Pope, 5 vols. (Cambridge, Mass., 1963).

HAZLITT, WILLIAM, *A View of the English Stage; or, a Series of Dramatic Criticisms* (London, 1821).

HEARTZ, DANIEL, 'Thomas Attwood's Lessons in Composition with Mozart', *PRMA* 100 (1973–4), 175–83.

HIGHFILL, PHILIP H., Jr., BURNIM, KALMAN A., and LANGHANS, EDWARD A., *A Biographical Dictionary of Actors, Actresses, Musicians, Dancers, Managers and Other Stage Personnel in London, 1660–1800* (Carbondale, Ill., 1973–93).

The History of The Times, i: *'The Thunderer' in the Making 1785–1841* (London, 1935).

HOGARTH, GEORGE, *Musical History, Biography and Criticism* (1st pub. London, 1835; New York, 1845).

HUGHES, LEO, *The Drama's Patrons: A Study of the Eighteenth-Century London Audience* (Austin, Tex., 1971).

HUME, ROBERT D., *The Rakish Stage: Studies in English Drama, 1660–1800* (Carbondale, Ill., 1983).

HUMPHRIES, CHARLES, and SMITH, WILLIAM C., *Music Publishing in the British Isles from the Beginning until the Middle of the Nineteenth Century: A Dictionary of Engravers, Printers, Publishers and Music Sellers, with a Historical Introduction* (2nd edn., Oxford, 1970).

HUNTER, DAVID, 'Music Copyright in Britain to 1800', *ML* 67 (1986), 269–82.

International Genealogical Index, microfiche (Salt Lake City, Ut., 1992).

JOHNSON, DAVID, 'The 18th-Century Glee', *MT* 120 (1979), 200–2.

JOHNSTONE, H. DIACK, and FISKE, ROGER (eds.), *The Blackwell History of Music in Britain*, iv: *The Eighteenth Century* (Oxford, 1990).

JONES, THOMAS, *Memoirs of Thomas Jones: Penkerrig, Radnorshire, 1803* (London, 1951).

KELLY, MICHAEL, *Reminiscences of Michael Kelly of the King's Theatre and Theatre Royal Drury Lane*, 2 vols. (2nd edn., London, 1826, repr. New York, 1968; ed. Roger Fiske, London, 1975).

KEMBLE, FRANCES ANN, *Records of a Girlhood* (2nd edn., New York, 1883).

KING, ALEC HYATT, 'Music Circulating Libraries in Britain', *MT* 119 (1978), 134–48.

—— NEIGHBOUR, OLIVER W., and TYSON, ALAN, 'Great Britain', in Donald W. Krummel (comp.), *Guide for Dating Early Published Music: A Manual of Bibliographic Practices* (Hackensack, NJ, 1974).

KINNE, WILLARD A., *Revivals and Importations of French Comedies in England, 1749–1800* (New York, 1939).

KITCHINER, WILLIAM, 'Observations on Vocal Music', *Ivanhoe or the Knight Templar* (London [1820]).

KNAPP, J. MERRILL, 'Samuel Webbe and the Glee', *ML* 33 (1952), 346–51.

KOCH, CHARLES E., Jr., 'The Dramatic Ensemble Finale in the Opéra Comique of the Eighteenth Century', *Acta Musicologica*, 39 (1967), 72–83.

KOURY, DANIEL J., *Orchestral Performance Practices in the Nineteenth Century: Size, Proportions, and Seating* (Ann Arbor, Mich., 1986).

KRUMMEL, D. W. (comp.), *Guide for Dating Early Published Music: A Manual of Bibliographical Practices* (Hackensack, NJ, 1974).

—— *English Music Printing 1553–1700* (London, 1975).

—— and SADIE, STANLEY, *Music Printing and Publishing* (Norton/Grove Handbooks in Music; New York, 1990).

LACKINGTON, JAMES, *Memoirs of the First Forty-Five Years of the Life of James Lackington, the Present Bookseller in Chiswell-street, Moorfields, London. Written by Himself. In a Series of Letters to a Friend* (London [1791]).

LANDON, H. C. ROBBINS, *Haydn: Chronicle and Works*, iii: *Haydn in England 1791–1795* (Bloomington, Ind., 1976).

LARUE, JAN, 'British Music Paper 1770–1820: Some Distinctive Characteristics', *MMR* 87 (1957), 177–80.

LAWRENCE, W. J., 'Early Irish Ballad Opera and Comic Opera', *MQ* 8 (1922), 397–412.

LIESENFELD, VINCENT J., *The Licensing Act of 1737* (Madison, Wis., 1984).

LOEWENBERG, ALFRED (comp.), *Annals of Opera 1597–1940* (Totowa, NJ, 1978).

The London Stage; a Collection of the Most Reputed Tragedies, Comedies, Operas, Melo-Dramas, Farces, and Interludes. Accurately Printed from Acting Copies, as Performed at the Theatres Royal, and Carefully Collated and Revised, 4 vols. (London [1824–7]).

The London Stage 1660–1800: A Calendar of Plays, Entertainments & Afterpieces Together with Casts, Box-Receipts and Contemporary Comment Compiled from the Playbills, Newspapers and Theatrical Diaries of the Period, pt. 4: *1747–1776*, ed. George W. Stone, jun.; pt. 5: *1776–1800*, ed. Charles B. Hogan (Carbondale, Ill., 1962–8).

LYSONS, DANIEL, *et al.*, *Origin and Progress of the Meeting of the Three Choirs of Gloucester, Worcester & Hereford, and of the Charity Connected with it* (Gloucester, 1895).

BIBLIOGRAPHY

MacMillan, Dougald, *Drury Lane Calendar 1747–1776* (Oxford, 1938).

—— (comp.), *Catalogue of the Larpent Plays in the Huntington Library* (San Marino, Ca., 1939).

Matthews, Betty, 'J. C. Bach in the West Country', *MT* 108 (1967), 702–3.

—— 'The Childhood of Nancy Storace', *MT* 110 (1969), 733–5.

—— (comp.), *The Royal Society of Musicians of Great Britain: List of Members 1738–1984* (London, 1985).

—— 'Nancy Storace and the Royal Society of Musicians', *MT* 128 (1987), 325–7.

—— *The Royal Society of Musicians of Great Britain: A History 1738–1988* (London, 1988).

Maxted, Ian, *The London Book Trades, 1775–1800: A Preliminary Checklist of Members* (Folkestone, 1977).

'Memoir of Stephen Storace', *The Harmonicon*, 6 (1828), 1–3.

Meyer, Eve R., '*Turquerie* and Eighteenth-Century Music', *Eighteenth-Century Studies*, 7 (1973–4), 474–88.

Michtner, Otto, *Das alte Burgtheater als Opernbühne von der Einführung des Deutschen Singspiels (1778) bis zum Tod Kaiser Leopolds II (1792)* (Vienna, 1970).

Milhous, Judith, and Hume, Robert D., 'Opera Salaries in Eighteenth-Century London', *JAMS* 46 (1993), 26–83.

Milligan, Thomas B., *The Concerto and London's Musical Culture in the Late Eighteenth Century* (Ann Arbor, Mich., 1983).

Moore, Robert E., 'The Music to *Macbeth*', *MQ* 47 (1961), 22–40.

Moore, Thomas, *Memoirs of the Life of the Right Honourable Richard Brinsley Sheridan*, 2 vols. (5th edn., London, 1827).

Mozart, W. A., *The Letters of Mozart and His Family*, trans. Emily Anderson (3rd edn., London, 1985).

—— *W. A. Mozart: Neue Ausgabe sämtlicher Werke*, 10th ser., 30/1: *Thomas Attwoods Theorie- und Kompositionsstudien bei Mozart*, ed. Erich Hertzmann and Cecil B. Oldman (Kassel, 1965).

'Musical Biography No. X: Stephen Storace', *The Musical World*, ns 7/41 (July–Dec. 1840), 212–15.

Neighbour, Oliver W., and Tyson, Alan, *English Music Publishers' Plate Numbers in the First Half of the Nineteenth Century* (London, 1965).

Nicoll, Allardyce, *A History of Late Eighteenth Century Drama, 1750–1800* (Cambridge, 1937).

Oldman, C. B., 'Watermark Dates in English Paper', *Library*, 4/25 (1944–5), 70–1.

Orrell, John, 'The Lincoln's Inn Fields Playhouse in 1731', *Theatre Notebook*, 46 (1992), 144–54.

Oulton, Walley C., *The History of the Theatres of London: Containing an Annual Register of all the New and Revived Tragedies, Comedies, Operas, Farces, Pantomimes, &c. that have been Performed at the Theatres-Royal, in London, from the Year 1771 to 1795. With Occasional Notes and Anecdotes*, 2 vols. (London, 1796).

BIBLIOGRAPHY

OWENS, EVAN, 'La serva padrona in London, 1750–1783', Pergolesi Studies, 2 (1988), 204–21.

OXBERRY, WILLIAM, Oxberry's Dramatic Biography, and Histrionic Anecdotes, 6 vols. (London, 1825).

PARKE, WILLIAM T., Musical Memoirs; Comprising an Account of the General State of Music in England, from the First Commemoration of Handel, in 1784, to the Year 1830. Interspersed with Numerous Anecdotes, Musical, Histrionic, &c, 2 vols. (London, 1830; repr. 2 vols. in 1, New York, 1970).

PASQUIN, ANTHONY [John Williams], The Pin Basket to the Children of Thespis. A Satire (London, 1796).

Patents for Inventions: Abridgments of Specifications Relating to Music and Musical Instruments. A.D. 1694–1966 (2nd edn., London, 1871).

PEAKE, RICHARD B., Memoirs of the Colman Family, Including their Correspondence with the Most Distinguished Personages of Their Time, 2 vols. (London, 1841).

PEDICORD, HARRY W., 'By their Majesties' Command': The House of Hanover at the London Theatres, 1714–1800 (London, 1991).

PETTY, FREDERICK C., Italian Opera in London 1760–1800 (Ann Arbor, Mich., 1980).

PHILLIPS, JAMES W., 'A Bibliographical Inquiry into Printing and Bookselling in Dublin from 1670 to 1800', Ph.D. diss. (Trinity College, Dublin, 1952).

PICKERING, JENNIFER M., Music in the British Isles 1700 to 1800: A Bibliography of Literature (Edinburgh, 1990).

PLANCHÉ, JAMES ROBINSON, Recollections and Reflections: A Professional Auto-biography (1st edn., 1872; rev. edn. London, 1901).

PLATOFF, JOHN, 'Music and Drama in the Opera buffa Finale: Mozart and His Contemporaries in Vienna, 1781–1790', Ph.D. diss. (University of Pennsylvania, 1984).

—— 'Tonal Organization in "Buffo" Finales and the Act II Finale of "Le Nozze di Figaro"', ML 72 (1991), 387–403.

Playbills from the Harvard Theatre Collection: Theatre Royal Drury Lane, microfilm series (Woodbridge, Conn., n.d.).

PORTER, ROY, English Society in the Eighteenth Century (Harmondsworth, 1982).

PRICE, CURTIS, 'Italian Opera and Arson in Late Eighteenth-Century London', JAMS 42 (1989), 55–107.

—— 'Unity, Originality, and the London Pasticcio', Harvard Library Bulletin, NS 2/4: Bits and Pieces: Music for Theater (1991), 17–30.

PRICE, CURTIS, MILHOUS, JUDITH, and HUME, ROBERT D., 'The Rebuilding of the King's Theatre, Haymarket, 1789–1791', Theatre Journal, 43 (1991), 421–44.

—— —— —— Italian Opera in Late Eighteenth-Century London, i: The King's Theatre Haymarket, 1778–1791 (Oxford, 1995).

RABIN, RONALD J., and ZOHN, STEVEN, 'Arne, Walsh, and Music as Intellectual Property: Two Eighteenth-Century Lawsuits', Royal Musical Association Research Journal, 120 (1995), 112–45.

BIBLIOGRAPHY

RANGER, PAUL, *'Terror and Pity Reign in Every Breast': Gothic Drama in the London Patent Theatres, 1750–1820* (London, 1991).

RANSOM, HARRY, *The First Copyright Statute: An Essay on 'An Act for the Encouragement of Learning, 1710'* (Austin, Tex., 1956).

Répertoire international des sources musicales, series A/I, 11 vols. (Kassel, 1971–86).

RENWICK, WILLIAM L., *English Literature 1789–1815* (Oxford, 1963).

RISHTON, TIMOTHY J., 'Plagiarism, Fiddles and Tarantulas', *MT* 125 (1984), 325–7.

RITCHEY, LAWRENCE I., 'The Untimely Death of Samuel Wesley; or, the Perils of Plagiarism', *ML* 60 (1979), 45–59.

RODWELL, G. HERBERT, *A Letter to the Musicians of Great Britain: Containing a Prospectus of Proposed Plans for the Better Encouragement of Native Musical Talent, and for the Erection and Management of a Grand National Opera in London* (London, 1833).

ROSENFELD, SYBIL, *Georgian Scene Painters and Scene Painting* (Cambridge, 1981).

RYAN, RICHARD, *Dramatic Table Talk; or Scenes, Situations, & Adventures, Serious & Comic, in Theatrical History & Biography*, 3 vols. (London, 1825).

SACHS, JOEL, 'English and French Editions of Hummel', *JAMS* 25 (1972), 203–29.

—— 'Hummel and the Pirates: The Struggle for Musical Copyright', *MQ* 59 (1973), 31–60.

SADIE, STANLEY (ed.), *The New Grove Dictionary of Music and Musicians*, 20 vols. (London, 1980).

—— *The New Grove Dictionary of Musical Instruments*, 3 vols. (London, 1984).

—— *The New Grove Dictionary of Opera*, 4 vols. (London, 1992).

[SAINSBURY, JOHN S.], *Dictionary of Musicians, from the Earliest Ages to the Present Time*, 2 vols. (London, 1825; repr. New York, 1966).

SANDS, MOLLIE, 'Some Haymarket and Drury Lane Singers in the Last Decade of the 18th Century', *MMR* 89 (1959), 175–9.

—— *The Eighteenth-Century Pleasure Gardens of Marylebone 1737–1777* (London, 1987).

SCHNAPPER, EDITH B. (ed.), *The British Union-Catalogue of Early Music Printed before the Year 1801*, introd. Cecil B. Oldman, 2 vols. (London, 1957).

SCOTT, ALEXANDER, 'Arne's "Alfred"', *ML* 55 (1974), 385–97.

SHELDON, ESTHER K., *Thomas Sheridan of Smock-Alley: Recording His Life as Actor and Theater Manager in both Dublin and London; and Including a Smock-Alley Calendar for the Years of His Management* (Princeton, NJ, 1967).

SHERIDAN, RICHARD B., *The Letters of Richard Brinsley Sheridan*, ed. Cecil Price, 3 vols. (Oxford, 1966).

SMALL, JOHN, 'J. C. Bach Goes to Law', *MT* 126 (1985), 526–9.

SMITH, JOHN T., *Nollekens and His Times: Comprehending a Life of that Celebrated Sculptor; and Memoirs of Several Contemporary Artists, from the Time of Roubiliac, Hogarth, and Reynolds, to that of Fuseli, Flaxman, and Blake*, 2 vols. (London, 1828).

STORACE, STEPHEN, *No Song, No Supper*, ed. Roger Fiske, Musica Britannica, xvi (London, 1959; 2nd edn., London, 1975).

STORACE, STEPHEN, sen., Letter to *The Gentleman's Magazine*, 23 (1753), 433–4.

STOWELL, ROBIN, ' "Good Execution and Other Necessary Skills": The Role of the Concertmaster in the Late 18th Century', *Early Music*, 16 (1988), 21–33.

STROUD, DOROTHY, *Sir John Soane, Architect* (London, 1984).

The Thespian Dictionary; or, Dramatic Biography of the Present Age (1st edn., London, 1802; 2nd edn., London, 1805).

TREFMAN, SIMON, *Sam. Foote, Comedian, 1720–1777* (New York, 1971).

TROUBRIDGE, ST VINCENT, *The Benefit System in the British Theatre* (London, 1967).

TRUSLER, JOHN, *The London Adviser and Guide* (2nd edn., London, 1790).

—— *Memoirs of the Life of the Rev. Dr. Trusler, with His Opinions on a Variety of Interesting Subjects, and His Remarks, Through a Long Life, on Men and Manners, Written by Himself. Replete with Humour, Useful Information and Entertaining Anecdote* (Bath, 1806); a second volume of this work exists in manuscript at Bath Central Library.

TYSON, ALAN, *The Authentic English Editions of Beethoven* (London, 1963).

VELIMIROVIĆ, MILOŠ, 'Belgrade as Subject of Musical Compositions', *Muzikološki Zbornik*, 17/1 (1981), 147–63.

WALSH, THOMAS J., *Opera in Dublin 1705–1797: The Social Scene* (Dublin, 1973).

WATKINS, JOHN, *Memoirs of the Public and Private Life of the Right Honorable Richard Brinsley Sheridan, with a Particular Account of His Family and Connexions*, 2 vols. (London, 1817).

WERKMEISTER, LUCYLE, *A Newspaper History of England 1792–1793* (Lincoln, Nebr., 1967).

WHITE, ERIC W., *A History of English Opera* (London, 1983).

—— (comp.), *A Register of First Performances of English Operas and Semi-Operas from the 16th Century to 1980* (London, 1983).

WILKINSON, TATE, *The Wandering Patentee; or, A History of the Yorkshire Theatres, from 1770 to the Present Time: Interspersed with Anecdotes Respecting Most of the Performers in the Three Kingdoms, from 1765 to 1795*, 4 vols. (New York, 1795).

WINSTON, JAMES, *Drury Lane Journal: Selections from James Winston's Diaries, 1819–1827*, ed. Alfred L. Nelson and Gilbert B. Cross (London, 1974).

WOLFE, RICHARD J., *Secular Music in America 1801–1825: A Bibliography*, 3 vols. (New York, 1964).

—— *Early American Music Engraving and Printing: A History of Music Publishing in America from 1787 to 1825 with Commentary on Earlier and Later Practices* (Urbana, Ill., 1980).

WOOD, FREDERICK T., 'Pirate Printing in the XVIII Century', *Notes and Queries*, 159 (1930), 381–4, 400–3.

BIBLIOGRAPHY

WROTH, WARWICK, and WROTH, ARTHUR E., *The London Pleasure Gardens of the Eighteenth Century* (London, 1896).

YOUNG, PERCY M. (ed.), *The English Glee* (Oxford, 1990).

ZASLAW, NEAL, 'Toward the Revival of the Classical Orchestra', *PRMA* 103 (1976–7), 158–87.

INDEX

263

INDEX

INDEX

INDEX